John Adams Library, Jean-A.-N. Condorcet

Outlines of an Historical View of the Progress of the Human Mind

John Adams Library, Jean-A.-N. Condorcet

Outlines of an Historical View of the Progress of the Human Mind

ISBN/EAN: 9783337367503

Printed in Europe, USA, Canada, Australia, Japan

Cover: Foto ©Andreas Hilbeck / pixelio.de

More available books at **www.hansebooks.com**

OUTLINES

OF AN

HISTORICAL VIEW

OF THE

PROGRESS OF THE HUMAN MIND:

BEING A POSTHUMOUS WORK OF THE LATE

M. DE CONDORCET.

TRANSLATED FROM THE FRENCH.

LONDON:

PRINTED FOR J. JOHNSON, IN ST. PAUL'S CHURCH-YARD.

1795.

CONTENTS.

CONTENTS.

EIGHTH

CONTENTS.

PREFACE.

PREFACE.

CONDORCET, profcribed by a fanguinary faction, formed the idea of addreffing to his fellow-citizens a fummary of his principles, and of his conduct in public affairs. He fet down a few lines in execution of this project : but when he recollected, as he was obliged to do, thirty years of labour directed to the public fervice, and the multitude of fugitive pieces in which, fince the revolution, he had uniformly attacked every inftitution inimical to liberty, he rejected the idea of a ufelefs juftification. Free as he was from the dominion of the paffions, he could not confent to ftain the purity of his mind by recollecting his perfecutors; perpetually and fublimely inattentive to himfelf, he determined to confecrate the fhort fpace that remained between him and death to a work of general

b   and

and permanent utility. That work is the performance now given to the world. It has relation to a number of others, in which the rights of men had previoufly been difcuffed and eftablifhed; in which fuperftition had received its laft and fatal blow; in which the methods of the mathematical fciences, applied to new objects, have opened new avenues to the moral and political fciences; in which the genuine principles of focial happinefs have received a developement, and kind of demonftration, unknown before; laftly, in which we every where perceive marks of that profound morality, which banifhes even the very frailties of felf-love—of thofe pure and incorruptible virtues within the influence of which it is impoffible to live without feeling a religious veneration.

May this deplorable inftance of the moft extraordinary talents loft to the country—to the caufe of liberty—to the progrefs of fcience, and its beneficial application to the wants

of

of civilized man, excite a bitternefs of regret that fhall prove advantageous to the public welfare! May this death, which will in no fmall degree contribute, in the pages of hiftory, to characterife the era in which it has taken place, infpire a firm and dauntlefs attachment to the rights of which it was a violation! Such is the only homage worthy the fage who, the fatal fword fufpended over his head, could meditate in peace the melioration and happinefs of his fellow-creatures; fuch the only confolation thofe can experience who have been the objects of his affection, and have known all the extent of his virtue. ◆⌐◢

OUTLINES

OF AN

HISTORICAL VIEW, &c.

INTRODUCTION.

MAN is born with the faculty of receiving
fenfations. In thofe which he receives, he is
capable of perceiving and of diftinguifhing
the fimple fenfations of which they are compofed. He can retain, recognife, combine
them. He can preferve or recal them to his
memory; he can compare their different
combinations; he can afcertain what they
poffefs in common, and what characterifes
each; laftly, he can affix figns to all thefe
objects, the better to know them, and the
more eafily to form from them new combinations.

This faculty is developed in him by the
action of external objects, that is, by the

B   prefence

prefence of certain complex fenfations, the conftancy of which, whether in their identical whole, or in the laws of their change, is independent of himfelf. It is alfo exercifed by communication with other fimilarly organifed individuals, and by all the artificial means which, from the firft developement of this faculty, men have fucceeded in inventing.

Senfations are accompanied with pleafure or pain, and man has the further faculty of converting thefe momentary impreffions into durable fentiments of a correfponding nature, and of experiencing thefe fentiments either at the fight or recollection of the pleafure or pain of beings fenfitive like himfelf. And from this faculty, united with that of forming and combining ideas, arife, between him and his fellow creatures, the ties of intereft and duty, to which nature has affixed the moft exquifite portion of our felicity, and the moft poignant of our fufferings.

Were we to confine our obfervations to an enquiry into the general facts and unvarying laws which the developement of thefe faculties prefents to us, in what is common to the

different

different individuals of the human fpecies, our enquiry would bear the name of metaphy-*Metaphy* fics.

But if we confider this developement in its refults, relative to the mafs of individuals co-exifting at the fame time on a given fpace, and follow it from generation to generation, it then exhibits a picture of the progrefs of human intellect. This progrefs is fubject to the fame general laws, obfervable in the individual developement of our faculties ; being the refult of that very developement confidered at once in a great number of individuals united in fociety. But the refult which every inftant prefents, depends upon that of the preceding inftants, and has an influence on the inftants which follow.

This picture, therefore, is hiftorical ; fince, *Hiftori* fubjected as it will be to perpetual variations, it is formed by the fucceffive obfervation of human focieties at the different eras through which they have paffed. It will accordingly exhibit the order in which the changes have taken place, explain the influence of every paft period upon that which follows it, and thus fhow, by the modifications which the

human

human fpecies has experienced, in its inceffant renovation through the immenfity of
ages, the courfe which it has purfued, and
the fteps which it has advanced towards
knowledge and happinefs. From thefe obfervations on what man has heretofore been, and
what he is at prefent, we fhall be led to the
means of fecuring and of accelerating the ftill
further progrefs, of which, from his nature,
we may indulge the hope.

Such is the objeƈt of the work I have undertaken ; the refult of which will be to
fhow, from reafoning and from faƈts, that no
bounds have been fixed to the improvement
of the human faculties ; that the perfeƈtibility
of man is abfolutely indefinite ; that the progrefs of this perfeƈtibility, henceforth above
the control of every power that would impede it, has no other limit than the duration
of the globe upon which nature has placed us.
The courfe of this progrefs may doubtlefs be
more or lefs rapid, but it can never be retrograde ; at leaft while the earth retains its
fituation in the fyftem of the univerfe, and
the laws of this fyftem fhall neither effeƈt
upon the globe a general overthrow, nor introduce

troduce fuch changes as would no longer permit the human race to preferve and exercife therein the fame faculties, and find the fame refources.

The firft ftate of civilization obfervable in the human fpecies, is that of a fociety of men, few in number, fubfifting by means of hunting and fifhing, unacquainted with every art but the imperfect one of fabricating in an uncouth manner their arms and fome houfehold utenfils, and òf conftructing or digging for themfelves an habitation ; yet already in poffeffion of a language for the communication of their wants, and a fmall number of moral ideas, from which are deduced their common rules of conduct, living in families, conforming themfelves to general cuftoms that ferve inftead of laws, and having even a rude form of government.

In this ftate it is apparent that the uncertainty and difficulty of procuring fubfiftance, and the unavoidable alternative of extreme fatigue or an abfolute repofe, leave not to man the leifure in which, by refigning himfelf to meditation, he might enrich his mind with new combinations. The means of fatisfying

fying his wants are even too dependent upon chance and the feafons, ufefully to excite an induftry, the progreffive improvement of which might be tranfmitted to his progeny; and accordingly the attention of each is confined to the improvement of his individual fkill and addrefs.

For this reafon, the progrefs of the human fpecies muft in this ftage have been extremely flow; it could make no advance but at diftant intervals, and when favoured by extraordinary circumftances. Meanwhile, to the fubfiftance derived from hunting and fifhing, or from the fruits which the earth fpontaneoufly offered, fucceeds the fuftenance afforded by the animals which man has tamed, and which he knows how to preferve and multiply. To thefe means is afterwards added an imperfect agriculture; he is no longer content with the fruit or the plants which chance throws in his way; he learns to form a ftock of them, to collect them around him, to fow or to plant them, to favour their reproduction by the labour of culture.

Property, which, in the firft ftate, was confined to his houfehold utenfils, his arms,

his

his nets, and the animals he killed, is now extended to his flock, and next to the land which *land*,
he has cleared and cultivated. Upon the death
of its head, this property naturally devolves to
the family. Some individuals poffefs a fuperfluity capable of being preferved. If it be abfolute, it gives rife to new wants. If confined to a fingle article, while the proprietor
feels the want of other articles, this want
fuggefts the idea of exchange. Hence moral
relations multiply, and become complicate.
A greater fecurity, a more certain and more
conftant leifure, afford time for meditation,
or at leaft for a continued feries of obfervations. The cuftom is introduced, as to fome
individuals, of giving a part of their fuperfluity in exchange for labour, by which they
might be exempt from labour themfelves.
There accordingly exifts a clafs of men whofe
time is not engroffed by corporeal exertions,
and whofe defires extend beyond their fimple wants. Induftry awakes; the arts already *Induftry*
known, expand and improve; the facts which *Arts*,
chance prefents to the obfervation of the moft *experiment*
attentive and beft cultivated minds, bring to
light new arts; as the means of living be-

come

come lefs dangerous and lefs precarious, population increafes; agriculture, which can
provide for a greater number of individuals
upon the fame fpace of ground, fupplies the
place of the other fources of fubfiftance; it
favours the multiplication of the fpecies, by
which it is favoured in its turn; in a fociety
become more fedentary, more connected, more
intimate, ideas that have been acquired communicate themfelves more quickly, and are
perpetuated with more certainty. And now
the dawn of the fciences begins to appear;
man exhibits an appearance diftinct from the
other claffes of animals, and is no longer like
them confined to an improvement purely individual.

The more extenfive, more numerous and
more complicated relations which men now
form with each other, caufe them to feel the
neceffity of having a mode of communicating
their ideas to the abfent, of preferving the
remembrance of a fact with more precifion
than by oral tradition, of fixing the conditions
of an agreement more fecurely than by the
memory of witneffes, of ftating, in a way
lefs liable to change, thofe refpected cuftoms

to

to which the members of any fociety agree to
fubmit their conduct.

Accordingly the want of writing is felt, and *Writing.*
the art invented. It appears at firft to have
been an abfolute painting, to which fucceeded
a conventional painting, preferving fuch traits
only as were characteriftic of the objects.
Afterwards, by a kind of metaphor analogous
to that which was already introduced into *Hieroglyphicks*
their language, the image of a phyfical object
became expreffive of moral ideas. The origin
of thofe figns, like the origin of words, were
liable in time to be forgotten; and writing
became the art of affixing figns of convention
to every idea, every word, and of confequence
to every combination of ideas and words.

There was now a language that was written,
and a language that was fpoken, which it was
neceffary equally to learn, between which
there muft be eftablifhed a reciprocal corre-
fpondence.

Some men of genius, the eternal benefactors *Genius is*
of the human race, but whofe names and *now deified*
even country are for ever buried in oblivion, *and fubftitute*
obferved that all the words of a language were *for Heathen*
only the combinations of a very limited num- *gods and*
ber *Roman Catholic Saints. Genius*
is now the Mythology of french
Philosophers. Becaufe men of
Genius want to be worshipped.

Natural History of Speech.
Brightland
Harris
Court de Gebelin.

ber of primitive articulations; but that this number, fmall as it was, was fufficient to form a quantity almoft infinite of different combinations. Hence they conceived the idea of reprefenting by vifible figns, not the ideas or the words that anfwered to them, but thofe fimple elements of which the words are compofed.

Alphabet

Alphabetical writing was then introduced. A fmall number of figns ferved to exprefs every thing in this mode, as a fmall number of founds fufficed to exprefs every thing orally. The language written and the language fpoken were the fame; all that was neceffary was to be able to know, and to form, the few given figns; and this laft ftep fecured for ever the progrefs of the human race.

Scientific Language.

It would perhaps be defirable at the prefent day, to inftitute a written language, which, devoted to the fole ufe of the fciences, expreffing only fuch combinations of fimple ideas as are found to be exactly the fame in every mind, employed only upon reafonings of logical ftrictnefs, upon operations of the mind precife and determinate, might be underftood by men of every country, and be tranflated

tranflated into all their idioms, without being, like thofe idioms, liable to corruption, by paffing into common ufe.

Then, fingular as it may appear, this kind of writing, the prefervation of which would only have ferved to prolong ignorance, would become, in the hands of philofophy, an ufeful inftrument for the fpeedy ·propagation of knowledge, and advancement of the fciences.

It is between this degree of civilization and that in which we ftill find the favage tribes, that we muft place every people whofe hiftory has been handed down to us, and who, fome-times making new advancements, fometimes plunging themfelves again into ignorance, fometimes floating between the two alter-natives or ftopping at a certain limit, fome-times totally difappearing from the earth under the fword of conquerors, mixing with thofe conquerors, or living in flavery ; laftly, fometimes receiving knowledge from a more enlightened people, to tranfmit it to other nations,—form an unbroken chain of con-nection between the earlieft periods of hiftory and the age in which we live, between the

firſt people known to us, and the preſent nations of Europe.

In the picture then which I mean to
ſketch, three diſtinct parts are perceptible.

In the firſt, in which the relations of travellers exhibit to us the condition of mankind in the leaſt civilized nations, we are
obliged to gueſs by what ſteps man in an
iſolated ſtate, or rather confined to the ſociety
neceſſary for the propagation of the ſpecies,
was able to acquire thoſe firſt degrees of improvement, the laſt term of which is the uſe
of an articulate language : an acquiſition that
preſents the moſt ſtriking feature, and indeed
the only one, a few more extenſive moral
ideas and a ſlight commencement of ſocial
order excepted, which diſtinguiſhes him from
animals living like himſelf in regular and permanent ſociety. In this part of our picture,
then, we can have no other guide than an inveſtigation of the developement of our faculties.

To this firſt guide, in order to follow man
to the point in which he exerciſes arts, in
which the rays of ſcience begin to enlighten.
him,

him, in which nations are united by commercial intercourfe ;- in which, in fine, alphabetical writing is invented, we may add the hiftory of the feveral focieties that have been obferved in almoft every intermediate ftate : though we can follow no individual one through all the fpace which feparates thefe two grand epochs of the human race.

Here the picture begins to take its colouring in great meafure from the feries of facts tranfmitted to us by hiftory: but it is neceffary to felect thefe facts from that of different nations, and at the fame time compare and combine them, to form the fuppofed hiftory of a fingle people, and delineate its progrefs.

From the period that alphabetical writing was known in Greece, hiftory is connected by an uninterrupted feries of facts and obfervations, with the period in which we live, with the prefent ftate of mankind in the moft enlightened countries of Europe ; and the picture of the progrefs and advancement of the human mind becomes ftrictly hiftorical. Philofophy has no longer any thing to guefs, has no more fuppofitious combinations to form ;

all

all it has to do is to collect and arrange facts, and exhibit the useful truths which arise from them as a whole, and from the different bearings of their several parts.

There remains only a third picture to form,—that of our hopes, or the progress reserved for future generations, which the conftancy of the laws of nature seems to secure to mankind. And here it will be neceffary to shew by what steps this progress, which at present may appear chimerical, is gradually to be rendered possible, and even easy; how truth, in spite of the transient success of prejudices, and the support they receive from the corruption of governments or of the people, must in the end obtain a durable triumph; by what ties nature has indissolubly united the advancement of knowledge with the progress of liberty, virtue, and respect for the natural rights of man; how these blessings, the only real ones, though so frequently seen apart as to be thought incompatible, must necessarily amalgamate and become inseparable, the moment knowledge shall have arrived at a certain pitch in a great number of nations at once, the moment it shall have penetrated
the

the whole mafs of a great people, whofe language fhall have become univerfal, and whofe
commercial intercourfe fhall embrace the
whole extent of the globe. This union having
once taken place in the whole enlightened
clafs of men, this clafs will be confidered as
the friends of human kind, exerting themfelves
in concert to advance the improvement and
happinefs of the fpecies.

We fhall expofe the origin and trace the
hiftory of general errors, which have more or
lefs contributed to retard or fufpend the advance of reafon, and fometimes even, as much
as political events, have been the caufe of
man's taking a retrograde courfe towards
ignorance.

Thofe operations of the mind that lead to
or retain us in error, from the fubtle para-
logifm, by which the moft penetrating mind
may be deceived, to the mad reveries of en-
thufiafts, belong equally, with that juft mode
of reafoning that conducts us to truth, to the
theory of the developement of our individual
faculties ; and for the fame reafon, the manner in which general errors are introduced,
propagated, tranfmitted, and rendered per-

manent

manent among nations, forms a part of the
picture of the progrefs of the human mind.
Like truths which improve and enlighten it,
they are the confequence of its activity, and
of the difproportion that always exifts between what it actually knows, what it has
the defire to know; and what it conceives
there is a neceffity of acquiring.

It is even apparent, that, from the general
laws of the developement of our faculties,
certain prejudices muft neceffarily fpring up
in each ftage of our progrefs, and extend
their feductive influence beyond that ftage;
becaufe men retain the errors of their infancy, their country, and the age in which
they live, long after the truths neceffary to
the removal of thofe errors are acknowledged.

In fhort, there exift, at all times and in all
countries, different prejudices, according to
the degree of illumination of the different
claffes of men, and according to their profeffions. If the prejudices of philofophers be
impediments to new acquifitions of truth,
thofe of the lefs enlightened claffes retard the
propagation of truths already known, and
thofe

thofe of efteemed and powerful profeffions oppofe like obftacles. - Thefe are the three kinds of enemies which reafon is continually obliged to encounter, and over which fhe frequently does not triumph till after a long and painful ftruggle. The hiftory of thefe contefts, together with that of the rife, triumph, and fall of prejudice, will occupy a confiderable place in this work, and will by no means form the leaft important or leaft ufeful part of it.

If there be really fuch an art as that of forefeeing the future improvement of the human race, and of directing and haftening that improvement, the hiftory of the progrefs it has already made muft form the principal bafis of this art. Philofophy, no doubt, ought to profcribe the fuperftitious idea, which fuppofes no rules of conduct are to be found but in the hiftory of paft ages, and no truths but in the ftudy of the opinions of antiquity. But ought it not to include in the profcription, the prejudice that would proudly reject the leffons of experience? Certainly it is meditation alone that can, by happy combinations, conduct us to the general prin-

C   ciples

ciples of the science of man. But if the study
of individuals of the human species be of
use to the metaphysician and moralist, why
should that of societies be less useful to them ?
And why not of use to the political philo-
sopher ? If it be advantageous to observe the
societies that exist at one and the same period, and to trace their connection and re-
semblance, why not to observe them in a suc-
ceffion of periods ? Even suppofing that such
obfervation might be neglected in the inveftigation of speculative truths, ought it to be
neglected when the question is to apply thofe
truths to practice, and to deduce from science
the art that should be the useful refult ? Do
not our prejudices, and the evils that are the
confequence of them, derive their fource from
the prejudices of our anceftors ? And will it
not be the fureft way of undeceiving us re-
specting the one, and of preventing the other,
to develope their origin and effects ?

Are we not arrived at the point when there
is no longer any thing to fear, either from
new errors, or the return of old ones ; when
no corrupt inftitution can be introduced by
hypocrify, and adopted by ignorance or enthufiafm ;

thufiafm ; when no vicious combination can effect the infelicity of a great people ? Accordingly would it not be of advantage to know how nations have been deceived, corrupted, and plunged in mifery.

Every thing tells us that we are approach- *grand in deed, but will it be for better or worfe?* ing the era of one of the grand revolutions of the human race. What can better enlighten us as to what we may expect, what can be a furer guide to us, amidft its commotions, than the picture of the revolutions that have preceded and prepared the way for it ? The prefent ftate of knowledge affures us that it will be happy. But is it not upon condition that we know how to affift it with all our ftrength ? *Aye. Sir.* And, that the happinefs it promifes may be lefs dearly bought, that it may fpread with more rapidity over a greater fpace, that it may be more complete in its effects, is it not requifite to ftudy, in the hiftory of the human mind, what obftacles remain to be feared, and by what means thofe obftacles are to be *Aye. Sir.* furmounted?

I fhall divide the fpace through which I mean to run, into nine grand epochs ; and fhall prefume, in a tenth, to advance fome

con-

conjectures upon the future deftiny of mankind.

I fhall confine myfelf to the principal features that characterife each ; I fhall give them in the group, without troubling myfelf with exceptions or detail. I fhall indicate the objects, of the refults of which the work itfelf will prefent the developements and the proofs.

FIRST

FIRST EPOCH.

Men united into Hordes.

WE have no direct information by which
to afcertain what has preceded the ftate of
which we are now to fpeak; and it is only
by examining the intellectual or moral faculties, and the phyfical conftitution of man,
that we are enabled to conjecture by what
means he arrived at this firft degree of civilization.

Accordingly an inveftigation of thofe phyfical qualities favourable to the firft formation
of fociety, together with a fummary analyfis
of the developement of our intellectual or
moral faculties, muft ferve as an introduction
to this epoch.

A fociety confifting of a family appears
to be natural to man. Formed at firft by the
want which children have of their parents,
and by the affection of the mother, as well as
that of the father, though lefs general and
lefs lively, time was allowed, by the long

con-

continuance of this want, for the birth and growth of a fentiment which muft have excited the defire of perpetuating the union. The continuance of the want was alfo fufficient for the advantages of the union to be felt. A family placed upon a foil that afforded an eafy fubfiftance, might afterwards have multiplied and become a horde.

Hordes

Hordes that may have owed their origin to the union of feveral diftinct families, muft have been formed more flowly and more

united Families

rarely, the union depending on motives lefs urgent and the concurrence of a greater number of circumftances.

Primitive Arts.

The art of fabricating arms, of preparing aliments, of procuring the utenfils requifite for this preparation, of preferving thefe aliments as a provifion againft the feafons in which it was impoffible to procure a frefh fupply of them—thefe arts, confined to the moft fimple wants, were the firft fruits of a continued union, and the firft features that diftinguifhed human fociety from the fociety obfervable in many fpecies of beafts.

Woman's Garden

In fome of thefe hordes, the women cultivate round the huts plants which ferve for
food

food and fuperfede the neceffity of hunting and fifhing. In others, formed in places where the earth fpontaneoufly offers vegetable nutriment, a part of the time of the favages is occupied by the care of feeking and gathering it. In hordes of the laft defcription, where the advantage of remaining united is lefs felt, civilization has been obferved very little to exceed that of a fociety confifting of a fingle family. Meanwhile there has been found in all the ufe of an articulate language.

More frequent and more durable con-nections with the fame individuals, a fimi-larity of interefts, the fuccour mutually given, whether in their common hunting or againft an enemy, muft have equally produced both the fentiment of juftice and a reciprocal af-fection between the members of the fociety. In a fhort time this affection would transform itfelf into attachment to the fociety.

The neceffary confequence was a violent enmity, and a defire of vengeance not to be extinguifhed, againft the enemies of the horde.

The want of a chief, in order to act in common, and thereby defend themfelves the

better,

C 4

better, and procure with greater eafe a more certain and more abundant fubfiftance, introduced the firft idea of public authority into thefe focieties. In circumftances in which the whole horde was interefted, refpecting which a common refolution muft be taken, all thofe concerned in executing the refolution were to be confulted. The weaknefs of the femalcs, which exempted them from the diftant chace and from war, the ufual fubjects of debate, excluded them alike from thefe confultations. As the refolutions demanded experience, none were admitted but fuch as were fuppofed to poffefs it. The quarrels that arofe in a fociety difturbed its harmony, and were calculated to deftroy it: it was natural to agree that the decifion of them fhould be referred to thofe whofe age and perfonal qualities infpired the greateft confidence. Such was the origin of the firft political inftitutions.

The formation of a language muft have preceded thefe inftitutions. The idea of expreffing objects by conventional figns appears to be above the degree of intelligence attained in this ftage of civilization; and it is probable they were only brought into ufe by

length

length of time, by degrees, and in a manner in fome fort imperceptible.

The invention of the bow was the work *The Bow* of a fingle man of genius; the formation of a language that of the whole fociety. Thefe two *Language* kinds of progrefs belong equally to the human fpecies. The one, more rapid, is the refult of thofe new combinations which <u>men favoured</u> *The God* <u>by nature</u> are capable of forming; is the fruit *Genius again* of their meditations and the energies they difplay: the other, more flow, arifes from the reflections and obfervations that offer themfelves to all men, and from the habits contracted in their common courfe of life.

Regular movements adjufted to each other in due proportion, are capable of being executed with a lefs degree of fatigue; and they who fee, or hear them, perceive their order and relation with greater facility. For both thefe reafons, they form a fource of pleafure. Thus the origin of the dance, of mufic and *Dance, Mufic* of poetry, may be traced to the infant ftate *Poetry* of fociety. They were employed for the amufement of youth and upon occafions of public feftivals. There were at that period love fongs and war fongs; and even mufical *Songs* inftru-

Instrument inftruments were invented. Neither was the
Eloquence. art of eloquence abfolutely unknown in thefe
hordes; at leaft they could affume in their fet
fpeeches a more grave and folemn tone, and
were not ftrangers to rhetorical exaggeration.

The errors that diftinguifh this epoch of
Revenge & civilization are the converfion of vengeance
Cruelty, Virtue and cruelty towards an enemy into virtue,;
the prejudice that configns the female part of
Seperation of fociety to a fort of flavery; the right of
Women commanding in war confidered as the pre-
Royalty rogative of an individual family; together
with the firft dawn of various kinds of fuper-
Superstition ftition. Of thefe it will be neceffary to trace
the origin and afcertain the motives. For
man never adopts without reafon any errors,
except what his early education have in a
manner rendered natural to him: if he embrace any new error, it is either becaufe it is
connected with thofe of his infancy, or becaufe his opinions, paffions, interefts, or other
circumftances, difpofe him to embrace it.

The only fciences known to favage hordes,
Astronomy are a flight and crude idea of aftronomy, and
Medicine the knowledge of certain medicinal plants
employed in the cure of wounds and difeafes;

and even thefe are already corrupted by a *Superstition* mixture of fuperftition.

Meanwhile there is prefented to us in this epoch one fact of importance in the hiftory of the human mind. We can here perceive the *Schools/gall* beginnings of an inftitution, that in its pro- *edges Acade* grefs has been attended with oppofite effects, *miss, Priest* accelerating the advancement of knowledge, *Nobles* at the fame time that it diffeminated error; enriching the fciences with new truths, but precipitating the people into ignorance and religious fervitude, and obliging them to pur- chafe a few tranfient benefits at the price of a long and fhameful tyranny.

I mean the formation of a clafs of men the *Are not the* depofitaries of the elements of the fciences or *Pretenfions* proceffes of the arts, of the myfteries or cere- *of Genius,* monies of religion, of the practices of fuper- ftition, and frequently even of the fecrets of *Lett up by* legiflation and polity. I mean that feparation *this Vifionary* of the human race into two portions; the one *as dangerous* deftined to teach, the other to believe; the *and indeed* one proudly concealing what it vainly boafts *in the end* of knowing, the other receiving with refpect *a useful fys*- whatever its teachers fhall condefcend to re- *tem ?* veal; the one wifhing to raife itfelf above

reafon,

reafon, the other humbly renouncing reafon, and debafing itfelf below humanity, by acknowledging in its fellow men prerogatives fuperior to their common nature.

This diftinction, of which, at the clofe of the eighteenth century, we ftill fee the remains in our priefts, is obfervable in the leaft civilized tribes of favages, who have already their quacks and forcerers. It is too general, and too conftantly meets the eye in all the ftages of civilization, not to have a foundation in nature itfelf: and we fhall accordingly find in the ftate of the human faculties at this early period of fociety, the caufe of the credulity of the firft dupes, and of the rude cunning of the firft impoftors.

Thefe were your Men of Genius, the Ethereal Spirits of Bolingbroke, Condorcet. There never was a more flagrant one, among them all than yourfelf. nor one who opened wider the Box of Pandora. The Credulity of Dupes and the Cunning of Impostors was never more grofs or glaring than in The French Revolution.

SECOND

SECOND EPOCH.

*Paſtoral State of Mankind.—Tranſition from
that to the Agricultural State.*

THE idea of preferving certain animals *Keeping*
taken in hunting, muſt readily have oc- *Animals*
curred, when their docility rendered the prefervation of them a taſk of no difficulty, when
the foil round the habitations of the hunters
afforded thefe animals an ample fubfiſtance,
when the family poffeffed a greater quantity
of them than it could for the prefent confume, and at the fame time might have reafon to apprehend the being expofed to want,
from the ill fuccefs of the next chace, or the
intemperature of the feafons.

From keeping thefe animals as a fimple *young.*
fupply againſt a time of need, it was obferved
that they might be made to multiply, and
thus furnifh a more durable provifion. Their
milk afforded a farther refource : and thofe *Milk*
fruits of a flock, which, at firſt, were regarded
only as a fupplement to the produce of the

chace,

chace, became the moſt certain, moſt abundant and leaſt painful means of ſubſiſtance.
Accordingly the chace ceaſed to be conſidered
as the principal of theſe reſources, and ſoon
as any reſource at all ; it was purſued only
as a pleaſure, or as a neceſſary precaution for
keeping beaſts of prey from the flocks, which,
become more numerous, could no longer find
round the habitations of their keepers a ſufficient nouriſhment.

Shepherds   A more ſedentary and leſs fatiguing life
afforded leiſure favourable to the developement of the mind. Secure of ſubſiſtance, no
longer anxious reſpecting their firſt and indiſ-
penſible wants, men ſought, in the means of
providing for thoſe wants, new ſenſations.

The arts made ſome progreſs : new light
was acquired reſpecting that of maintaining
domeſtic animals, of favouring their reproduction, and even of improving their breed.

wool   Wool was uſed for apparel, and cloth ſub-
ſtituted in the place of ſkins.

Family ſocieties became more urbane, without being leſs intimate. As the flocks of each
could not multiply in the ſame proportion,
This difference a difference of wealth was eſtabliſhed. Then
existed, equally in the hunting and fishing life. was
one Man had more and better bows and Nets, and greater Skill
in using them.

was fuggefted the idea of one man fharing the *Unequal Wealth.* produce of his flocks with another who had no flocks, and who was to devote his time and ftrength to the care they required. Then it was found that the labour of a young and able individual was of more value than the expence of his bare fubfiftance ; and the cuf- tom was introduced of retaining prifoners of *Prisoners preferved.* war as flaves, inftead of putting them to death.

Hofpitality, which is practifed alfo among *Hospitality* favages, affumes in the paftoral ftate a more *improves but* decided and important character, even among *begins not* thofe wandering hordes that dwell in their *with Pastoral* waggons or in tents. More frequent occa- *life. it exist* fions occur for the reciprocal exercife of this *among all* act of humanity between man and man, be- *favages,* tween individual families, and between one people and another. It becomes a focial duty, and is fubjected to laws.

As fome families poffeffed not only a fure fubfiftance, but a conftant fuperfluity, while others were deftitute of the neceffaries of life, natural compaffion for the fufferings of the latter gave birth to the fentiment and practice of beneficence. *Beneficence.*

Manners

Manners soften
Manners muſt of courſe have ſoftened. The ſlavery of women became leſs ſevere, and the wives of the rich were no longer condemned to fatiguing labours.

A greater variety of articles employed in ſatisfying the different wants, a greater number of inſtruments to prepare theſe wants, and a greater inequality in their diſtribution, gave energy to exchange, and converted it into actual commerce: it was impoſſible it ſhould extend without the neceſſity of a common meaſure and a ſpecies of money being felt.

Exchange
Barter Common
meaſure.
Meaſure Weight
Money.

Hordes became more numerous. At the ſame time, in order the more eaſily to maintain their flocks, they placed their habitations, when fixed, more apart from each other; or changed them into moveable encampments, as ſoon as they had diſcovered the uſe of certain ſpecies of animals they had tamed, in drawing or carrying burthens.

Military Chief
Each nation had its chief for the conduct of war; but being divided into tribes, from the neceſſity of ſecuring paſturage, each tribe had alſo its chief. This ſuperiority was attached almoſt univerſally to certain families. The heads however of families in poſſeſſion

Chiefs of Tribes

of

of numerous flocks, a multitude of flaves, and *Nobility*. who employed in their fervice a great number of poor, partook of the authority of the chiefs of the tribe, as thefe alfo fhared in that of the chiefs of the nation; at leaft when, from the refpect due to age, to experience, and the exploits they had performed, they were conceived to be worthy of it. And it is at this epoch of fociety that we muft place the origin of flavery, and inequality of political rights between men arrived at the age of maturity.

The counfels of the chiefs of the family or tribe decided, from ideas of natural juftice or of eftablifhed ufage, the numerous and intricate difputes that already prevailed. The tradition of thefe decifions, by confirming and perpetuating the ufage, foon formed a kind of jurifprudence more regular and coherent *Jurisprudence* than the progrefs of fociety had rendered in other refpects neceffary. The idea of property and its rights had acquired greater extent and precifion. The divifion of inhe- *Inheritances* ritances becoming more important, there was a neceffity of fubjecting it to fixed regulalations. The agreements that were entered

D   into

into being more frequent, were no longer confined to such simple objects; they were to be subjected to forms; and the manner of verifying them, to secure their execution, had also its laws.

The utility of observing the stars, the occupation which in long evenings they afforded to the mind, and the leisure enjoyed by the shepherds, effected a slight degree of improvement in astronomy.

Astronomy

But we observe advancing at the same time the art of deceiving men in order to rob them, and of assuming over their opinions an authority founded upon the hopes and fears of the imagination. More regular forms of worship begin to be established, and systems of faith less coarsely combined. The ideas entertained of supernatural powers, acquire a sort of refinement: and with this refinement we see spring up in one place pontiff princes, in another sacerdotal families or tribes, in a third colleges of priests; a class of individuals uniformly affecting insolent prerogatives, separating themselves from the people, the better to enslave them, and seizing exclusively upon medicine and astronomy, that

Religion
Man is by Nature a religious Animal, a religious Man will say: and that The Philosophers have taught the People Atheism and Irreligion in order to rob them. Invisible Powers produce Sun Moon and Stars Animals Vegetables Fruits Flowers and Blossoms force themselves on the human Mind as soon as it can think. A Sense of his own Weakness, Wants and Dependance forces him to think whence he came and what produced him and all Things.

that they may poffefs every hold upon the
mind for fubjugating it, and leave no means
by which to unmafk their hypocrify, and
break in pieces their chains.

Languages were enriched without becoming *Languages*
lefs figurative or lefs bold. The images employed were more varied and more pleafing.
They were acquired in paftoral life, as well as
in the favage life of the forefts, from the regular phenomena of nature, as well as from
its wildnefs and eccentricities. Song, poetry, *Poetry*
and inftruments of mufic were improved. *Music*
during a leifure that produced an audience
more peaceable, and at the fame time more
difficult to pleafe, and allowed the artift to
reflect on his own fentiments, examine
his firft ideas, and form a felection from
them.

It could not have efcaped obfervation that *Botany.*
fome plants yielded the flocks a better and
more abundant fubfiftance than others. The
advantage was accordingly felt of favouring
the production of thefe, of feparating them
from plants lefs nutritive, unwholfome, and
even dangerous; and the means of effecting
this were difcovered.

In

In like manner, where plants, grain, the spontaneous fruits of the earth, contributed, with the produce of the flocks, to the subsistance of man, it muft equally have been obferved how thofe vegetables multiplied; and the care muft have followed of collecting them nearer to the habitations; of feparating them from ufelefs vegetables, that they might occupy a foil to themfelves; of fecuring them from untamed beafts, from the flocks, and even from the rapacity of other men.

Thefe ideas muft have equally occurred, and even fooner, in more fertile countries, where the fpontaneous productions of the earth almoft fufficed of themfelves for the fupport of men; who now began to devote themfelves to agriculture.

agriculture In fuch a country, and under a happy climate, the fame fpace of ground produces, in corn, roots, and fruit, wherewith to maintain a greater number of men than if employed as pafturage. Accordingly, when the nature of the foil rendered not fuch cultivation too laborious, when the difcovery was made of employing therein thofe fame animals ufed by paftoral tribes for the tranfport

from

from place to place of themselves and their
effects, agriculture became the moft plentiful
fource of fubfiftance, the firft occupation of
men ; and the human race arrived at the third ₃ *Epoch*.
epoch of its progrefs.

There are people who have remained, from *Indians*
time immemorial, in one of the two ftates we *Negroes*
have defcribed. They have not only not *Tartars*.
rifen of themfelves to any higher degree of *Arabs*.
improvement, but the connections and commercial intercourfe they have had with nations
more civilized have failed to produce this
effect. Such connections and intercourfe have
communicated to them fome knowledge, fome
induftry, and a great many vices, but have
never been able to draw them from their ftate
of mental ftagnation.

The principal caufes of this phenomenon
are to be found in climate ; in habit; in the
fweets annexed to this ftate of almoft complete independence, an independence not to *Sweets of*
be equalled but in a fociety more perfect even *Independence*
than our own ; in the natural attachment of
man to opinions received from his infancy,
and to the cuftoms of his country; in the
averfion that ignorance feels to every fort of

novelty;

novelty; in bodily and more efpecially mental indolence, which fupprefs the feeble and as yet fcarcely exifting fpark of curiofity; and laftly, in the empire which fuperftition already exercifes over thefe infant focieties. To thefe caufes muft be added the avarice, cruelty, corruption and prejudices of polifhed nations, who appear to thefe people more powerful, more rich, more informed, more active, but at the fame time more vicious, and particularly lefs happy than themfelves. They muft frequently indeed have been lefs ftruck with the fuperiority of fuch nations, than terrified at the multiplicity and extent of their wants, the torments of their avarice, the never ceafing agitations of their ever active, ever infatiable paffions. This defcription of people has by fome philofophers been pitied, and by others admired and applauded: thefe have confidered as wifdom and virtue, what the former have called by the names of ftupidity and floth.

The queftion in debate between them will be refolved in the courfe of this work. It will there be feen why the progrefs of the mind has not been at all times accompanied

with

with an equal progrefs towards happinefs and virtue ; and how the leaven of prejudices and errors has polluted the good that fhould flow from knowledge, a good which depends more upon the purity of that knowledge than its extent. Then it will be found that the ftormy and arduous tranfition of a rude fo-ciety to the ftate of civilization of an en-lightened and free people, implies no degene-ration of the human fpecies, but is a neceffary crifis in its gradual advance towards abfolute perfection. Then it will be found that it is not the increafe of knowledge, but its de-cline, that has produced the vices of polifhed nations, and that, inftead of corrupting, it has in all cafes foftened, where it has been unable to correct or to change the manners of men.

civilization

a benefit.

D 4   THIRD

THIRD EPOCH.

Progrefs of Mankind from the Agricultural State to the Invention of Alphabetical Writing.

THE uniformity of the picture we have hitherto drawn will foon difappear; and we fhall no longer have to delineate thofe indiftinct features, thofe flight fhades of difference, that diftinguifh the manners, characters, opinions and fuperftitions of men, rooted, as it were, to their foil, and perpetuating almoft without mixture a fingle family.

Invafions, conquefts, the rife and overthrow of empires, will fhortly be feen mixing and confounding nations, fometimes difperfing them over a new territory, fometimes covering the fame fpot with different people.

Fortuitous events will continually interpofe, and derange the flow but regular movement of nature, often retarding, fometimes accelerating it.

The appearances we obferve in a nation in any particular age, have frequently their caufe

in

in a revolution happening ten ages before *True enough*
it, and at a diftance of a thoufand leagues; *but trite.*
and the night of time conceals a great portion
of thofe events, the influence of which we fee
operating upon the men who have preceded us, and fometimes extending to ourfelves.

But we have firft to confider the effects of
the change of which we are fpeaking, in a
fingle people, and independently of the influence that conquefts and the intermixture of
nations may have exercifed.

Agriculture attaches man to the foil which *Husbandry*
he cultivates. It is no longer his perfon, his *attaches men*
family, his implements for hunting, that it *to the Soil*
would fuffice him to tranfport; it is no longer
even his flocks which he might drive before
him. The ground not belonging in common
to all, he would find in his flight no fubfiftance, either for himfelf or the animals from
which he derives his fupport.

Each parcel of land has a mafter, to whom
alone the fruits of it belong. The harveft
exceeding the maintenance of the animals
and men by whom it has been prepared, furnifhes the proprietor with an annual wealth, *Surplus or*
that *due.*

that he has no neceſſity of purchaſing with
his perſonal labour.

In the two former ſtates of ſociety, every
individual, or every family at leaſt, practiſed
nearly all the neceſſary arts.

*operation
of the arts.
or
diviſion of
labour.*

But when there were men, who, without
labour, lived upon the produce of their land,
and others who received wages ; when occupations were multiplied, and the proceſſes
of the arts become more extenſive and complicate, common intereſt ſoon enforced a ſe-
paration of them. It was perceived, that the
induſtry of an individual, when confined to
fewer objects, was more complete ; that the
hand executed with greater readineſs and preciſion a ſmaller number of operations that
long habit had rendered more familiar ; that
a leſs degree of underſtanding was required
to perform a work well, when that work had
been more frequently repeated.

Accordingly, while one portion of men devoted themſelves to the labours of huſbandry,
others prepared the neceſſary inſtruments.
The care of the flocks, domeſtic economy,
and the making of different articles of apparel, became in like manner diſtinct em-
ployments.

ployments. As, in families poffeffing but
little property, one of thefe occupations was
infufficient of itfelf to engrofs the whole time
of an individual, feveral were performed by
the fame perfon, for which he received the
wages only of a fingle man. Soon the materials ufed in the arts increafing, and their
nature demanding different modes of treatment, fuch as were analogous in this refpect
became diftinct from the reft, and had a particular clafs of workmen. Commerce ex-
panded, embraced a greater number of objects, and derived them from a greater extent
of territory : and then was formed another
clafs of men, whofe fole occupation was the
purchafe of commodities for the purpofe of
preferving, tranfporting, or felling them again
with profit.

Thus to the three claffes of men before
diftinguifhable in paftoral life, that of pro-*Proprietors*
prietors, that of the domeftics of their family, *Domesties*
and laftly, that of flaves, we muft now add, *Slaves*
that of the different kinds of artifans, and *Artifans*
that of merchants. *Merchants*

Then it was, that, in a fociety more fixed,
more compact, and more intricate, the neceffity was felt of a more regular and more
ample

Laws ample code of legiflation; of determining
Punishment with greater precifion the punifhments for
crimes, and the forms to be obferved as to
Contract contracts; of fubjecting to feverer rules the
means of afcertaining and verifying the facts
Evidence. to which the law was to be applied.

This progrefs was the flow and gradual
work of neceffity and concurring circumftances: it is but a ftep or two farther in the
route we have already traced in paftoral
nations.

Education In the firft two epochs, education was
purely domeftic. The children were inftructed
by refiding with the father, in the common
labours that were followed, or the few arts
that were known. From him they received
the fmall number of traditions that formed
the hiftory of the horde or of the family, the
fables that had been tranfmitted, the knowledge of the national cuftoms, together with
the principles and prejudices that compofed
their petty code of morality. Singing, dancing
and military exercifes they acquired in the
fociety of their friends.

In the epoch at which we are arrived, the
children of the richer families received a fort
Common of common education, either in towns, from
con-

converfation with the old and experienced, or
in the houfe of a chief, to whom they attached themfelves. Here it was they were
inftructed in the laws, cuftoms and prejudices
of the country, and learned to chant poems
defcriptive of the events of its hiftory.

A more fedentary mode of life had introduced a greater equality between the fexes.
The wives were no longer confidered as fimple
objects of utility, as only the more familiar
flaves of their mafter. Man looked upon them
as companions, and faw how conducive
they might be made to his happinefs. Meanwhile, even in countries where they were
treated with moft refpect, where polygamy *Polygamy*
was profcribed, neither reafon nor juftice extended fo far as to an entire reciprocity as to
the right of divorce, and an equal infliction *Divorce*
of punifhment in cafes of infidelity.

The hiftory of this clafs of prejudices, and
of their influence on the lot of the human
fpecies, muft enter into the picture I have
propofed to draw; and nothing can better
evince how clofely man's happinefs is connected with the progrefs of reafon.

Some nations remained difperfed over the
country. Others united themfelves in towns,
which

which became the refidence of the common chief, called by a name anfwering to the word *king*, of the chiefs of tribes who partook his power, and of the elders of every great family. There the common affairs of the fociety were decided, as well as individual difputes. There the rich brought together the moft valuable part of his wealth, that it might be fecure from robbers, who muft of courfe have multiplied with fedentary riches. When nations remained difperfed over a territory, cuftom determined the time and place where the chiefs were to meet for deliberation upon the general interefts of the community, and the adjudication of fuits.

Nations who acknowledged a common origin, who fpoke the fame language, without abjuring war with each other, entered almoft univerfally into a confederacy more or lefs clofe, and agreed to unite themfelves, either againft foreign enemies, or mutually to avenge their wrongs, or to difcharge in common fome religious duty.

Hofpitality and commerce produced even fome lafting ties between nations different in origin, cuftoms and language; ties that by robbery and war were often diffolved, but

which

which neceffity, ftronger than the love of pillage or a thirft for vengeance, afterwards renewed.

To murder the vanquifhed, or to ftrip and reduce them to flavery, was no longer the only acknowledged right between nations inimical to each other. Ceffions of territory, ranfoms, tribute, in part fupplied the place of thefe barbarous outrages.

At this epoch every man that poffeffed arms was a foldier. He who had the beft, and beft knew how to exercife them, who could furnifh arms for others, upon condition that they followed him to the wars, and from the provifion he had amaffed was in a capacity to fupply their wants, neceffarily became a chief. But this obedience, almoft voluntary, did not involve them in a fervile dependence.

As there was feldom occafion for new laws; as there were no public expences to which the citizens were obliged to contribute, and fuch as it became neceffary to incur were defrayed out of the property of the chiefs, or the lands that were preferved in common; as the idea of reftricting induftry and commerce

by

by regulations was unknown; as offenſive war was decided by general conſent, or undertaken by thoſe only who were allured by the love of glory or deſire of pillage;—man believed himſelf free in theſe rude governments, notwithſtanding the hereditary ſucceſſion, almoſt univerſal, of their firſt chiefs or kings, and the prerogative, uſurped by other ſubordinate chiefs, of ſharing alone the political authority, and exerciſing the functions of government as well as of magiſtracy.

But frequently a king ſurrendered himſelf to the impulſe of perſonal vengeance, to the commiſſion of arbitrary acts of violence; frequently, in theſe privileged families, pride, hereditary hatred, the fury of love and thirſt for gold, engendered and multiplied crimes, while the chiefs aſſembled in towns, the inſtruments of the paſſions of kings, excited therein factions and civil wars, oppreſſed the people by iniquitous judgments, and tormented them by the enormities of their ambition and rapacity.

In many nations the exceſſes of theſe families exhauſted the patience of the people, who accordingly extirpated, baniſhed, or ſubjected

jected them to the common law; it was rarely that their title, with a limited authority, was preferved to them; and we fee take place what has fince been called by the name of *Republics* republics.

In other places, thefe kings, furrounded with minions, becaufe they had arms and treafures to beftow on them, exercifed an abfolute authority: and fuch was the origin *Defpotifms.* of tyranny.

Elfewhere, particularly in countries where the fmall nations did not unite together in towns, the firft forms of thofe crude infti-tutions were preferved, till the period in which thefe people, either fell under the yoke of a conqueror, or, inftigated by the fpirit of robbery, fpread themfelves over a foreign territory.

This tyranny, compreffed within too narrow a fpace, could have but a fhort duration. The people foon threw off a yoke which force alone impofed, and opinion had been unable to maintain. The monfter was feen too nearly not to excite more horror than dread: and force as well as opinion could forge no durable chains, if tyrants did not extend their

E   empire

empire to a diftance fufficiently great to be able, by dividing the nation they oppreffed, to conceal from it the fecret of its own power and of their weaknefs.

The hiftory of republics belongs to the next epoch: but that which we are confidering will prefently exhibit a new fpectacle.

olonies An agricultural people, fubjected to a foreign power, does not abandon its hearths: neceffity obliges it to labour for its mafters.

Sometimes the ruling nation contents itfelf with leaving, upon the conquered territory, chiefs to govern, foldiers to defend it, and efpecially to keep in awe the inhabitants, and with exacting from the fubmiffive and dif-armed fubjects a tribute in money or in pro-vifion.

Sometimes it feizes upon the territory it-felf, diftributing the property of it to the officers and foldiers: in that cafe it annexes to each eftate the old occupiers that culti-vated it, and fubjects them to this new kind of flavery, which is regulated by laws more or lefs rigorous. Military fervice, and a tri-bute from the individuals of the conquered people, are the conditions upon which the

enjoy-

enjoyment of thefe lands is granted to them.

Sometimes the ruling nation referves to it-felf the property of the territory, and diftri-butes only the ufufruct upon the fame con-ditions as in the preceding inftance.

Commonly, however, all thefe modes of re-compenfing the inftruments of conqueft, and of robbing the vanquifhed, are adopted at the fame time.

Hence we fee new claffes of men fpring up ; the defcendants of the conquering na-tion and thofe of the oppreffed ; an hereditary *Nobility* nobility, not however to be confounded with the patrician dignity of republics ; a people *Patricians* condemned to labour, to dependence, to a *A People* ftate of degradation, but not to flavery ; and laftly, flaves attached to the glebe, a clafs dif- *Slaves* fering from that of domeftic flaves, whofe fervitude is lefs arbitrary, and who may ap-peal againft the caprices of their mafters to the law.

It is here alfo we may obferve the origin of the feodal fyftem, a peft that has not been *Feodal fys* peculiar to our own climate, but has found a *tem* footing in almoft every part of the globe, at

the

the fame periods of civilization, and whenever a country has been occupied by two
people between whom victory has eftablifhed
an hereditary inequality.

potifm In fine, defpotifm was alfo the fruit of conqueft. By defpotifm I here mean, in order
to diftinguifh it from tyrannies of a tranfient
duration, the oppreffion of a people by a
fingle man, who governs it by opinion, by
habit, and above all, by a military force, over
the individuals of which he exercifes himfelf
an arbitrary authority, but at the fame time is
obliged to refpect their prejudices, flatter their
caprices, and footh their avidity and pride.

Perfonally guarded by a numerous and
felect portion of this armed force, taken from
the conquering nation or confifting of foreigners ; immediately furrounded by the moft
powerful military chiefs ; holding the provinces in awe by means of generals who have
the control of inferior detachments of this
gns by term fame armed body, the defpot reigns by terror:
nor is the poffibility conceived, either by the
depreffed people, or any of thofe difperfed
d to him chiefs, rivals as they are to each other, of
in their bringing againft this man a force, which the
t.   armies

armies he has at his command would not be
able to crush at the inftant.

A mutiny of the guards, an infurrection in *Mutiny*
the capital, may be fatal to the defpot, without *Sedition*
crushing defpotifm. The general of an army,
by deftroying a family rendered facred by prejudice, may eftablish a new dynafty, but it is *Dynafty.*
only to exercife a fimilar tyranny.

In this third epoch, the people who have *When? When*
yet not experienced the misfortune, either of *not fuch a*
conquering, or of being conquered, exhibit a *People? when*
picture of thofe fimple but ftrong virtues of *is their Hiſto*
agricultural nations, thofe manners of heroic *their hrale*
times, rendered fo interefting by a mixture of *tim, or hable*
greatnefs and ferocity, of generofity and bar- *This is all*
barifm, that we are ftill fo far feduced as to *fiction.*
admire and even regret them.

On the contrary, in empires founded by *Empire.s*
conquerors, we are prefented with a picture *founded by*
containing all the gradations and fhades of *Conquerors*
that abafement and corruption, to which defpotifm and fuperftition can reduce the human
fpecies. There we fee fpring up taxes upon *all this*
induftry and commerce, exactions obliging a *fee in*
man to purchafe the right of employing as he *every from*
pleafes his own faculties, laws reftricting him *mervil the*

E 3 *in tim, however*

*founded, – and fhall fee it, Thou art a Quack, for
dov ut.*

in the choice of his labour and ufe of his property, other laws compelling the children to
follow the profeffion of their parents, confif-
cations, cruel and atrocious punifhments, in
fhort, all thofe acts of arbitrary power, of le-
galized tyranny, of fuperftitious wickednefs,
that a contempt of human nature has been
able to invent. *and that wickednefs like yours*
on does it has accufed it not justified In hordes that have not undergone any
confiderable revolution, we may obferve the
progrefs of civilization ftopping at no very
elevated point. Meanwhile men already felt
the want of new ideas or fenfations ; a want   *'ant of*
which is the firft moving power in the pro-   *'ovelty.*
grefs of the human mind, equally awakening
a tafte for the fuperfluities of luxury, inciting
induftry and a fpirit of curiofity, and piercing
with an eager eye the veil with which nature has concealed her fecrets. But it has
happened, almoft univerfally, that, to efcape
this want, men have fought, and embraced
with a kind of phrenzy, phyfical means of
procuring fenfations that may be continually
renewed. Such is the practice of ufing fer-
mented liquors, hot drinks, opium, tobacco,   *'pirits, Opium*
and betel. There are few nations among   *'obacco Betel*
whom

whom one or other of thefe practices is not
obferved, from which is derived a pleafure
that occupies whole days, or is repeated at
every interval, that prevents the weight of
time from being felt, fatisfies the neceffity of
having the faculties roufed or employed, and
at laft blunting the edge of this neceffity, thus
prolongs the duration of the infancy and inac-
tivity of the human mind. Thefe practices,
which have proved an obftacle to the progrefs of ignorant and enflaved nations, produce alfo their effects in wifer and more civilized countries, preventing truth from dif-
fufing through all claffes of men a pure and
equal light.

I doubt. Some are faid to one all their genii to them. Guard from Paine & others.

By expofing what was the ftate of the arts
in the firft two periods of fociety, it will be
feen how to thofe of working wood, ftone,
or the bones of animals, of preparing fkins,
and weaving cloths, thefe infant people were
able to add the more difficult ones of dyeing,
of making earthen ware, and even their firft
attempts upon metals.

In ifolated nations the progrefs of thefe
arts muft have been flow ; but the intercourfe,
flight as it was, which took place between

them,

them, ferved to haften it. A new method of
proceeding, a better contrivance, difcovered
by one people, became common to its neighbours. Conqueft, which has fo often deftroyed the arts, began with extending, and
contributed to the improving of them, before
it ftopped their progrefs, or was inftrumental
to their fall.

We obferve many of thefe arts carried to
the higheft degree of perfection in countries,
where the long influence of fuperftition and
defpotifm has completed the degradation of
all the human faculties. But, if we fcrutinife
the wonderful productions of this fervile induftry, we fhall find nothing in them which
The God Ge- announces the <u>infpiration of genius</u>; all the
nius again. improvements appear to be the flow and
painful work of reiterated practice; every
where may be feen, amidft this labour which
aftonifhes us, marks of ignorance and ftupidity that difclofe its origin.

Aftronomy In fedentary and peaceable focieties, aftro-
Medicine nomy, medicine, the moft fimple notions of
Anatomy anatomy, the knowledge of plants and mine-
Botany rals, the firft elements of the ftudy of the
Mineralogy phenomena of nature, acquired fome im-
prove-

provement, or rather extended themfelves by the mere influence of time, which, increafing the ftock of obfervations, led, in a manner flow, but fure, to the eafy and almoft inftant perception of fome of the general confequences to which thofe obfervations were calculated to lead.

Meanwhile this improvement was extremely flender; and the fciences would have remained for a longer period in a ftate of earlieft infancy, if certain families, and efpecially particular cafts, had not made them the firft foundation of their reputation and power.

Already the obfervation of man and of focieties had been connected with that of nature. Already a fmall number of moral maxims, of a practical, as well as a political kind, had been tranfmitted from generation to generation. Thefe were feized upon by thofe cafts : religious ideas, prejudices, and different fuperftitions contributed to a ftill farther increafe of their power. They fucceeded the firft affociations, or firft families, of empirics and forcerers ; but they practifed more art to deceive and feduce the mind, which was now lefs rude and ignorant. The knowledge they
actually

actually poffeffed, the apparent aufterity of
their lives, an affected contempt for what
was the object of the defircs of vulgar men,
end to their gave weight <u>to their impoftures,</u> while thefe
honeſt from impoftures at the fame time rendered facred,
munications in the eyes of the people, their flender ftock
of uſeful knew of knowledge, and their hypocritical virtues.
edge too. The members of thefe focieties purfued at
firft, almoft with equal ardour, two very dif-
you omit ferent objects: one, that of acquiring for
all the good themfelves new information ; the other, that
and take only of employing fuch as they had already ac-
the evil. quired in <u>deceiving</u> the people, and gaining
informing the an afcendancy over their minds.
People and do Their fages devoted their attention particu-
ing them good. larly to aftronomy : and, as far as we can
judge from the fcattered remains of the monuments of their labours, they appear to have
carried it to the higheft poffible pitch to which,
without the aid of telefcopes, without the affiftance of mathematical theories fuperior to
the firft elements, it can be fuppofed to arrive.

In reality, by means of a continued courfe
of obfervations, an idea fufficiently accurate of
the motion of the ftars may be acquired, by
which

which to calculate and predict the phenomena
of the heavens. Thofe empirical laws, fo
much the eafier attained as the attention becomes extended through a greater fpace of
time, did not indeed lead thefe firft aftronomers to the difcovery of the general laws of
the fyftem of the univerfe ; but they fufficiently fupplied their place for every purpofe
that might intereft the wants or curiofity of
man, and ferve to augment the credit of thefe
ufurpers of the exclufive right of inftructing *There never*
him. *was one of them more arrogant or more mischie-*
vous than they self, or on derict, or more empirical.

It fhould feem that to them we are indebted for the ingenious idea of arithmetical
fcales, that happy mode of reprefenting all
poffible numbers by a fmall quantity of figns, *Thofe more*
and of executing, by technical operations of *Benefactors*
a very fimple nature, calculations which the *indeed, to*
human intellect, left to itfelf, could not have *Man,*
reached. This is the firft example of thofe
contrivances that double the powers of the
mind, by means of which it can extend indefinitely its limits, without its being poffible to
fay to it, thus far fhalt thou go, and no farther.

But they do not appear to have extended
the fcience of arithmetic beyond its firft opera- *Arithmetic*
tions.

Their

Geometry Their geometry, including what was neceffary for furveying, as well as for the practice
of aftronomy, is bounded by that celebrated
problem which Pythagoras carried with him
into Greece, or difcovered anew.

Machines The conftructing of machines they refigned
to thofe by whom the machines were to be
ufed. Some recitals, however, in which there
is a mixture of fable, feem to indicate their
having cultivated themfelves this branch of
the fciences, and employed it as one of the
means of ſtriking upon the mind by a femblance of prodigy.

The laws of motion, the fcience of the mechanical powers, attracted not their notice.

If they ftudied medicine and furgery, that
part efpecially the object of which is the
treatment of wounds, anatomy was neglected
by them.

Their knowledge in botany, and in natural hiftory, was confined to the articles ufed
as remedies, and to fome plants and minerals,
the fingular properties of which might affift
their projects.

Their chymiftry, reduced to the moft fimple proceffes, without theory, without method, without analyfis, confifted in the making
certain

certain preparations, in the knowledge of a
few fecrets relative to medicine or the arts, or
in the acquifition of fome noftrums calculated
to dazzle an ignorant multitude, fubjected to *In this they*
chiefs not lefs ignorant than itfelf. *refembled thee and*

The progrefs of the fciences they confidered *thy Parifian*
but as a fecondary object, as an inftrument *Philosophes.*
of perpetuating or extending their power. *This is as*
They fought Truth only to diffufe errors; and *applicable to*
it is not to be wondered they fo feldom found *thee as to thee*
her.

In the mean time, flow and feeble as was
this progrefs of every kind, it would not
have been attainable, if thefe men had not
known the art of writing, the only way by *Writing.*
which traditions can be rendered fecure and
permanent, and knowledge, in proportion as
it increafes, be communicated and tranfmitted
to pofterity.

Accordingly, hieroglyphic writing was *Hieroglyphics.*
either one of their firft inventions, or had
been difcovered prior to the formation of
cafts affuming to themfelves the prerogative *Cafts.*
of inftruction.

As the view of thefe cafts was not to en- *This also*
lighten, but to govern the mind, they not *was thy*
only *View, and*
that of thy affociates & Colleagues.

only avoided communicating to the people the whole of their knowledge, but adulterated with errors fuch portions as they thought proper to difclofe. They taught not what they believed to be true, but what they thought favourable to their own ends.

Just as you intended to Illuminations & Inspirations of Genius Superior to other Men. Every thing which the people received from them had in it a ftrange mixture of fomething fupernatural, facred, celeftial, which led thefe men to be regarded as beings fuperior to humanity, as invefted with a divine character, as deriving from heaven itfelf information prohibited to the reft of mankind.

Thefe men had therefore two doctrines, one for themfelves, the other for the people. Frequently even, as they were divided into many orders, each order referved to itfelf its own *As you and your friends were Knaves & Dupes to orleans* myfteries. All the inferior orders were at once both knaves and dupes ; and it was only by a few adepts that all the mazes of this hypocritical fyftem were underftood and developed.

No circumftance proved more favourable to *Double Doctrine* the eftablifhment of this double doctrine, than the changes which time, and the intercourfe and mixture of nations, introduced into language.

guage. The double-doctrine men, preferving *Catholic Chh.*
the old language, or that of another nation,
thereby fecured the advantage of having one
that was underftood only by themfelves.

The firft mode of writing, which reprefented things by a painting more or lefs
accurate, either of the thing itfelf or of an
analogous object, giving place to a more
fimple mode, in which the refemblance of
thefe objects was nearly effaced, in which
fcarcely any figns were employed, but fuch as
were in a manner purely conventional, the
fecret doctrine came to have a writing, as it
had before a language to itfelf.

In the origin and upon the firft introduction of language, almoft every word is a
metaphor, and every phrafe an allegory. The
mind catches at once both the figurative and
natural fenfe; the word fuggefts at the fame
inftant with the idea, the analogous image by
which it has been expreffed. But from the habit
of employing a word in a figurative fenfe, the
mind alternately fixed upon that alone, heed-
lefs of the original meaning: and thus the
figurative fenfe of a word became gradually
its proper and ordinary fignification.

The

The priests by whom the first allegorical language was preserved, employed it with the people, who were no longer capable of discovering its true meaning; and who, accustomed to take words in one acceptation only, that generally received, pictured to themselves I know not what absurd and ridiculous fables, in expressions that conveyed to the minds of the priests but a plain and simple truth. The same use was made by the priests of their sacred writing. The people saw men, animals, monsters, where the priests meant only to represent an astronomical phenomenon, an historical occurrence of the year.

Thus, for example, the priests, in their contemplations, invented, and introduced almost every where, the metaphysical system of a great, immense and eternal ALL, of which the whole of the beings that existed were only parts, of which the various changes observable in the universe were but modifications. The heavens struck them in no other light than as groupes of stars dispersed through the immensity of space, planets describing motions more or less complicate, and phenomena

2   purely

purely phyſical reſulting from their reſpective poſitions. They affixed names to theſe conſtellations and planets, as well as to the fixed or moveable circles, invented with a view to repreſent their ſituation and courſe, and explain their appearances.

But the language, the memorials, employed in expreſſing theſe metaphyſical opinions, theſe natural truths, exhibited to the eyes of the people the moſt extravagant fyſtem of mythology, and became the foundation of *Mythology* creeds the moſt abſurd, modes of worſhip the moſt ſenſelefs, and practices the moſt ſhameful and barbarous.

Such is the origin of almoſt all the re- *Religious* ligions that are known to us, and which the hypocriſy or the extravagance of their inventors and their proſelytes afterwards loaded with new fables.

Theſe caſts ſeized upon education, that they might faſhion man to a more patient endurance of chains, embodied as it were with his exiſtence, and extirpate the poſſibility of his deſiring to break them. But, if we would know to what point, even without the aid of ſuperſtitious terrors, theſe inſtitutions, ſo de-

F   ſtructive

ſtructive to the human faculties, can extend
their baneful power, we muſt look for a moment to China; to that people who ſeem to
have preceded all others in the arts and
ſciences, only to ſee themſelves ſucceſſively
eclipſed by them all; to that people whom
the knowledge of artillery has not prevented
from being conquered by barbarous nations;
where the ſciences, of which the numerous
ſchools are open to every claſs of citizens,
alone lead to dignities, and at the ſame time,
fettered by abſurd prejudices, are condemned
to an eternal mediocrity; laſtly, where even
the invention of printing has remained an inſtrument totally uſeleſs in advancing the progreſs of the human mind.

Men, whoſe intereſt it was to deceive, ſoon
felt a diſlike to the purſuit of truth. Content
with the docility of the people, they conceived there was no need of further means to
ſecure its continuance. By degrees they for-
got a part of the truths concealed under their
allegories; they preſerved no more of their
ancient ſcience than was ſtrictly neceſſary to
maintain the confidence of their diſciples; and
at laſt they became themſelves the _dupes of
their own fables._

the Dupes of your own Atheiſm Then
*gaety, your nonsensical Notions of Liberty
and Fraternity. — You were all as ignorant
and Government and much more
so than thoſe you censure so much.*

Then was all progrefs of the fciences at a *God grant*
ftand; fome even of thofe which had been *that your*
enjoyed by preceding ages, were loft to the *extravagance*
generations that followed; and the human *may not intro*
mind, a prey to ignorance and prejudice, was *duce another*
condemned, in thofe vaft empires, to a fhame- *fuch age of*
ful ftagnation, of which the uniform and un- *Darkne/s.*
varied continuance has fo long been a dif-
honour to Afia.

The people who inhabit thefe countries are *Europe will*
the only inftance that is to be met with of *be another*
fuch civilization and fuch decline. Thofe who *if your*
occupy the reft of the globe either have been *Plans are pur-*
ftopped in their career, and exhibit an ap- *sued.*
pearance that again brings to our memory the
infant days of the human race, or they have
been hurried by events through the periods
of which we have ftill to illuftrate the
hiftory.

At the epoch we are confidering, thefe
very people of Afia had invented alphabetical *Afia invented*
writing, which they fubftituted in the place *Alphabet.*
of hieroglyphics, probably after having employed that other mode, in which conventional
figns are affixed to every idea, which is the
only one that the Chinefe are at prefent acquainted with.

Hiftory

Hiſtory and reflection may throw ſome light upon the manner in which the gradual tranſition from hieroglyphics to this intermediary ſort of art, muſt have taken place ; but nothing can inform us with preciſion either in what country, or at what time, alphabetical writing was firſt brought into uſe.

The diſcovery was in time introduced into Greece, among a people who have exerciſed ſo powerful and happy an influence on the progreſs of the human ſpecies, whoſe genius has opened all the avenues to truth, whom nature had prepared, whom fate had deſtined to be the benefactor and guide of all nations and all ages : an honour in which no other people has hitherto ſhared. One only nation has ſince dared to entertain the hope of preſiding in a revolution new in the deſtiny of mankind. And this glory both nature and a concurrence of events ſeem to agree in reſerving for her. But let us not ſeek to penetrate what an uncertain futurity as yet conceals from us.

[handwritten marginal notes:] Greece. as much as I love, esteem and admire the Greeks, I believe the Hebrews have done more to enlighten and civilize the world. Moses did more than their legislators & others together. Ah! let us conceal a veil over this awful scene.

FOURTH

Progrefs of the Human Mind in Greece, till the Divifion of the Sciences about the Age of Alexander.

THE Greeks, difgufted with thofe kings, who, calling themfelves the children of the Gods, difgraced humanity by their paffions and crimes, became divided into republics, of which Lacedemonia was the only one that *Lacedemon* acknowledged hereditary chiefs : but thefe chiefs were kept in awe by other magiftracies, were fubjected, like citizens, to the laws, and were weakened by the divifion of royalty be-tween the two branches of the family of the Heraclides.

The inhabitants of Macedonia, of Theffaly, and of Epirus, allied to the Greeks by a common origin and the ufe of a fimilar lan-guage, and governed by princes weak, and divided among themfelves, though unable to opprefs Greece, were yet fufficient to pre-ferve it at the north from the incurfions of Scythian nations.

F 3   At

At the weſt, Italy, divided into ſmall and unconnected ſtates, could occaſion no apprehenſions ; and already nearly the whole of Sicily, and the moſt delightful parts of the ſouth of Italy, were occupied by Greek colonies, forming independent republics, but preſerving at the ſame time ties of filiation with their mother countries. Other colonies were eſtabliſhed in the iſlands of the Ægean ſea, and upon part of the coaſts of Aſia-Minor.

Greek Colonies

Accordingly the union of this part of the Aſiatic continent to the vaſt empire of Cyrus, was in the ſequel the only real danger that could threaten the independence of Greece, and the freedom of its inhabitants.

Tyranny, though more durable in ſome colonies, and in thoſe particularly the eſtabliſhment of which had preceded the extirpation of the royal families, could be conſidered only as a tranſient and partial evil, that inflicted miſery on the inhabitants of a few towns, but without influencing the general ſpirit of the nation.

The Greeks had derived from the eaſtern nations their arts, a part of their information, the uſe of alphabetical writing, and their ſyſtem

tem of religion : but it was in confequence of *Greeks brought* the intercourfe eftablifhed between herfelf and *these laby* thefe nations by exiles, who fought an afy-*from the East.* lum in Greece, and by Greek travellers, who brought back with them from the Eaft knowledge and errors.

The fciences, therefore, could not become *law in (country* in this country the occupation and patrimony *has it been so* of an individual caft. The functions of the *in Wales?. in* priefts were confined to the worfhip of the *China?* Gods. Genius might difplay all its energies, *Aye the God* without being fettered by the pedantic ob-*Genius could* fervances, the fyftematic hypocrify of a fa-*govern: but has* cerdotal college. All men poffeffed an equal right to the knowledge of truth. All might engage in the purfuit of it, and communicate it to all, not in fcraps and parcels, but in its whole extent.

This fortunate circumftance, ftill more than political freedom, wrought in the human mind, among the Greeks, an independance, the fureft pledge of the rapidity and greatnefs of its future progrefs.

In the mean time their learned men, their fages, as they were called, but who foon *Sages* took the more modeft appellation of philofo- *O. ilosophus*

F 4   phers,

They had not the Presumption and the Conduct and go to claim a Monopoly of Genius. phers, or friends of fcience and wifdom, wan-dered in the immenfity of the too vaſt and comprehenſive plan which they had embraced. They were defirous of penetrating both the na-ture of man, and that of the Gods ; the origin of the world, as well as of the human race. They endeavoured to reduce all nature to one principle only, and the phenomena of the univerſe to one law. They attempted to in-*+ or is this? the golden rule?* clude, in a fingle rule of conduct, all the du-ties of morality, and the fecret of true happi-neſs.

Thus, inſtead of difcovering truths, they forged fyſtems ; they neglected the obferva-tion of facts, to purfue the chimeras of their imagination ; and being no longer able to fupport their opinions with proofs, they fought to defend them by fubtleties.

Geometry and aſtronomy, however, were cultivated with fuccefs by thefe men. Greece owed to them the firſt elements of thefe fci-ences, and even fome new truths, or at leaſt the knowledge of fuch as they had brought with them from the Eaſt, not as eſtabliſhed creeds, but as theories, of which they under-ſtood the principles and proofs.

We

We even perceive, in the midft of the
darknefs of thofe fyftems, two happy ideas
beam forth, which will again make their appearance in more enlightened ages.

Democritus confidered all the phenomena *Democritus*
of the univerfe as the refult of the combinations and motion of fimple bodies, of a fixed
and unalterable form, having received an original impulfe, and thence derived a quantity
of action that undergoes modifications in the
individual atoms, but that in the entire mafs
continues always the fame.

Pythagoras was of opinion that the uni- *Pythagoras*
verfe was governed by a harmony, the principles of which were to be unfolded by the
properties of numbers ; that is, that the whole
phenomena of nature depended upon general
laws capable of being afcertained by calculation.

In thefe two doctrines we readily perceive
the bold fyftems of Defcartes, and the philo- *Defcartes*
fophy of Newton. *Newton*

Pythagoras either difcovered by his own *Pythagoras*
meditation, or learned from the priefts of
Egypt or of Italy, the actual difpofition of
the heavenly bodies, and the true fyftem of the
world.

world. This he communicated to the Greeks. But the fyftem was too much at variance with the teftimony of the fenfes, too oppofite to the vulgar opinions, for the feeble proofs by which it could then be fupported to gain much hold upon the mind. Accordingly it was confined to the Pythagorean fchool, and afterwards forgotten with that fchool, again to appear at the clofe of the fixteenth century, ftrengthened with more certain proofs, by which it now triumphed not only over the repugnance of the fenfes, but over the prejudices of fuperftition, ftill more powerful and dangerous.

The Pythagorean fchool was chiefly prevalent in Upper Greece, where it formed legiflators, and intrepid defenders of the rights of mankind. It fell under the power of the tyrants, one of whom burnt the Pythagoreans in their own fchool. This was fufficient, no doubt, to induce them not to abjure philofophy, not to abandon the caufe of the people, but to bear no longer a name become fo dangerous, or obferve forms that would ferve only to wake the lion rage of the enemies of liberty and of reafon.

A

. A grand bafis of every kind of found philofophy is to form for each fcience a precife
and accurate language, every term of which
fhall reprefent an idea exactly determined and *Locke*
circumfcribed; and to enable ourfelves to determine and circumfcribe the ideas with which
the fcience may be converfant, by the mode of
a rigorous analyfis.

The Greeks on the contrary took advantage
of the corruptions of their common language
to play upon the meaning of words, to embarrafs the mind by contemptible equivoques,
and lead it aftray by exprefling fuccellively
different ideas by the fame fign : a practice
which gave acutenefs to the mind, at the
fame time that it weakened its ftrength againft
chimerical difficulties. Thus this philofophy
of words, by filling up the fpaces where
human reafon feems to ftop before fome obftacle above its ftrength, did not affift immediately its progrefs and advancement, but it
prepared the way for them ; as we fhall have
farther occafion to obferve.

The courfe of philofophy was ftopped from
its firft introduction by an error at that time
indeed excufable. This was the fixing the
attention

attention upon queſtions incapable perhaps
for ever of being ſolved ;. ſuffering the
mind to be led away by the importance or
ſublimity of objects, without thinking whether
the means exiſted of compaſſing them ; wiſh-
ing to eſtabliſh theories, before facts had been
collected, and to frame the univerſe, before
it was yet known how to ſurvey it. Accordingly we ſee Socrates, while he combated
the ſophiſts and expoſed their vain ſubtleties
to ridicule, crying to the Greeks to recal to
the earth this philoſophy which had loſt itſelf in the clouds. Not that he deſpiſed
either aſtronomy, or geometry, or the obſervation of the phenomena of nature ; not
that he entertained the puerile and falſe idea
of reducing the human mind to the ſtudy of
morality alone : on the contrary, it was to
his ſchool and his diſciples that the mathematical and phyſical ſciences were indebted for
their progreſs ; in the ridicule attempted to
be thrown upon him in theatrical repreſen-
tations, the reproach which afforded moſt
pleaſantry was that of his cultivating geometry, ſtudying meteors, drawing geographical charts, and making experiments upon
burning,

(77)

burning-glaſſes, of which, it is pleaſant to *burning glaſs* remark, the earlieſt mention that has been tranſmitted to us, we owe to a buffoonery *Ariſtophanes* of Ariſtophanes.

Socrates merely wiſhed by his advice to induce men to confine themſelves to objects which nature ,has placed within their reach ; to be ſure of every ſtep already taken before they attempted any new one, and to ſtudy the ſpace that ſurrounded them, before they precipitated themſelves at random into an unknown ſpace.

The death of this man is an important *death of* event in the hiſtory of the human mind. It is *Socrates.* the firſt crime that the war between philoſo-*war bet.* phy and ſuperſtition conceived and brought *Superſtition* forth. *and Philoſophy.*

The burning of the Pythagorean ſchool *Tyranny v.* had already ſignalized the war, not leſs an-*Philoſophy.* cient, not leſs eager, of the oppreſſors of mankind againſt philoſophy. The one and *your Philo-* the other will continue to be waged as long *ſophy, (on* as there ſhall exiſt priefts or kings upon the *dorſet, has* earth ; and theſe wars will occupy a conſpi-*waged a more* cuous place in the picture that we have ſtill *cruel war* to delineate. *againſt Ink*

there war was attempted by Priefts *King or*

Priest.

Priefts faw with grief the appearance of men, who, cultivating the powers of reafon, afcending to firft principles, could not but difcover all the abfurdity of their dogmas, all the extravagance of their ceremonies, all the delufion and fraud of their oracles and pro-digies. This difcovery they were afraid thefe philofophers would communicate to the difci-ples that frequented their fchools ; from whom it might pafs to all thofe who, to obtain autho-rity or credit, were obliged to pay attention to the improvement of their minds ; and thus the prieftly empire be reduced to the moft ig-norant clafs of the people, which might at laft be itfelf alfo undeceived.

Hypocrify, alarmed and terrified, haftened to bring accufations, againft the philofophers, of impiety to the Gods, that they might not have time to teach the people that thofe Gods were the work of their priefts. The philo-fophers thought to efcape perfecution by adopting, in imitation of the priefts them-felves, the practice of a double doctrine, and they confided to fuch of their difciples only whofe fidelity had been proved, doctrines' that too openly offended vulgar prejudices.

But

But the priefts reprefented to the people
the moft fimple truths of natural philofophy
as blafphemies; and Anaxagoras was profe- *Anaxagoras*.
cuted for having dared to affert, that the fun
was larger than Peloponnefus.

Socrates could not efcape their fury. There *Socrates*
was in Athens no longer a Pericles to watch *Pericles, and was*
over the fafety of genius and of virtue. Be- *not a good*
fides, Socrates was ftill more culpable. His *Sans culotte*
enmity to the fophifts, and his zeal to bring- *view he protects*
back the attention of mifguided philofophy *the God Genius.*
to the moft ufeful objects, announced to the
priefts that truth alone was the end he had in *Truth*
view; that he did not wifh to enforce upon
men a new fyftem, and fubject their imagination to his; but that he was defirous of
teaching them to make ufe of their own rea- *Reason*
fon: and of all crimes this is what facerdotal pride knows leaft how to pardon.

It was at the very foot of the tomb of Socrates that Plato dictated the leffons which *Plato*
he had received from his mafter.

His enchanting ftile, his brilliant imagination, the cheerful or dignified colouring, the
ingenious and happy traits, that, in his dialogues, difpel the drynefs of philofophical
difcuffion;

2

difcuffion ; the maxims of a mild and pure morality which he knew how to infufe into them ; the art with which he brings his per- fonages into action, and preferves to each his diftinct character ; all thofe beauties, which time and the revolutions of opinion have been unable to tarnifh, muft doubtlefs have obtained a favourable reception for the vifion- ary ideas that too often form the bafis of his works, and that abufe of words which his mafter had fo much cenfured in the fophifts, but from which he could not preferve the firft of his difciples.

In reading thefe dialogues we are aftonifhed at their being the production of a philofopher who, by an infcription placed on the door of his fchool, forbad the entrance of any one who had not ftudied geometry ; and that he, who maintains with fuch confidence fyftems fo far fetched and fo frivolous, fhould have been the founder of a fect by whom, for the firft time, the foundations of the certainty of human knowledge were fubjected to a fevere examination, and even others made to trem- ble that a more enlightened reafon might have been induced to refpect.

But

But the contradiction difappears when we
confider that in his dialogues Plato never fpeaks
in his own perfon ; that Socrates, his mafter,
is made to exprefs himfelf with the modefty of
doubt ; that the fyftems are exhibited in the
names of thofe who were, or whom Plato
fuppofed to be, the authors of them ; that
hereby thefe dialogues are a fchool of pyrrho- *Pyrrhonifm*
nifm, and that Plato has known how to dif-
play in them at once the adventurous imagination of a learned man, amufing himfelf
with combining and diffecting fplendid hypothefes, and the referve of a philofopher, giving
fcope to his fancy, but without fuffering himfelf to be hurried away by it ; becaufe his
reafon, armed with a falutary doubt, had
wherewithal to defend itfelf againft illufions,
however feducing might be their charms.

The fchools, in which were perpetuated *Schools*
the doctrine, and efpecially the principles and
forms of a firft inftitutor, to which however
the refpective fucceffors by no means obferved
a fervile adherence, thefe fchools poffeffed
the advantage of uniting together, by the
ties of a liberal fraternity, men intent upon
penetrating the fecrets of nature. If the opi-

nion of the mafter had frequently an influence
in them that ought to belong only to the
province of reafon, and the progrefs of knowledge was thereby fufpended; yet did they
ftill more contribute to its fpeedy and extenfive propagation, at a time when, printing
being unknown, and manufcripts exceedingly
rare, thefe inftitutions, the fame of which attracted pupils from every part of Greece,
were the only powerful means of cherifhing
in that country a tafte for philofophy, and
of difleminating new truths.

The rival fchools contended with a degree
of animofity that produced a fpirit of party
or fect; and not feldom was the intereft of
truth facrificed to the fuccefs of fome tenet,
in which every member of the fect confidered
his pride in a manner as concerned. The perfonal paffion of making converts corrupted
the more generous one of enlightening mankind. But at the fame time, this rivalfhip
kept the mind in a ftate of activity that was
not without its ufe. The continual fight of
fuch difputes, the intereft that was taken in
thefe combats of opinion, awakened and attached to the ftudy of philofophy a multitude

of

of men, whom the mere love of truth could
neither have allured from their bufinefs and
pleafure, nor even have roufed from their
indolence.

In fhort, as thefe fchools, thefe fects, which
the Greeks had the wifdom never to introduce into the public inftitutions, remained
perfectly free; as every one had the power
of opening another fchool, or forming a new
fect, at his pleafure, there was no caufe to
apprehend that abafement of reafon, which,
with the majority of other nations, was an
infurmountable obftacle to the advancement
of the human mind.

Let us confider what was the influence of
the philofophers of Greece on the underftanding, manners, laws and governments of
that country; an influence that muft be afcribed
in great meafure to their not having, and
even not wifhing to have, a political exiftence; to its being held as a rule of conduct
common to almoft all their fects, voluntarily
to keep aloof from public affairs; and laftly,
to their affecting to diftinguifh themfelves
from other men by their lives, as well as
their opinions.

G 2　　　　　　　In

In delineating thefe different fects, we fhall attend lefs to the fyftems, and more to the principles of their philofophy; we fhall not attempt, as has frequently been done, to exhibit a precife view of the abfurd doctrines which a language become almoft unintelligible conceals from us ; but fhall endeavour to fhew by what general errors they were feduced into thofe deceitful paths, and to find the origin of thefe in the natural courfe of the human mind.

Above all things we fhall be careful to difplay the progrefs of thofe fciences that really deferved the appellation, and the fucceffive improvements that were introduced into them.

At this epoch philofophy embraced them all, medicine excepted, which was already *'Ippocrates* feparated from it. The writings of Hippocrates will fhew us what was at that period the ftate of this fcience, as well as of thofe naturally connected with it, but which had yet no exiftence diftinct from that connection.

The mathematical fciences had been culti*Thales* vated with fuccefs in the fchools of Thales and of Pythagoras. Meanwhile they rofe

there

there very little above the point at which they
had ftopped in the facerdotal colleges of the
eaftern nations. But from the birth of Plato's
fchool they foared infinitely above that barrier, which the idea of confining them to an
immediate utility and practice had erected.

This philofopher was the firft who folved
the problem of the duplication of the cube, by
the hypothefis, indeed, of a continued motion; but the procefs was ingenious, and
ftrictly accurate. His early difciples difcovered the conic fections, and demonstrated *Conic Sections.*
their principal properties; thereby opening
upon the human mind that vaft horifon of
knowledge, where, as long as the world
fhall endure, it may exercife its powers without ceafing, while at every ftep the horifon
retires as the mind advances.

The fciences connected with politics did *Politicks.*
not derive from philofophy alone their progrefs among the Greeks. In thefe fmall republics, jealous of preferving both their independence and their liberty, the practice was
almoft generally prevalent of confiding to one
man, not the power of making laws, but
the function of digefting and prefenting them

to the people, by whom they were examined, and from whom they received their direct ſanction.

Thus the people impoſed a taſk on the philoſopher, whoſe wiſdom or whoſe virtues had recommended him to their confidence, but they conferred on him no authority; they exerciſed alone and of themſelves what we have ſince called by the name of legiſlative power. But the practice, ſo fatal, of calling ſuperſtition to the aid of political inſtitutions, has too often corrupted the execution of an idea ſo admirably fitted to give that ſyſtematic unity to the laws of a country which alone can render their operation ſure and eaſy, as well as maintain the duration of them. Nor had politics yet acquired principles ſufficiently invariable not to fear that the legiſlators might introduce into theſe inſtitutions their prejudices and their paſſions.

Religion ought always to aid Gov.t You, & Co. were obliged to call in aid the Worships of Genius and Reason.

Their object could not be, as yet, to found upon the baſis of reaſon, upon the rights which all men have equally received from nature, upon the maxims of univerſal juſtice, the ſuperſtructure of a ſociety of men equal and free; but merely to eſtabliſh laws by

All authority in one Center and that Center the Nation. Fool!

which

which the hereditary members of a society, already exifting, might preferve their liberty, live fecure from injuftice, and, by exhibiting an impofing appearance to their neighbours, continue in the enjoyment of their independence.

As it was fuppofed that thefe laws, almoft univerfally connected with religion, and confecrated by oaths, were to endure for ever, *Oaths* it was lefs an object of attention to fecure to a people the means of effecting, in a peaceable manner, their reform, than to guard from every poffible change fuch as were fundamental, and to take care that the reforms of detail neither incroached upon the fyftem, nor corrupted the fpirit of them.

Such inftitutions were fought for as were *in fault* calculated to cherifh and give energy to the *do you find* love of country, in which was included a *in this?* love of its legifiation and even ufages; fuch an organization of powers, as would fecure the execution of the laws againft the negligence or corruption of magiftrates, and the reftlefs difpofition of the multitude.

The rich, who alone were in a capacity *Will not* of acquiring knowledge, by feizing on the *knowledge* reins *always be*

confined, chiefly to the rich?

G 4

reins of authority might oppreſs the poor, and compel them to throw themſelves into the arms of a tyrant. The ignorance and fickleneſs of the people, and its jealouſy of powerful citizens, might ſuggeſt to ſuch citizens both the deſire and the means of eſtabliſhing ariſtocratic deſpotiſm, or of ſurrendering an enfeebled ſtate to the ambition of its neighbours. Obliged to guard at once againſt both theſe rocks, the Greek legiſlators had recourſe to combinations more or leſs happy, but always bearing the ſtamp of this ſagacity, this artifice, which accordingly charaċteriſed the general ſpirit of the nation.

It would be difficult to find in modern republics, or even in the plans ſketched by philoſophers, a ſingle inſtitution of which the Greek republics did not ſuggeſt the outlines, or furniſh the example. For, in the Amphiċtyonic league, as well as in that of the Ætolians, Arcadians, Achæans, we have inſtances of federal conſtitutions, of a union more or leſs cloſe ; and there were eſtabliſhed a leſs barbarous right of nations, and more liberal rules of commerce between theſe different people, conneċted by a common origin,

3

gin, by the ufe of the fame language, and by
a fimilarity of manners, opinions and religious
perfuafions.

The mutual relations of agriculture, induftry and commerce, with the laws and conftitution of a ftate, their influence upon its
profperity, power, freedom, could not have
efcaped the obfervation of a people ingenious
and active, and at the fame time watchful of
the public intereft : and accordingly among
them are perceived the firft traces of that
fcience, fo comprehenfive and ufeful, known
at prefent by the name of political economy. *political Econ-*

omy. The obfervation alone of eftablifhed governments was therefore fufficient fpeedily to
convert politics into an extenfive fcience.
Thus in the writings even of the philofo-
phers, it is a fcience rather of facts, and, if I *Is there any*
may fo fpeak, empirical, than a true theory *fcience not of*
founded upon general principles, drawn from *facts? Now=*
nature, and acknowledged by reafon. Such *this Science*
is the point of view in which we ought to *is empirical.*
regard the political ideas of Ariftotle and *Principles*
Plato, if we would difcover their meaning, *drawn from*
and form of them a juft eftimate. *Nature, are drawn from*
Facts. It is Nature but
Almoft Fact? How
can reafon acknowledge any thing but facts and
Inferences from facts? Behmen and Sweedenbourg
were not more myftical and unintelligible than
this philofophical and mathematical charlatan.

Almoft all the Greek inftitutions fuppofe the exiftence of flavery, and the poffibility of uniting together, in a public place, the whole community of citizens: two moft important diftinctions, of which we ought never to lofe fight, if we would judge rightly of the effect of thofe inftitutions, particularly on the extenfive and populous nations of modern times. But upon the firft we cannot reflect without the painful idea, that at that period the moft perfect forms of government had for object the liberty or happinefs of at moft but half the human fpecies.

With the Greeks, education was an important part of polity. Men were formed for their country, much more than for themfelves, or their family. This principle can only be embraced by communities little populous, in which it is more pardonable to fuppofe a national intereft, feparate from the common intereft of humanity. It is practicable only in countries where the moft painful labours of culture and of the arts are performed by flaves. This branch of education was reftricted almoft entirely to fuch bodily exercifes, fuch manners and habits as were

calcu-

calculated to excite an exclufive patriotifm: *exclufive Da-*
the other branches were acquired, as a mat- *triotifm*
ter of free choice, in the fchools of the philofophers or rhetoricians, and the fhops of the
artifts; and this freedom was a farther caufe
of the fuperiority of the Greeks,

In their polity, as in their philofophy, a *Does He*
general principle is obfervable, to which hif- *know what*
tory fcarcely furnifhes any exceptions: they *he means*
aimed lefs in their laws at <u>extirpating the</u> *here.*
<u>caufes of an evil, than deftroying its effects,</u>
<u>by oppofing thefe caufes one to another;</u>
<u>they wifhed rather to take advantage of pre-</u>
<u>judices and vices, than to difperfe or fupprefs</u>
<u>them;</u> they attended more frequently to the
means by which to deform and brutalize
man, to inflame, to miflead his fenfibility,
than to refine and purify the inclinations and
defires which are the neceffary refult of his
moral conftitution; errors occafioned by the
more general one of miftaking for the man of
nature, him who exhibited in his character
the actual ftate of civilization, that is to
fay, man corrupted by prejudices, by the intereft of factitious paffions, and by focial habits.

This obfervation is of the more import-ance, and it will be the more neceffary to develope its origin, in order the better to de-ftroy it, as it has been tranfmitted to our own age, and ftill too often corrupts both our mo-rals and our politics.

If we compare the legiflation, and parti-cularly the form and rules of judicature in the Greek, or in the eaftern nations, we fhall find that, in fome, the laws are a yoke to which force has bowed the necks of flaves; in others, the conditions of a common com-pact between the members of the fociety. In fome the object of legal forms is, that the will of the mafter be executed; in others that the liberty of the citizens be not oppreffed. In fome the law is made for the party that im-pofes it; in others for the party that is to fubmit to it. In fome the fear of the law is enforced, in others the love of it inculcated. And thefe diftinctions we alfo find in modern nations, between the laws of a free people, and thofe of a country of flaves. In Greece we fhall find that man poffeffed at leaft a confcioufnefs of his rights, if he did not yet know them, if he could not fathom the na-

ture,

ture, and embrace and circumfcribe the extent of them.

At this epoch, of the firft dawn of philofophy and firft advance of the fciences among
the Greeks, the fine arts rofe to a degree of *Fine Arts*
perfeftion known at that time to no other
people, and fcarcely equalled fince by almoft
any nation. Homer lived at the period of *Homer*
thofe diffentions which accompanied the fall
of the tyrants, and the formation of republics. Sophocles, Euripides, Pindar, Thucydides, Demofthenes, Phidias, Apelles, were
the contemporaries of Socrates or of Plato. *Socrates.*

We fhall give a delineation of the progrefs
of thofe arts ; we fhall enquire into its caufes ;
we fhall diftinguifh between what may be
confidered as a perfeftion of the art itfelf,
and what is to be afcribed only to the happy
genius of the artift : a diftinftion calculated to
deftroy thofe narrow limits to which the improvement of the fine arts has been reftrifted.
We fhall explain the influence that forms of
government, fyftems of legiflation, and the
fpirit of religious obfervances have exercifed
on their progrefs, and fhall examine what
they have derived from the advances of philofophy,

lofophy, and what philofophy itfelf has derived from them.

We fhall fhew that liberty, arts, knowledge, have contributed to the fuavity and
melioration of manners; that the vices of the
Greeks, fo often afcribed to their civilization,
were thofe of ruder ages, and which the ac-
quirements we have mentioned have in all
inftances qualified, when they have proved
unable to extirpate them. We fhall demon-
ftrate that the eloquent declamations which
have been made againft the arts and fciences,
are founded upon a miftaken application of
hiftory; and that, on the contrary, the progrefs of virtue has ever accompanied that of
knowledge, as the progrefs of corruption has
always followed or announced its decline.

In this Para-
graph, I am
inclined to
agree with him
rather than
Rousseau.

This is
capable of
much dis-
cussion: many distinctions: limitations: and Expla-
nations,

FIFTH

FIFTH EPOCH.

Progreſs of the Sciences, from their Diviſion to their Decline.

PLATO was ſtill living when Ariſtotle, his *Aristotle* diſciple, opened, in Athens itſelf, a ſchool, the rival of that of his maſter.

He not only embraced all the ſciences, but applied the method obſerved in philoſophy to the arts of eloquence and poetry. He was the firſt whoſe daring genius conceived the propriety of extending this method to every thing attainable by human intelligence ; ſince, as this intelligence exerciſed in all caſes the ſame faculties, it ought invariably to be governed by the ſame laws.

The more comprehenſive was the plan he formed, the more he felt the neceſſity of ſeparating the different parts of it, and of fixing with greater preciſion the limits of each. And from this epoch the majority of philoſophers, and even whole ſects, are feen

feen confining their attention to fome only of thofe parts.

Mathematics & The mathematical and phyfical fciences
Phyfichs formed of themfelves a grand divifion. As they were founded upon calculation and the obfervance of the phenomena of nature, as what they taught was independent of the opinions which embroiled the fects, they fe-
Philofophy parated themfelves from philofophy, over which thefe fects ftill reigned. They accordingly became the ftudy of the learned, who had the wifdom almoft univerfally to keep aloof from the difputes of the fchools, which were conducted in a manner calculated rather to promote the tranfient fame of the profeffors, than aid the progrefs of philofophy itfelf. And foon this word ceafed to be employed, except for the purpofe of expreffing
Syftem of the the general principles of the fyftem of the
World world, metaphyfics, logic, and morals, of which the fcience of politics formed a part.

Fortunately the era of this divifion preceded the period in which Greece, after long ftruggles, was deftined to lofe her freedom. The fciences found, in the capital of Egypt, an afylum, which, by the defpots who governed

verned it, would probably have been refufed to philofophy. But as the princes derived no inconfiderable portion of their riches and power from the united commerce of the Mediterranean and Afiatic feas, it was their intereft to encourage fciences ufeful to navigation and commerce.

Accordingly, they efcaped the fpeedy decline that was foon experienced by philo- fophy, the fplendour of which vanifhed with the departure of liberty. The tyranny of the Romans, fo regardlefs of the progrefs of knowledge, did not extend to Egypt till a late period, and when the town of Alexandria was *Alexandria* become neceffary to the fubfiftance of Rome. By its population, its wealth, the great influx of ftrangers, the eftablifhments formed by the Ptolemies, and which the conquerors did not *Ptolemies* give themfelves the trouble to deftroy, this town, the centre of commerce, and already poffeffing wherewith to be the metropolis of the fciences, was fufficient of itfelf to the prefervation of their facred flame.

The fect of Academics, in which, from its *Academics* origin, the mathematics had been cultivated, and which confined its philofophical inftruc-

H   tion

tion almoſt entirely to proving the utility of doubt, and aſcertaining the narrow limits of certainty, muſt of courſe have been a ſect of men of learning; and as the doctrine had nothing in it calculated to give alarm to deſpots, it flouriſhed in the ſchool of Alexandria.

doubt
certainly

The theory of conic ſections, with the method of employing it, whether for the conſtructing of geometrical loci, or for the ſolution of problems, and the diſcovery of ſome other curves, extended the limits, hitherto ſo narrow, of the ſcience of geometry.

Conic Sections

Archimedes diſcovered the quadrature of the parabola, and meaſured the ſurface of the ſphere. Theſe were the firſt advances in the theory of limits which determines the ultimate value of a quantity, or, in other words, the value to which the quantity in an infinite progreſſion inceſſantly approaches, but never attains; that theory which teaches how to determine the ratios of evaneſcent quantities, and by other proceſſes to deduce from theſe ratios the propoſitions of finite magnitudes; in a word, that very calculus which the moderns, with more pride than juſtice, have termed the calculus of infinities. It was Archimedes

Archimedes

chimedes who firſt determined the proportion
of the diameter of a circle to its circum-
ference in numbers nearly true; who taught
us how to obtain values approaching nearer
and nearer to accuracy, and made known the
methods of approximation, that happy remedy for the defects of the known methods,
and frequently of the ſcience itſelf.

He may, in ſome reſpect, be conſidered as
the father of rational or theoretical mechanics.*Mechanics*
To him we are indebted for the theory of the
lever, as well as the diſcovery of that principle
of hydroſtatics, that a body immerſed in any
fluid, loſes a portion of its weight equal to the
maſs of fluid it has diſplaced.

The ſcrew that bears his name, his burning
glaſſes, the prodigies of the ſiege of Syracuſe,
atteſt his ſkill in the art of conſtructing mechanical inſtruments, which the learned had
neglected, becauſe the principles of the theory
at that time known were inadequate to the
attainment. Theſe grand diſcoveries, theſe
new ſciences, place Archimedes among thoſe
happy geniuſes whoſe life forms an epoch in
the hiſtory of man, and whoſe exiſtence may
be conſidered as one of the munificent gifts of *gift of Na-*
nature. *ture.*

It

Alexandria
Algebra
It is in the fchool of Alexandria that we find the firft traces of algebra; that is to fay, of the calculation of quantities confidered fimply as fuch. The nature of the problems propofed and refolved in the work of Dio-
Diophantus
phantus, made it neceffary that numbers fhould be confidered as having a general value, undetermined in their particular relations, and fubject only to certain conditions.

But this fcience had not then, as at prefent, its appropriate figns, methods and technical operations. The general value of quantities was reprefented by words; and it was only by means of a feries of reafonings that the folution of problems was difcovered and developed.

Chaldeans
The obfervations of the Chaldeans, tranf-mitted to Ariftotle by Alexander, accelerated the progrefs of aftronomy. The moft brilliant portion of them was due to the genius
Hipparchus
of Hipparchus. And if, after him in aftronomy, as after Archimedes in geometry and mechanics, we no longer perceive thofe difcoveries and acquifitions which change, as it were, the whole face of a fcience, they yet for a long time continued to improve, expand,

pand, and enrich themfelves by the truths of
detail.

In his hiftory of animals, Ariftotle had *Animals*
laid down the principles and furnifhed an
excellent model for obferving with accuracy,
and defcribing according to fyftem, the objects of nature, as well as for clafling thofe
obfervations, and catching with readinefs the
general refults which they exhibited. The
hiftory of plants and of minerals were treated
afterwards by others, but with inferior precifion, and with views lefs extenfive and lefs
philofophical.

The progrefs of anatomy was very flow, *Anatomy*
not only becaufe religious prejudices would *religious Preju*
not admit of the diffection of dead bodies, *dices*
but from the vulgar opinion which regarded *vulgar opinion*
the touch of fuch bodies as a fort of moral
defilement.

The medical fyftem of Hippocrates was *Hippocrates*
nothing more than a fcience of obfervation,
which as yet had led only to empirical methods. The fpirit of fect, and the love of hypothetical pofitions foon infected it. But if
the number of errors was greater than that of
new truths, if the prejudices or fyftems of the

H 3   prac-

practitioners did more harm than their obfervations were calculated to do good, yet it
cannot be denied that the fcience made,
during this epoch, a real, though very flight
progrefs.

Ariftotle introduced into natural philofophy
neither the accuracy nor the prudent referve
which characterife his hiftory of animals.
He paid tribute to the cuftoms of his age, to
Hypothefes. the tafte of the fchools, by disfiguring it with
thofe hypothetical data, which, from their
vague nature, explain every thing with a fort
of readinefs, becaufe they are able to explain
nothing with precifion.

Befides, obfervation alone was not enough;
Experiments experiments were neceffary : thefe demanded
Inftruments inftruments ; and it appears that at that time
men had not fufficiently collected facts, had
not examined them with the proper minute-
nefs, to feel the want, to conceive the idea
Interrogating of this mode of interrogating nature, and
Nature obliging her to anfwer us.

At this epoch alfo, the hiftory of the progrefs of natural philofophy is confined to a
fmall number of truths, acquired by chance,
and derived from obfervations furnifhed by
the

the practice of the arts, rather than from the researches of the learned. Hydraulics, and *Hydraulics* especially optics, prefent us with a harveft *Opticks* fomewhat lefs fterile ; but thefe alfo confift rather of facts, which were remarked becaufe they fell in the way and forced attention, than of theories or phyfical laws difcovered by experiments, or obtained by meditation and ftudy.

Agriculture had hitherto been confined to *Agriculture* the fimple routine and a few regulations, which priefts, in tranfmitting them to the people, had corrupted with their fuperftition. It became with the Greeks, and ftill more with the Romans, an important and refpected art ; and men of greateft learning employed themfelves in collecting its ufages and precepts. Thefe collections of facts, precifely defcribed and judicioufly arranged, were ufeful to enlighten the practical cultivator, and to extend fuch methods as had proved valuable ; but the age of experiment and regular deduction was ftill very far off.

The mechanic arts began to connect them- *Mechanic Art* felves with the fciences. Philofophers examined the labours, fought the origin, and

ftudied

ſtudied the hiſtory of theſe arts ; at the ſame time they deſcribed the proceſſes and fruits of thoſe which were cultivated in different countries, and were induced to collect together their obſervations, and tranſmit them to poſterity.

Thus Pliny, in the comprehenſive plan of his natural hiſtory, includes man, nature and the arts. This work is a valuable and complete inventory of what at that time conſtituted the true ſtores of the human mind : nor can his claims to our gratitude be ſuperſeded by the charge, however merited, of his having collected with too little diſcrimination and too much credulity, what the ignorance or lying vanity of hiſtorians preſented to his avidity, not to be ſatiated, of knowing every thing.

In the midſt of the decline of Greece, Athens, which, in the days of its power, had ·honoured philoſophy and letters, owed to them, in its turn, the preſerving for a longer period ſome remains of its ancient ſplendour. In its tribune, indeed, the deſtinies of Greece and Aſia were no longer decided ; it was, however, in the ſchools of Athens that the

Romans

Romans acquired the fecrets of eloquence; and it was at the feet of Demofthenes' lamp that the firft of their orators was formed.

The academy, the lyceum, the portico, the *Academy* gardens of Epicurus, were the nurfery and *Lyceum* principal fchool of the four fects that difputed *Portico* the empire of philofophy. *Gardens of Epicurus.*

It was taught in the academy, that every thing is doubtful; that man can attain, as to any object, neither abfolute certainty nor a true comprehenfion; in fine, and it was difficult to go farther, that he could not be fure of this very impoffibility of knowing any thing, and that it was proper to doubt even of the neceffity of doubting.

The opinions of different philofophers were explained, defended and oppofed in this fchool, but merely as hypothefes calculated to exercife the mind and illuftrate more fully, by the uncertainty which accompanied thefe difputes, the vanity of human knowledge *Vanity of hu-* and abfurdity of the dogmatical confidence of *man knowledge* the other fects.

This doctrine, if it go no farther than to difcountenance reafoning upon words to which we can affix no clear and precife ideas;

than

than to proportion our belief in any propofition to the degree of probability it bears;
than to afcertain, as to every fpecies of knowledge, the bounds of certainty we are able to
acquire,—this fcepticifm is then rational; but
when it extends to demonftrated truths; when
it attacks the principles of morality, it becomes either weaknefs or infanity; and fuch
is the extreme into which the fophifts have
fallen, who fucceeded in the academy the
firft difciples of Plato.

Sophists

We fhall follow the fteps of thefe fceptics,
and exhibit the caufe of their errors. We
fhall examine what, in the extravagance of
their doctrine, is to be afcribed to the paffion,
fo prevalent, of diftinguifhing themfelves by
whimfical opinions; and fhall fhew, that,
though fufficiently refuted by the inftinct of
other men, by the inftinct which directed
thefe fophifts themfelves in the ordinary conduct of life, they were neither properly refuted, nor even underftood, by the philofophers of the day.

Scepticks

a modern no left than an ancient paffion

Meanwhile this fceptical mania did not
poffefs the whole fect of academics; and the
doctrine of an eternal idea, juft, comely,
honeft,

eternal Idea

honeft, independent of the interefts and conventions of men, and even of their exiftence,
an idea that, imprinted on the foul, becomes
the principle of duty and the law of our *law written*
actions, this doctrine, derived from the Dia- *on our hearts.*
logues of Plato, was ftill inculcated in his
fchool, and conftituted the bafis of moral inftruction,

Ariftotle was no better fkilled than his *Aristotle*
mafter in the art of analyfing ideas; that
is, of afcending ftep by ftep to the moft
fimple ideas that have entered into their combination, of obferving the formation of thefe
fimple ideas themfelves, of following in thefe
operations the regular procedure of the mind,
and developement of its faculties.

His metaphyfics, like thofe of the other
philofophers, confifted of a vague doctrine,
founded fometimes upon an abufe of words,
and fometimes upon mere hypothefes.

To him, however, we owe that important
truth, that firft ftep in the fcience of the
human mind, that OUR IDEAS, EVEN SUCH *Sensation*
AS ARE MOST ABSTRACT, MOST STRICTLY
INTELLECTUAL, fo to fpeak, HAVE THEIR
ORIGIN IN OUR SENSATIONS. But this
truth

truth he failed to fupport by any demonftration. It was rather the intuitive perception of a man of genius, than the refult of a
feries of obfervations accurately analyfed,
and fyftematically combined, in order to derive from them fome general truth. Accordingly, this germ, caft in an ungrateful
foil, produced no ufeful fruit till after a period of more than twenty centuries.

Ariftotle, in his dialectics, having reduced
all demonftrations to a train of arguments
drawn up in a fyllogiftical form, and then
divided all imaginable propofitions under four
heads, teaches us to difcover, among the
poffible combinations of propofitions of thefe
four claffes in collections of three and three,
thofe which anfwer to the nature of con-
clufive fyllogifms, and may be admitted without apprehenfion. In this way we may judge
of the cogency or weaknefs of an argument,
merely by knowing to what clafs it belongs ;
and thus the art of right reafoning is fubjected in fome meafure to technical rules.

This ingenious idea has hitherto remained
ufelefs; but perhaps it may one day become
the leading ftep towards a perfection which

the

the art of reafoning and difcuffion feems ftill
to expect.

Every virtue, according to Ariftotle, is *virtue bet,*
placed between two vices, of which one is its *2 Vius*
defect, and the other its excefs ; it is only, as
it were, one of thofe natural inclinations
which reafon equally forbids us too ftrongly
to refift, and too flavifhly to obey.

This general principle muft have been
fuggefted to him by one of thofe vague ideas
of order and conformity, fo common at that
time in philofophy ; but he proved its truth,
by applying it to the vocabulary of words
which, in the Greek language, expreffed what
were called the virtues.

About the fame period, two new fects,
founding their fyftems of morality, at leaft in
appearance, upon two contrary principles,
divided the general mind, extended their influence beyond the limits of their fchools,
and haftened the fall of Greek fuperftition ;
but, unhappily, a fuperftition more gloomy,
more dangerous, more inimical to knowledge,
was foon to fucceed it.

The ftoics made virtue and happinefs con-*Stoics*
fift in the poffeffion of a foul alike infenfible

to pleafure and to pain, free from all the paffions, fuperior to every fear, every weaknefs, knowing no abfolute good but virtue, no real evil but remorfe. They believed that man was capable of raifing himfelf to this elevation, if he poffeffed a ftrong and conftant defire of doing fo ; and that then, independent of fortune, always mafter of himfelf, he was equally inacceffible to vice and calamity.

Anima. Mundi An individual mind animates the world : it is prefent in every thing, if it be not every thing, if there exift any other thing than itfelf. The fouls of human beings are emanations of it. That of the fage, who has not defiled the purity of his origin, is re-united, at the inftant of death, to this univerfal fpirit. Accordingly, to the fage, death would be a bleffing, if, fubmiffive to nature, hardened againft what vulgar men call evils, it was not more glorious in him to regard it with indifference.

Epicurus By Epicurus, happinefs is placed in the enjoyment of pleafure, and in freedom from pain. Virtue, according to him, confifts in following the natural inclinations of the heart, at the fame time taking care to purify and direct

direct them. The practice of temperance,
which prevents pain, and, by preferving our
faculties in their full force, fecures all the enjoyments that nature has provided for us;
the care to guard ourfelves againft hateful
and violent paffions that torment and rend
the foul delivered up to their bitternefs and
fury; the farther care to cultivate, on the
contrary, the mild and tender affections; to
be frugal of pleafures that flow from benevolence; to preferve the foul in purity, that we
may avoid the fhame and remorfe which
punifh vice, and enjoy the delicious fentiment that is the reward of laudable actions:
fuch is the road that conducts at once both to
happinefs and virtue.

Epicurus regarded the univerfe only as
a collection of atoms, the different combina-*Atoms.*
tions of which were fubjected to neceffary *Molecules.*
laws. The human foul was itfelf one of thofe
combinations. The atoms which compofed it,
united when the body began to live, were
difperfed at the moment of death, to unite
themfelves again to the common mafs, and
enter into new combinations.

Unwilling too violently to fhock popular
prejudices, he admitted of Gods; but, indifferent

different to the actions of men, strangers to
the order of the univerfe, and governed, like
other beings, by the general laws of its mechanifm, they were a fort of excrefcence of
the fyftem.

Men of morofe, proud, and unjuft characters, fcreened themfelves under the mafk
of ftoicifm, while voluptuous and corrupt
men frequently ftole into the gardens of Epicurus. Some calumniated the principles of
the Epicureans, who were accufed of placing
the fovereign good in the gratification of
fenfual appetites. Others turned into ridicule
Zeno the pretenfions of the fage Zeno, who, whether
a flave at the mill, or tormented with the gout,
was equally happy, free, and independent.

The philofophy that pretended to foar
above nature, and that which wifhed only to
obey nature; the morality which acknowledged no other good than virtue, and that
which placed happinefs in the indulgence of
the natural inclinations, led to the fame practical confequences, though departing from
fuch oppofite principles, and holding fo contrary a language. This refemblance between
Morality the moral precepts of all fyftems of religion,
all Sects and Systems, the Same. and

and all fects of philofophy, would be fufficient
to prove that they have a foundation independent of the dogmas of thofe religions, or
the principles of thofe fects; that it is in the
moral conftitution of man we muft feek the *Moral Senfe*
bafis of his duties, the origin of his ideas of
juftice and virtue: a truth which the fect of
Epicureans approached more nearly than any
other; and no circumftance perhaps fo much
contributed to draw upon it the enmity of all
claffes of hypocrites, with whom morality was
a commercial object of which they ambi-
tioufly contended for the monopoly.

The fall of the Greek republics involved *Politicks not*
that of the political fciences. After Plato, *tolerated*
Ariftotle, and Xenophon, they almoft ceafed
to be included in the fyftem of philofophy.

But it is time to fpeak of an event that-
changed the lot of a confiderable part of the
world, and exercifed on the progrefs of the
mind an influence that has reached even to
ourfelves.

If we except India and China, the city of *Is Paris*
Rome had extended its empire over every. *pray, to be*
nation in which human intelligence had rifen *another Rome*
above the weaknefs of its earlieft infancy. *It 1798*

I

It gave laws to all the countries into which the Greeks had introduced their language, their fciences, and their philofophy; and thefe nations, held by a chain which victory had faftened to the foot of the capitol, no longer exifted but by the will of Rome, and for the paffions of its chiefs.

A true picture of the conftitution of this fovereign city will not be foreign to the object *Such a Rank* of this work. We fhall there fee the origin of *exists in every* hereditary patrician rank, and the artful means *Nation und./..* that were adopted to give it greater ftability *Sem. & will it* and force, by rendering it lefs odious; we *it forms.* fhall there fee a people inured to arms, but *never drew* never employing them in domeftic diffentions; *blood, till* uniting real power to legal authority, yet *the Gracchi.* fcarcely defending themfelves againft a haughty fenate, that, while it rivetted the chains of fuperftition, dazzled them at the fame time with the fplendor of their victories; a great nation, the fport in turn both of its tyrants and its de- *Saved, however,* fenders, and the patient dupe, for four centu- *by this mode,* ries, of a mode of taking votes, abfurd but confecrated.

We fhall fee this conftitution, made for a fingle city, change its nature without changing

its

its form, when it was neceſſary to extend it to
a great empire, unable to maintain itſelf but
by continual wars, and preſently deſtroyed by
its own armies ; and laſtly, the people, the
ſovereign people, debaſed by the habit of
being maintained at the expence of the public
treaſury, and corrupted by the bounty of the
ſenators, ſelling to an individual the imaginary
remains of their uſeleſs freedom.

The ambition of the Romans led them to
ſearch in Greece for maſters in the art of elo- *Eloquence*
quence, which in Rome was one of the roads
to fortune. That taſte for excluſive and refined enjoyments, that want of new plea-
ſures, which ſprings from wealth and idleneſs,
made them court other arts of the Greeks,
and even the converſation of their philoſophers. But the ſciences, philoſophy, and the *ſciences*
arts connected with painting, were plants fo- *Painting*
reign to the ſoil of Rome. The avarice of the
conquerors covered Italy with the maſter- *The Tuſcans*
pieces of Greece, taken by violence from the *had little*
temples, from cities of which they conſtituted *imitated the*
the ornament, and where they ſerved as a *in Spain*
conſolation under ſlavery. But the produc- *Italy of all*
tio ns of no Roman dared mix with them. *it Glorie*

Cicero

Cicero
Lucretius
Seneca

Cæsar

Cicero, Lucretius and Seneca wrote eloquently in their language upon philofophy, but it was upon Grecian philofophy ; and to reform the barbarous calendar of Numa, Cæfar was obliged to employ a mathematician from Alexandria.

Rome, long torn by the factions of ambitious generals, bufied in new conquefts, or agitated by civil difcords, fell at laft from its

esclefs liberty
1.

reftlefs liberty into a military defpotifm ftill more reftlefs. And where, among the chiefs that afpired to tyranny, and foon after under the defpots who feared truth, and equally hated both talents and virtue, were the tranquil meditations of philofophy and the fciences to find a place ? Befides, the fciences and philofophy are neceffarily neglected as barren and unprofitable in every country where fome honourable career, leading to wealth and dignities, is open to all whom their natural inclination may difpofe to ftudy : and

jurifprudence

fuch at Rome was that of jurifprudence.

When laws, as in the eaft, are allied to religion, the right of interpreting them becomes one of the ftrongeft fupports of facerdotal tyranny. In Greece they had conftituted a part of the code given to each city by its refpective

legifla-

legiflator, who had aſſimilated them to the
ſpirit of the conſtitution and government
which he eſtabliſhed. They experienced but
few alterations. The magiſtrates frequently
abuſed them, and individual inſtances of in-
juſtice were not leſs frequent ; but the vices of
the laws never extended in Greece to a regular ſyſtem of robbery, reduced to the cold
forms of calculation. In Rome, where for a
long time no other authority was known but
the tradition of cuſtoms, where the judges declared every year by what principles diſputes
would be 'decided during the continuance of
their magiſtracy, where the firſt written laws
were a compilation from the Greek laws,
drawn up by the decemvirs, more anxious
to preſerve their power than to honour it
by preſenting a found code of legiſlation :
in Rome, where, after that period, laws,
dictated at one time by the party of the
ſenate, and at another by the party of the
people, ſucceeded each other with rapidity,
and were inceſſantly either deſtroyed or confirmed, meliorated or aggravated by new declarations, the multiplicity, the complication
and the obſcurity of the laws, an inevitable

I 3   con-

confequence of the fluctuation of the language, foon made of this ftudy a fcience apart. The fenate, taking advantage of the refpect of the people for the ancient inftitutions, foon felt that the privilege of interpreting laws was nearly equivalent to that of making new ones ; and accordingly this body abounded with lawyers. Their power furvived that of the fenate itfelf : it increafed under the emperors, becaufe it is neceffarily greater as the code of legiflation becomes more anomalous and un-certain.

Jurifprudence Jurifprudence then is the only new fcience for which we are indebted to the Romans. We fhall trace its hiftory, fince it is connected with the progrefs which the fcience of legifla-tion has made among the moderns, and parti-cularly with the obftacles which that legifla-tion has had to encounter.

We fhall fhow, that refpect for the pofitive law of the Romans has contributed to preferve fome ideas of the natural law of men, in or-der afterwards to prevent thefe ideas from in-creafing and extending themfelves ; and that, while we are indebted to their code for a fmall quantity of truths, it has furnifhed us

with

with a far greater portion of tyrannical prejudices.

The mildnefs of the penal laws, under the *Penal Laws*
republic, is worthy our notice. They in a
manner rendered facred the blood of a Roman
citizen. The penalty of death could not be
inflicted, without calling forth that extraordinary power which announced public calamities and danger to the country. The whole
body of the people might be claimed as
judge between a fingle individual and the republic. It was found that, with a free people,
this mildnefs was the only way to prevent *Mildnefs*
political diffentions from degenerating into
cruel maffacres ; the object was to correct, by
the humanity of the laws, the ferocious manners
of a people that, even in its fports, fquandered
profufely the blood of its flaves. Accordingly,
ftopping at the times of the Gracchi, in no
country have ftorms fo numerous and violent
been attended with fo few crimes, or coft fo
little blood.

No work of the Romans upon the fubject of
politics has defcended to us. That of Cicero *Cicero*
upon laws was probably but an embellifhed
extract from the books of the Greeks. It

was not amidſt the convulſions of expiring
liberty, that moral ſcience could refine and
perfect itſelf. Under the deſpotiſm of the
Cæſars. Cæſars, ſtudy would have experienced no
other conſtruction than a conſpiracy againſt
their power. In ſhort, nothing more clearly
proves how much the Romans were ignorant
of this ſcience, than the example they furniſh
us, not to be equalled in the annals of hiſtory,
Roman of an uninterrupted ſucceſſion, from Nerva to
Marc Antony, of five emperors, poſſeſſing at
Ignorance once virtue, talents, knowledge, a love of
of Utility. glory, and zeal for the public welfare, without a ſingle inſtitution originating from them
that has marked the deſire of fixing bounds to
deſpotiſm, of preventing revolutions, and of
cementing by new ties the parts of that huge
maſs, of which every thing predicted the approaching diſſolution.

The union of ſo many nations under one
ſovereignty, the ſpread of two languages
which divided the empire, and which were
alike familiar to almoſt every well-informed
mind, theſe cauſes, acting in concert, muſt
have contributed, no doubt, to the more equal
diffuſion of knowledge over a greater ſpace.

Another

Another natural effect muſt have been to weaken by degrees the differences which ſeparated the philoſophical ſects, and to unite them into one, that ſhould contain ſuch opinions of each as were moſt conformable to reaſon, and which a ſober inveſtigation had tended to confirm. This was the point to which reaſon could not fail to bring philoſophers, when, from the effect of time on the enthuſiaſm of ſectaries, her voice alone was ſuffered to be heard. Accordingly, we find already, in Seneca, marks of this philoſophy : *Seneca* indeed it was never entirely diſtinct from the ſect of the academics, which at length appeared to become entirely the ſame with it ; and the moſt modern of the diſciples of Plato were the founders of the ſect of eclectics. *Eclectics*

Almoſt every religion of the empire had *Religion* been national ; but they all poſſeſſed ſtrong lines of reſemblance, and in a manner a family likeneſs. No metaphyſical doctrines ; many ſtrange ceremonies, of the meaning of which the people, and frequently the prieſts, were ignorant ; an abſurd mythology, in *Mythology* which the multitude read the marvellous hiſtory of its Gods only, but which men better

enlightened

enlightened fufpected to be an allegory of doctrines more fublime; bloody facrifices; idols reprefenting Gods, and of which fome poffeffed a celeftial virtue; pontiffs devoted to the worfhip of each divinity, but without forming a political corps, and even without being united in a religious communion; oracular powers attached to certain temples, refiding in certain ftatues; and laftly, myfteries, which their hierophants never revealed without impofing an inviolable law of fecrefy. Thefe were the features of refemblance.

Let us add, that the priefts, arbiters of the religious confcience, had prefumed to affert no claim upon the moral confcience; that they directed the practice of worfhip, but not the actions of private life. They fold oracles and auguries to political powers; they could precipitate nations into war; they could dictate to them crimes; but they exercifed no influence either over the government or the laws.

When the different nations, fubjects now of the fame empire, enjoyed an habitual intercourfe, and knowledge had every where

made

made nearly an equal progrefs, it was foon
difcovered, by well-informed minds, that all
this multifarious worfhip was that of one only
God, of whom the numerous divinities, the *one god*
immediate objects of popular adoration, were *The Hebrew*
but the modifications or the minifters. *known this long before.*

Meanwhile, among the Gauls, and in fome *Gauls*
cantons of the eaft, the Romans had found *East*
religions of another kind. There the priefts
were the arbiters of morality; and virtue
confifted in obedience to a God, of whom
they called themfelves the fole interpreters.
Their power extended over the whole man;
the temple and the country were confounded:
without being previoufly an adorer of Jehova, '
or OEfus, it was impoffible to be a citizen or *OEfus.*
fubject of the empire; and the priefts determined to what human laws their God exacted
obedience.

Thefe religions were calculated to wound
the pride of the mafters of the world. That
of the Gauls was too powerful for them not
to feek immediately its deftruction. The
Jewifh nation was even difperfed. But the
vigilance of government either difdained, or
elfe was unable to reach, the obfcure fects that
fecretly

fecretly formed themfelves out of the wreck of the old fyftems of worfhip.

One of the benefits refulting from the propagation of the Greek philofophy, had been to put an end to a belief in the popular divinities in all claffes of men who had received any tolerable education. A vague kind *Vague Deifm* of deifm, or the pure mechanifm of Epicurus, was, even at the time of Cicero, the common doctrine of every enlightened mind, and of all thofe who had the direction of public affairs. This clafs of men was neceffarily attached to the old religion, which however it fought to purify from its drofs ; for the multiplicity of Gods of every country had tired *Credulity* out even the credulity of the people. Then *exhaufted* were feen philofophers forming fyftems upon the idea of interpofing genii, and fubmitting to preparatory obfervances, rites, and a religious difcipline, to render themfelves more worthy of approaching thefe fuperior effences ; *Plato* and it was in the dialogues of Plato they fought the principles of this doctrine.

The inhabitants of conquered nations, the children of misfortune, men of a weak but fanguine imagination, would from preference

attach

attach themfelves to the facerdotal religions ; *Sacerdotal*
becaufe the intereft of the ruling priefts dic-*dictated ons*,
tated to them that very doctrine of equality
in flavery, of the renunciation of temporal
enjoyments, of rewards in heaven referved for
blind fubmiffion, for fufferings, for mortifica-
tions inflicted voluntarily, or endured without
repining ; that doctrine fo attractive, fo con-*confolation*
folatory to oppreffed humanity ! But they
felt the neceffity of relieving, by metaphyfical *Metaphyfical*
fubtleties, their grofs mythology : and here *Subtletties*.
again they had recourfe to Plato. His dia- *Plato*
logues were the arfenal to which two oppofite
parties reforted to forge their theological arms.
In the fequel we fhall fee Ariftotle obtaining a *Ariftotle*
fimilar honour, and becoming at once the
mafter of the theologians, and chief of the
atheifts.

Twenty Egyptian and Jewifh fects, uniting *Egyptian & Jewifh fect*
their forces againft the religion of the empire,
but contending againft each other with equal
fury, were loft at length in the religion of
Jefus. From their wreck were compofed a *Jefus*
hiftory, a creed, a ritual, and a fyftem of morality, to which by degrees the mafs of thefe
fanatics attached themfelves.

They

Christ

They all believed in a Chrift, a Meffiah fent from God to reftore the human race. This was the fundamental doctrine of every fect that attempted to raife itfelf upon the ruins of the ancient fects. They difputed refpecting the time and place of his appearance, and his mortal name : but a prophet, *Prophet of Palestine* faid to have ftarted up in 'Paleftine, in the reign of Tiberius, eclipfed all the other expected prophets, and the new fanatics rallied under the ftandard of the fon of Mary.

In proportion as the empire weakened, the progrefs of this religion of Chrift became more rapid. The degraded ftate of the ancient conquerors of the world extended to their Gods, who, after prefiding in their victories, were no longer regarded than as the impotent witneffes of their defeat. The fpirit of the *Christianity Suited to Misfortune,* new fect was better fuited to periods of decline and misfortune. Its chiefs, in fpite of their impoftures and their vices, were enthu- *Who? What Chiefs?* fiafts ready to fuffer death for their doctrine. The religious zeal of the philofophers and of the great, was only a political devotion : and every religion which men permit themfelves to defend as a creed ufeful to be left to the

people,

people, can expect no other fate than a diſſolution more or leſs diſtant. Chriſtianity ſoon
became a powerful party; it mixed in the
quarrels of the Cæſars: it placed Conſtantine *Conſtantine*
on the throne; where it afterwards ſeated itſelf, by the ſide of his weak ſucceſſors.

In vain did one of thoſe extraordinary men
whom chance ſometimes exalts to ſovereign
power, Julian, wiſh to free the empire from *Julian*
this plague which was calculated to haſten its
fall. His virtues, his indulgent humanity,
the ſimplicity of his manners, the dignity of
his ſoul and his character, his talents, his
courage, his military genius, the ſplendor of
his victories, every thing ſeemed to promiſe
him ſucceſs. No other reproach could be
caſt upon him than that of ſhowing for a religion, become ridiculous, an attachment un-
worthy of him if ſincere, indiſcreet from its
extravagance if political: but he died in the
midſt of his glory, after a reign of two years.
The Coloſſus of the Roman empire found its
arms no longer ſufficiently ſtrong to ſupport
the weight of it; and the death of Julian broke
down the only mound that might yet have
oppoſed itſelf againſt the torrent of new ſu-
perſtitions,

perftitions, and the inundations of barbarians.

Contempt for human fciences was one of the
firft features of Chriftianity. It had to avenge
itfelf of the outrages of philofophy ; it feared
that fpirit of inveftigation and doubt, that
confidence of man in his own reafon, the peft
alike of all religious creeds. The light of the
natural fciences was even odious to it, and
was regarded with a fufpicious eye, as being
a dangerous enemy to the fuccefs of miracles : and there is no religion that does not
oblige its fectaries to fwallow fome phyfical
abfurdities. The triumph of Chriftianity was
thus the fignal of the entire decline both of
the fciences and of philofophy.

Had the art of printing been known, the
fciences would have been able to preferve
their ground ; but the exifting manufcripts
of any particular book were few in number ;
and to procure works that might form the entire body of a fcience, required cares, and often
journies and an expence to which the rich only
were competent. It was eafy for the ruling
party to fupprefs the appearance of books
which fhocked its prejudices, or unmafked its
impoftures.

impoftures. An incurfion of barbarians might, in one day, deprive for ever a whole country of the means of knowledge. The deftruction of a fingle manufcript was often an irreparable and univerfal lofs. Befides, no works were copied but fuch as were recommended by the names of the authors. All thofe inveftigations which can acquire importance only from their affemblage, thofe detached obfervations, thofe improvements of detail, that ferve to keep the fciences flowing in a level channel, and that prepare their future progrefs; all thofe materials which time amaffes, and which await the birth of genius, were condemned to an eternal obfcurity. That concert of learned men, that combination of all their forces, fo advantageous, fo indifpenfible at certain periods, had no exiftence. It was neceffary for the fame individual to begin and complete a difcovery; and he was obliged to combat with his fingle ftrength all the obftacles which nature oppofes to our efforts. The works which facilitate the ftudy of the fciences, which throw light upon difficulties, which exhibit truths under more commodious and more fimple forms, thofe details of obfer

K   vation,

vation, thofe developements which ferve to detect erroneous inferences, and in which the reader frequently catches what the author himfelf has not perceived ; fuch works would find neither copyifts nor readers.

It was then impoffible that the fciences, arrived at a point in which the progrefs, and even the ftudy of them were ftill difficult, fhould be able to fupport themfelves, and refift the current that bore them rapidly towards their decline. Accordingly it ought not to aftonifh us that Chriftianity, though unable in the fequel to prevent their re-appearance in fplendor, after the invention of printing, was at this period fufficiently powerful to accomplifh their ruin.

If we except the dramatic art, which flourifhed only in Athens, and muft have been involved in her fall, and eloquence, which cannot breathe but in a free air, the language and literature of the Greeks preferved for a long time their luftre. Lucian and Plutarch would not difparage the age of Alexander. Rome, it is true, rofe to a level with Greece in poetry, eloquence, hiftory, and the art of treating with dignity, elegance and fafcina-
tion,

tion, the dry fubjects of philofophy and the
fciences. Greece indeed had no poet, that
evinced fo fully as Virgil, the idea of perfec- *Virgil*
tion, and no hiftorian to be compared with
Tacitus. But this inftant of fplendor was *Tacitus*
followed by a fpeedy decline. From the time
of Lucian, Rome had fcarcely any writers
above barbarifm. Chryfiftom ftill fpeaks the *Chryfiftom*
language of Demofthenes. We recognife no
longer that of Cicero or of Livy, either in
Auftin, or even in Jerome, who has not to *Auftin Jerome*
plead in his excufe the influence of African
barbarity.

The caufe is, that at Rome the ftudy of
letters and love of the arts were never the real
tafte of the people; that the tranfient perfection of its language was the work, not of
the national genius, but of a few individuals
whom Greece had been the inftrument of
forming. The caufe is, that the Roman territory was always, as to letters, a foreign
foil, to which an affiduous culture had been
able to naturalife them, but where they muft
neceffarily degenerate the moment they were
abandoned to themfelves.

K 2   The

The importance fo long affixed, in Greece
and in Rome, to the tribune and the bar, increafed in thofe countries the clafs of rhetoricians. Their labours have contributed to
the progrefs of the art, of which they have
developed the principles and fubtleties. But
they taught another art too much neglected by
the moderns, and which at prefent it has been
thought proper to transfer from fpeeches for
the tribune, to compofitions for the prefs : I
mean that of preparing with facility, and in a
fhort fpace of time, difcourfes, which, from
the arrangement of their parts, from the method confpicuous in them, from the graces
with which they may be embellifhed, fhall at
leaft become fupportable : I mean the art of
being able to fpeak almoft inftantaneoufly,
without fatiguing the auditors with a medley
of ideas, or a diffufe ftyle ; without difgufting
them with idle declamation, quaint conceits,
nonfenfe and fopperies. How ufeful would
be this art in every country where the functions of office, public duty, or private intereft
may oblige men to fpeak and write, without
having time to ftudy their fpeeches or their
compofitions ? its hiftory is the more deferving

ing our attention, as the moderns, to whom
in the mean time it muft often be neceffary,
appear only to have known it on the fide of
abfurdity.

From the commencement of the epoch of
which I fhall here terminate the delineation,
manufcripts were tolerably numerous ; but
time had fpread over the performances of the
firft Greek writers a fufficient number of ob-
fcurities, for the ftudy of books and opinions,
known by the name of erudition, to form an *Erudition*
important portion of the occupations of the
mind ; and the Alexandrian library was
crowded with grammarians and critics.

In what has been tranfmitted to us of their
productions, we perceive a propenfity in thefe
critics to proportion their degree of confidence
and admiration of any book to its antiquity,
and the difficulty of underftanding and procuring it ; a difpofition to judge opinions not
by themfelves, not according to their merits,
but from the names of their authors ; to found
their belief upon authority, rather than upon
reafon ; in fhort, that falfe and deftructive
idea of the deterioration of the human race, and
fuperiority of ancient periods. The folution

K 3   and

and excufe of this error, an error in which the antiquarians of every country have had a greater or lefs fhare, are to be found in the importance which men affix to what has been the object of their attention, and called forth the energies of their mind.

quarians The Greek and Roman antiquarians, and even their literati and philofophers, are chargeable with a total neglect of that fpirit of doubt which fubjects to a rigorous invefligation both facts, and the proofs that eftablifh them. In reading their accounts of the hiftory of events or of manners, of the productions and phenomena of nature, or of the works and proceffes of the arts, we are aftonifhed at the compofure with which they relate the moft palpable abfurdities, and the moft fulfome and difgufting prodigies. A hearfay or rumour which they found tacked to any event, was fufficient, they conceived, to fcreen them from the cenfure of childifh credulity. This indifference, which fpoiled their ftudy of hiftory, and was an obftruction to their advancement in the knowledge of nature, is to be afcribed to the misfortune of the art of printing not being known. The certainty of our
havjng

having collected, refpecting any fact, all the
authorities for and againft it, a facility in
comparing the different teftimonies, the opportunity of throwing light upon the fubject
by the difcuffions to which that difference
may give rife, are means of afcertaining truth
which can only exift when it is poffible to
procure a great number of books, when copies of them may be indefinitely multiplied,
and when no fear is entertained of giving them
too extenfive a circulation.

How were the relations and defcriptions
of travellers, of which there frequently exifted
but a fingle copy, defcriptions that were not
fubjected to public judgment, to acquire that
ftamp of authority, founded upon the circumftance of fuch judgment not having, and not
being able, to contradict them ? Accordingly,
every thing was recorded alike, becaufe it was
impoffible to afcertain with any certainty what
was deferving of record. But we can have
no right to aftonifhment at this practice of
reprefenting with equal confidence, and as
founded upon equal authorities, facts the
moft natural, and miracles the moft ftupend-
ous; the fame error is ftill inculcated in our
K 4 fchools

ſchools as a principle of philoſophy, while, in another ſenſe, an overweening incredulity leads us to reject without examination whatever appears to us to be out of nature ; nor has the ſcience in our days begun to exiſt, that can alone teach us to find, between theſe two extremes, the point at which reaſon directs us to ſtop.

SIXTH

SIXTH EPOCH.

Decline of Learning, to its Restoration about the Period of the Crusades.

IN the difaftrous epoch at which we are now arrived, we fhall fee the human mind rapidly defcending from the height to which it had raifed itfelf, while Ignorance marches in triumph, carrying with her, in one place, barbarian ferocity ; in another, a more refined and accomplifhed cruelty ; every where, corruption and perfidy. A glimmering of talents, fome faint fparks of greatnefs or benevolence, of foul, will, with difficulty, be difcerned amidft the univerfal darknefs. Theological reveries, fuperftitious delufions, are become the fole genius of man, religious intolerance his only morality ; and Europe, crufhed between facerdotal tyranny and military defpotifm, awaits, in blood and in tears, the moment when the revival of light fhall reftore it to liberty, to humanity, and to virtue,

2   We

We fhall divide the picture into two diftinct parts. The firft will embrace the Weft, where the decline was more rapid and more abfolute, but where the light of reafon is again to make its appearance, never more to be extinguifhed. The fecond will be confined to the Eaft, where the decline was more flow, and, for a long time, lefs univerfal, but where the day of reafon has not yet dawned, that fhall enlighten it, and enable it to break in pieces its chains.

Chriftian piety had fcarcely overthrown the altars of victory, when the Weft became the prey of barbarians. They embraced the new religion, without adopting the language of the vanquifhed. This the priefts alone preferved; but, from their ignorance and contempt for human learning, they exhibited none of thofe appearances which might have been expected from a perufal of the Latin books, particularly when they only were capable of reading them.

The illiterate character, and rude manners of the conquerors, are fufficiently known: meanwhile, it was in the midft of this ferocious ftupidity that the deftruction of domeftic

meftic flavery took place ; a flavery that had *Domestic Slavery.* difgraced the beft days of Greece, when a country diftinguifhed for learning and liberty.

The rural flaves, ferfs of the glebe, culti-*Serfs.* vated the lands of the conquerors. By this oppreffed clafs of men, their houfes were fupplied with domeftics, whofe dependent fituation anfwered all the purpofes of their pride or their caprice. Accordingly, the object of their wars was not flaves, but lands and colonies.

Befide, the domeftic flaves which they found in the countries they invaded, were in a great meafure either prifoners taken from fome tribe of the victorious nation, or the children of thofe prifoners. Many, at the moment of conqueft, had fled, or elfe joined themfelves to the army of the conquerors.

The principles of general fraternity, which *Fraternity* conftituted a part of the Chriftian morals, alfo condemned flavery ; and, as the priefts faw no political reafon for contradicting, in this particular, maxims that did honour to their caufe, they contributed, by their difcourfes, to a downfall which otherwife events and manners would neceffarily have accomplifhed.

3   This

This change has proved the generative principle of a revolution in the deſtinies of mankind. To this men are indebted for the knowledge of true liberty. But its influence on the lot of individuals was at firſt almoſt infenſible. We ſhould form a very falſe idea of domeſtic ſlavery as it exiſted at this period and among the ancients, if we compared it to that of our negroes. The Spartans, the grandees of Rome, and the ſatraps of the Eaſt, were, no doubt, barbarous maſters. Avarice diſplayed all its brutality in the labours of the mines: but, on the other hand, intereſt had almoſt every where ſoftened the ſtate of ſlavery in private families. The impunity granted for violences committed againſt the rural ſlave, was carried to a high pitch, ſince the law had exactly fixed its price. His dependence was as great as that of the domeſtic, without being compenſated by the ſame attentions. He was leſs perpetually under the eye of his maſter; but he was treated with a more lordly arrogance. The domeſtic was a ſlave whom fortune had reduced to a condition to which a ſimilar fortune might one day reduce his maſter. The rural ſlave, on the contrary, was

con-

confidered as of a lower clafs, and in a ftate
of degradation.

It is principally, then, in its remote confequences that we muft confider this annihilation of domeftic flavery.

Thefe barbarian nations had all nearly the
fame form of government, confifting of a
common chief, called *king*, who, with a coun- *king*
cil, pronounced judgments, and gave decifions,
that it would have been dangerous to delay ;
of an affembly of private chiefs, confulted upon *chiefs*
all refolutions of a certain importance ; and,
laftly, of an affembly of the people, in which *People*
meafures interefting to the general community
were deliberated. The principal difference
was the greater or lefs degree of authority
affixed to thefe three powers, which were not
diftinguifhed by the nature of their functions,
but by the rank of affairs confided to them ;
and, above all, by the value of that rank in
the minds of the majority of the citizens.

Among the agricultural tribes of thefe barbarians, and particularly thofe who had already formed an eftablifhment on a foreign
territory, thefe conftitutions had affumed a
more regular and more folid form, than
among

among paftoral tribes. The individuals of
fuch tribes alfo were difperfed over the foil,
and did not live, like the others, in encampments more or lefs numerous. The king
therefore had not always an army affembled
about his perfon ; and defpotifm could not fo
immediately follow upon conqueft, as in the
revolutions of Afia.

The *victorious* nation was thus not enflaved.
At the fame time, thefe conquerors kept the
towns, but without inhabiting them. As they
were not held in awe by an armed force, no
permanent force of that kind exifting, they
acquired a fort of power ; and this power
was a point of fupport for the liberty of the
conquered nation.

Italy was often invaded by the barbarians ;
but they were able to form there no durable
eftablifhments, from its wealth continually
exciting the avarice of new conquerors, and
becaufe the Greeks entertained the hope, for a
confiderable period, of uniting it to the empire. It was never, by any people, entirely or
permanently fubdued. The Latin language,
which was there the only language of the
people, degenerated more flowly ; and igno-
                                        rance

rance alfo was lefs complete, fuperftition lefs
fenfelefs, than in the other parts of the
Weft.

Rome, which acknowledged mafters only *Rome*
to change them, maintained a fort of independence. This city was the refidence of *Pope*
the chief of the religion. Accordingly, while
in the Eaft, fubjected to a fingle prince, the
clergy, fometimes governing, and fometimes
confpiring againft the emperors, fupported
defpotifm, though refifting the defpot, and preferred availing themfelves of the whole power
of an abfolute mafter, to difputing a part of it;
we fee them, on the contrary, in the Weft,
united under a common head, erecting a
power, the rival of that of kings, and forming
in thefe divided ftates a fort of diftinct and
independent monarchy.

We fhall exhibit this ruling city trying the
experiment upon the univerfe of a new fpe-
cies of chains; its pontiffs fubjugating igno- *Pontiffs*
rant credulity by acts grofsly forged; mixing
religion with all the tranfactions of civil life,
to render them more fubfervient to their
avarice or their pride; punifhing by anathemas, from which the people fhrunk with
horror,

horror, the leaft oppofition to their laws, the fmalleft refiftance of their abfurd pretenfions; having an army of monks in every ftate, ready, by their impoftures, to enhance the terrors of fuperftition, thereby to feed the flame of fanaticifm; depriving nations of their worfhip and ceremonies, upon which depended their religious hopes, to kindle civil war; difturbing all, to govern all; commanding, in the name of God, treafon and perfidy, affaffination and parricide; making kings and warriors now the inftruments, and now the victims, of their revenge; difpofing of force, but never poffeffing it; terrible to their enemies, but trembling before their own defenders; omnipotent to the very extremities of Europe, yet infulted with impunity at the foot even of their altars; finding in heaven the point upon which to fix the lever for moving the world, but without difcovering on earth the regulator that is to direct and continue its motion at their will; in fhort, erecting a Coloffus, but with legs of clay, that, after firft oppreffing Europe, is afterwards to weary it, for a long period, with the weight of its ruins and fcattered fragments.

Conqueft

Conqueſt had introduced into the Weſt a tumultuous anarchy, in which the people groaned under the triple tyranny of kings, leaders of armies, and prieſts ; but this anarchy carried in its womb the feed of liberty. In this portion of Europe muſt be comprehended the countries into which the Romans had not penetrated. Partaking of the general commotion, conquering and conquered in turn, having the fame origin, the fame manners as the conquerors of the empire, thefe people were confounded with them in the common mafs. Their political ſtate muſt have experienced the fame alterations, and followed a fimilar route.

We ſhall give a ſketch of the revolutions of this feodal anarchy : a name that may feodal An furnifh an idea of its character.

Their legiſlation was incoherent and barbarous. If we find in its records many laws apparently mild, this mildnefs was nothing elfe than an unjuſt and privileged impunity. Meanwhile we trace among them fome inſtitutions of a true temper, which, though as being intended to confecrate the rights of the oppreſſor, were an additional outrage to

I. the

the rights of men, yet tended to preferve
fome feeble idea of thefe laft, and were
deftined one day to ferve as an index to their
recognition and reftoration.

In this legiflation two fingular cuftoms are
obfervable, charaćteriftic at once both of the
infancy of nations, and the ignorance of the
rude ages. A criminal might purchafe exemp-
tion from punifhment by means of a fum of
Fines money fixed by law, which eftimated the
lives of men according to their dignity or
their birth. Crimes were not confidered as a
violation of the fecurity and rights of citizens,
which the dread of punifhment was to prevent, but as an outrage committed on an individual, which himfelf or his family might
avenge, if they pleafed, but of which the law
offered a more advantageous reparation. Men
had fo little notion of afcertaining the proofs
by which a faćt might be fubftantiated, that
it was thought a more fimple mode of proceeding to requeft of Heaven a miracle, whenever the queftion was to difcriminate between
guilt and innocence; and the fuccefs of a
fuperftitious experiment, or the chance event
Combat of a combat, were regarded as the fureft
means

means of detecting falſhood and arriving at the truth.

With men who made no diſtinction be-tween independence and liberty, the quarrels ariſing among thoſe who ruled over a portion, however ſmall, of the territory, muſt degenerate into private wars; and theſe wars extending from canton to canton, from village to village, habitually delivered up the whole ſurface of each country to all thoſe horrors' which, even in great invaſions, are but tranſient, and in general wars deſolate only the frontiers.

Whenever tyranny aims at reducing the maſs of a people to the will of one of its portions, the prejudices and ignorance of the victims are counted among the means of effecting it: it endeavours to compenſate, by the compreſſion and activity of a ſmaller force, for the ſuperiority of real force, which, one might ſuppoſe, cannot fail to belong, at all times, to the majority of numbers. But the principal foundation of its hope, which how-ever it can ſeldom attain, is that of eſtabliſh-ing between the maſters and ſlaves a real dif-ference, which ſhall in a manner render na-ture herſelf an accomplice in the guilt of political inequality.

L 2   Such

Such was, in remote periods, the art of the *Priests* Eaftern priefts, who were at once, kings, pontiffs, judges, aftronomers, furveyors, artifts and phyficians. But what they owed to the exclufive poffeffion of intellectual powers, the groffer tyrants of our weak progenitors obtained by their inftitutions and their warlike habits. Clothed with an impenetrable armour, fighting only upon horfes as invulnerable as themfelves, acquiring, by dint of a long and painful difcipline, the neceffary ftrength and addrefs for guiding and governing them, they might opprefs with impunity, and murder without rifk, an individual of the commonalty, too poor to purchafe thefe expenfive accoutrements, and whofe youth, neceffarily occupied by ufeful labours, could not have been devoted to military exercifes.

Thus the tyranny of the few acquired, by the practice of this mode of fighting, a real fuperiority of force, which muft have excluded all idea of refiftance, and which rendered for a long time fruitlefs even the efforts of defpair. Thus the equality of nature difappeared before this factitious inequality of ftrength.

The

The morality of this period, which it was *Morality*
the province of the priefts alone to inculcate,
comprehended thofe univerfal principles which
no fect has overlooked ; but it gave birth to a
multitude of duties purely religious, and of *Duties,*
imaginary fins. Thefe duties were more *fins*
ftrongly enforced than thofe of nature ; and
actions indifferent, lawful, and even virtuous,
were cenfured and punifhed with greater feverity than actual crimes. Meanwhile a momentary repentance, confecrated by the abfo-
lution of a prieft, opened the gates of heaven
to the wicked ; and donations to the church,
with the obfervance of certain practices flat-
tering to its pride, fufficed to atone for a life
crowded with iniquity. Nor was this all :
abfolutions were formed into a regular tariff. *Priestcraft*
Care was taken to include in the catalogue of *indeed*
fins, all the degrees of human infirmity, from
fimple defires, from the moft innocent indulgences of love, to the refinements and
exceffes of the moft intemperate debauchery.
This was a frailty from which, it was well
known, few were able to efcape ; and it was
accordingly one of the moft productive
branches of the facerdotal commerce. There

L 3   was

was even a hell of a limited duration invented, which priefts had the power of abridging, and from which they could grant dif-
penfations; a favour which they firft obliged
the living to purchafe, and afterwards the
relations or friends of the deceafed. They
fold fo much land in heaven for an equal
quantity of land upon earth; and they had
the extreme modefty not to afk any thing to
boot.

The manners of this epoch were unfortunately worthy of a fyftem fo pregnant with
corruption, fo rootedly depraved. Their nature may be learned from the progrefs of this
very fyftem itfelf; from the monks, fometimes inventing old miracles, fometimes fabricating new ones, and nourifhing with prodigies and fables the ftupid ignorance of the
people, whom they deceived in order to rob
them; from the doctors of the church, employing the little imagination they poffeffed
in enriching their creed with farther abfurdities, and exceeding, if poffible, thofe which
had been tranfmitted to them; from the
priefts, obliging princes to confign to the
flames, not only the men who prefumed either

to

to doubt any of their dogmas, or inveſtigate
their impoſtures, or bluſh for their crimes,
but thoſe who ſhould depart for an inſtant from their blind obedience; and even
theologiſts themſelves, when they indulged in
dreams different from thoſe of the umpires of
the church, enjoying moſt influence and control. Such, at this period, are the only traits
which the manners of the Weſt of Europe
can furniſh to the picture of the human
ſpecies.

In the Eaſt, united under a ſingle deſpot, *laſt*
we ſhall obſerve a ſlower decline accompany-
ing the gradual debility of the empire; the
ignorance and depravity of every age advancing a few degrees above the ignorance
and depravity of the preceding one; while
riches diminiſh, the frontiers ally themſelves
more cloſely to the capital, revolutions become more frequent, and tyranny grows more
daſtardly and more cruel.

In following the hiſtory of this empire, in
reading the books that each age has produced, the moſt ſuperficial and leaſt attentive
obſerver cannot avoid being ſtruck with the
reſemblance we have mentioned.

L 4   The

The people there indulged themfelves more frequently in theological difputes. Thefe accordingly occupy a more confiderable portion of its hiftory, have a greater influence upon political events, and the dreams of priefts acquire a fubtlety which the jealoufy of the Weft could as yet not attain. Religious intolerance was equally oppreffive in both quarters of Europe ; but, in the country we are confidering, its afpect was lefs ferocious.

Intollerance

Meanwhile the works of Photius evince that a tafte for rational ftudy was not extinct. A few emperors, princes, and even fome female fovereigns, are found feeking laurels out of the boundaries of theological controverfy, and deigning to cultivate human learning.

Photius.

The Roman legiflation was but flowly corrupted by that mixture of bad laws which avarice and tyranny dictated to the emperors, or which fuperftition extorted from their weaknefs. The Greek language loft its purity and character; but it preferved its richnefs, its forms and its grammar; and the inhabitants of Conftantinople could ftill read Homer and Sophocles, Thucydides and Plato. Anthemius explained the conftruction of the

Anthemius.

burning

burning glaffes of Archimedes, which Proclus *Proclus*
employed with fuccefs in the defence of the
capital. Upon the fall of the empire, this city
contained fome literary characters, who took
refuge in Italy, and whofe learning was ufeful
to the progrefs of knowledge. Thus, even at
this period, the Eaft had not arrived at the
laft ftage of ignorance; but at the fame time
it furnifhed no hope of a revival of letters. It
became the prey of barbarians; the feeble remains of intellectual cultivation difppeared;
and the genius of Greece ftill waits the hand
of a deliverer.

At the extremities of Afia, and upon the
confines of Africa, there exifted a people, who,
from its local fituation and its courage, efcaped
the conquefts of the Perfians, of Alexander,
and of the Romans. Of its numerous tribes,
fome derived their fubfiftance from agriculture, while others obferved a paftoral life;
all purfued commerce, and fome addicted
themfelves to robbery. Having a fimilarity
of origin, of language and of religious habits,
they formed a great nation, the different parts
of which, however, were held together by no
political tie. Suddenly there ftarted up among
them

them a man of an ardent enthufiafm and moft
profound policy, born with the talents of a
poet, as well as thofe of a warrior. This man
conceived the bold project of uniting the
Arabian tribes into one body, and he had the
courage to execute it. To fucceed in impofing a chief upon a nation hitherto in-
vincible, he began with erecting upon the
ruins of the ancient worfhip a religion more
refined. At once legiflator, prophet, prieft,
judge, and general of the army, he was in
poffeffion of all the means of fubjugating the
mind ; and he knew how to employ them
with addrefs, but at the fame time with comprehenfion and dignity.

He promulgated a mafs of fables, which he
pretended to have received from heaven ; but
he alfo gained battles. Devotion and the
pleafures of love divided his leifure. After enjoying for twenty years a power without
bounds, and of which there exifts no other
example, he announced publicly, that, if he
had committed any act of injuftice, he was
ready to make reparation. All were filent :
one woman only had the boldnefs to claim a
fmall fum of money. He died; and the
enthu-

enthufiafm which he communicated to his people will be feen to change the face of three quarters of the globe.

The manners of the Arabians were mild and dignified ; they admired and cultivated poetry : and when they reigned over the fineft countries of Afia, and time had cooled the fever of fanaticifm, a tafte for literature and the fciences mixed with their zeal for the propagation of religion, and abated their ardour for conquefts.

They ftudied Ariftotle, whofe works they *Arabians* tranflated. They cultivated aftronomy, optics, all the branches of medicine, and enriched the fciences with fome new truths. To them we owe the general application of algebra, which *Algebra* was confined among the Greeks to a fingle clafs of queftions. If the chimerical purfuit of a fecret for the tranfmutation of metals, *Philosophers Stone.* and a draught for the perpetuating of life de- graded their chymical refearches, they were *Panacea* the reftorers, or more properly fpeaking the *Catholicon.* inventors, of this fcience, which had hitherto *Chymistry* been confounded with medicine and the ftudy of the proceffes of the arts. Among them it appeared for the firft time in its fimple form,

a ftrict

a ſtrict analyſis of bodies for the purpoſe of
aſcertaining their elements, a theory of the
combinations of matter and the laws to which
thoſe combinations are ſubjected.

The ſciences were free, and to that freedom
they owed their being able to revive ſome
ſparks of the Grecian genius; but the people
were ſubjected to the unmitigated deſpotiſm
of religion. Accordingly this light ſhone for
a few moments only to give place to a thicker
darkneſs; and theſe labours of the Arabs
would have been loſt to the human race, if
they had not ſerved to prepare that more
durable reſtoration, of which the Weſt will
preſently exhibit to us the picture.

a Pity! that We thus ſee, for the ſecond time, genius
is Man of abandoning nations whom it had enlightened;
enius, cannot but it was in this, as in the preceding in-
thing and ſtance, from before tyranny and ſuperſtition
niet for the that it was obliged to diſappear. Born in
whole human Greece, by the ſide of liberty, it was neither
use! able to arreſt the fall of that country, nor de-
as not Genius
een em fend reaſon againſt the prejudices of the
loyed to in people already degraded by ſlavery. Born
roduce tyran among the Arabs, in the midſt of deſpotiſm,
; and ſuper and, as it were, in the cradle of a fanatical
tition as
well as to introduce them! religion,

religion, it has only, like the generous and brilliant character of that people, furnished a tranfient exception to the general laws of nature, that condemn to brutality and ignorance enflaved and fuperftitious nations.

But this fecond example ought not to terrify us refpecting the future : it fhould operate only as a warning upon our contemporaries not to neglect any means of preferving and augmenting knowledge, if they wifh either to become or to remain free ; and to maintain their freedom, if they would not lofe the advantages which knowledge has procured them.

To the account of the labours of the Arabs, I fhall fuggeft the outlines of the fudden rife and precipitate fall of that nation, which, after reigning from the borders of the Atlantic ocean to the banks of the Indus, driven by the barbarians from the greater part of its conquefts, retaining the reft only to exhibit therein the fhocking fpectacle of a people degenerated to the loweft ftate of fervitude, corruption and wretchednefs, ftill occupies its ancient country, where it has preferved its manners, its fpirit and its character, and

learned

learned to regain and defend its former independence.

Mahomet

I fhall add that the religion of Mahomet,
the moft fimple in its dogmas, the leaft abfurd
in its practices, above all others tolerant
in its principles, feems to have condemned to
an eternal flavery, to an incurable ftupidity,
all that vaft portion of the earth in which it

Genius of Islam
beats the Genius
of Superftition,

has extended its empire ; while we are about
to fee the genius of fcience and of liberty
blaze forth anew under fuperftitions more
abfurd, and in the midft of the moft bar-

China

barous intolerance. China exhibits a fimilar
phenomenon, though the effects of this ftupe-
fying poifon have there been lefs fatal.

SEVENTH

SEVENTH EPOCH.

From the firſt Progreſs of the Sciences about the Period of their Revival in the Weſt, to the Invention of the Art of Printing.

A Variety of circumſtances have concurred to reſtore by degrees that energy to the human mind, which, from chains ſo degrading and ſo heavy, one might have ſuppoſed was cruſhed for ever.

The intolerance of prieſts, their eagerneſs *Intolerance* to graſp at political power, their abominable avarice, their diſſolute manners, rendered more diſguſting by their hypocriſy, excited againſt them every honeſt heart, every unbiaſſed un- *Unchriſtian* derſtanding, and every courageous character. *Character of* It was impoſſible not to be ſtruck with the *the Church.* contradiction between their dogmas, maxims and conduct, and thoſe of the evangeliſts, from which their faith and ſyſtem of morals had originated, and which they had been unable totally to conceal from the knowledge of the people.

Accord-

ation Accordingly, powerful outcries were raised againſt them. In the centre of France whole provinces united for the adoption of a more ſimple doctrine, a purer ſyſtem of Chriſtianity, in which, ſubjected only to the worſhip of a ſingle Divinity, man was permitted to judge, from his own reaſon, of what that Divinity had condeſcended to reveal in the books ſaid to have emanated from him.

Fanatic armies, conducted by ambitious chiefs, laid waſte the provinces. Executioners, under the guidance of legates and prieſts, put to death thoſe whom the ſoldiers had ſpared. A tribunal of monks was eſtabliſhed, with powers of condemning to the ſtake whoever ſhould be ſuſpected of making uſe of his reaſon.

Meanwhile they could not prevent a ſpirit of freedom and enquiry from making a ſilent and furtive progreſs. Cruſhed in one country, in which it had the temerity to ſhew itſelf, in which, more than once, intolerant hypo-criſy kindled the moſt ſanguinary wars, it ſtarted up, or ſpread ſecretly in another. It is ſeen at every interval, till the period, when, aided by the invention of the preſs, it gained
ſufficient

fufficient power to refcue a portion of Europe from the yoke of the court of Rome.

Even already there exifted a clafs of men, who, freed from the inglorious bondage of fuperftition, contented themfelves with fecretly indulging their contempt, or who at moft went no farther than to caft upon it, fortuitoufly as it were, fome traits of a ridicule, which was by fo much the more ftriking on account of the uniform refpect with which they took care to clothe it. The pleafantry of the writer obtained favour for the boldneffes of his pen. They were fcattered with moderation through works deftined for the amufement of men of rank or of letters, and which never reached the mafs of the people ; for which reafon they did not excite the refentment of the bigot.

Frederic the fecond was fufpected of being *Frederic 2* what our priefts of the eighteenth century have fince denominated a *philofopher*. He was accufed by the Pope, before all the nations of Europe, of having treated the religions of Mofes, Jefus, and Mahomet, as political fables. To his chancellor, Pierre des Vignes, *Pierre des Vig* was attributed the imaginary book of the

M   Three

Three Impostors Three Impoftors, which never had any exiftence but in the calumnies of fome, or the ingenious fportivenefs of others, but of which
the very title announced the exiftence of an
opinion, the natural refult of an examination
of thefe three creeds, which, derived from the
fame fource, were only a corruption of a lefs
impure worfhip rendered by the moft remote
Jehovah nations of antiquity to the univerfal foul of
the world.

Our collections of traditional tales, and the
Decameron Decameron of Bocace, are full of traits cha-
of racteriftic of this freedom of thought, this
Bocace contempt of prejudices, this inclination to
make them the fubject of fecret and acrimo-
nious derifion.

Thus we are furnifhed in this epoch, at one
and the fame period, with tranquil fatirifts of
all degrees of fuperftition, and enthufiaftical
reformers of its groffeft abufes ; and the hiftory
of thefe obfcure invectives, thefe protefts in
favour of the rights of reafon, may be almoft
connected with that of the moft modern difciples of the fchool of Alexandria.

We fhall enquire if, when philofophical
profelytifm was attended with fuch peril, fecret

cret focieties were not formed, whofe object
was to perpetuate, to fpread filently and without rifk, among fome difciples and adepts,
a few fimple truths which might operate as a
prefervative againft prevailing prejudices.

We fhall examine whether we ought not
to rank in the number of fuch focieties that
celebrated order, which popes and kings con- *Jesuits*
fpired againft with fuch meannefs, and deftroyed with fo much barbarity.

Priefts, either for felf-defence, or to invent *Priest*
pretexts by which to cover their ufurpations
over the fecular power, and to improve themfelves in the art of forging paffages of fcrip-
ture, were under the neceffity of applying
themfelves to ftudy. Kings, on the other
hand, to conduct with lefs difadvantage this
war, in which the claims were made to reft
upon authority and precedent, patronifed
fchools, that might furnifh civilians, of whom *Civilians*
they ftood in need to be on an equality with
the enemy.

In thefe difputes between the clergy and the
governments, between the clergy of each
country and the fupreme head of the church,
thofe of more honeft minds, and of a more

M 2   frank

frank and liberal character, vindicated the cause of men against that of priests, the cause of the national clergy against the despotism of the foreign chief. They attacked abuses and usurpations, of which they attempted to unveil the origin. To us this boldness scarcely appears at present superior to servile timidity ; we smile at seeing such a profusion of labour employed to prove what good sense alone was competent to have taught; but the truths to which I refer, at that time new, frequently decided the fate of a people : these men fought them with an independent mind ; they defended them with firmness ; and to their influence is it to be ascribed that human reason began to recover the recollection of its rights and its liberty.

Kings vs Nobles In the quarrels that took place between the kings and the nobles, the kings secured the support of the principal towns, either by granting privileges, or by restoring some of the natural rights of man : they endeavoured, by means of emancipations, to increase the number of those who enjoyed the common right of citizens. And these men, re-born as it were to liberty, felt how much it behoved

hoved them, by the ftudy of law and of hiftory, to acquire a fund of information, an authority of opinion, that might ferve to counterbalance the military power of the feodal tyranny.

The rivalfhip that exifted between the *Rivalry bet* emperors and the popes prevented Italy from *Emperor I Co*. uniting under a fingle mafter, and preferved there a great number of independent focieties. In thefe petty ftates, it was neceffary to add the power of perfuafion to that of force, and to employ negociation as often as arms : and as this political war was founded, in reality, in a war of opinion, and as Italy had never ab-folutely loft its tafte for ftudy, this country may be confidered, refpecting Europe, as a feedplot of knowledge, inconfiderable indeed as yet, but which promifed a fpeedy and vi-gorous increafe.

In fine, hurried on by religious enthu-*Crusades.* fiafm, the weftern nations engaged in the con-queft of places rendered holy, as it was faid, by the miracles and death of Chrift : and this zeal, at the fame time that it was favourable to liberty, by weakening and impoverifhing the nobles, extended the connection of the people of Europe with the Arabians, a con-

M 3   nection

nection which their mixture with Spain had before formed, and their commerce with Pifa, Genoa, and Venice cemented. Their language was ftudied, their books were read, part of their difcoveries was acquired ; and if the Europeans did not foar above the point in which the fciences had been left by the Arabians, they at leaft felt the ambition of rivaling them.

Arabians

Thefe wars, undertaken with fuperftitious views, ferved to deftroy fuperftition. The fpectacle of fuch a multitude of religions excited at length in men of fenfe a total indifference for creeds, alike impotent in refining the paffions, and curing the vices of mankind ; a uniform contempt for that attachment, equally fincere, equally obftinate, of fectaries, to opinions contradictory to each other.

Creeds

Republics were formed in Italy, of which fome were imitations of the Greek republics, while others attempted to reconcile the fervitude of a fubject people with the liberty and democratic equaity of a fovereign one. In Germany, in the north, fome towns, obtaining almoft entire independence, were governed by their own laws. In certain parts of Switzerland,

Republics in Italy.

Hans Towns

land, the people threw off the chains both of *Switzerland*
feodal and of royal power. In almoſt all
the great ſtates imperfect conſtitutions ſprung
up, in which the authority of raiſing ſubſi-
dies, and of making new laws, was divided
ſometimes between the king, the nobles, the *K. Nobles*
clergy and the people, and ſometimes between *Clergy, People*
the king, the barons and the commons ; in
which the people, though not yet exempt
from a ſtate of humiliation, were at leaſt ſecure from oppreſſion ; in which all that truly
compoſed a nation were admitted to the right
of defending its intereſts, and of being heard
by thoſe who had the regulation of its deſtiny.
In England a celebrated act, ſolemnly ſworn *Magna Charta*
by the king, and great men of the realm, ſecured the rights of the barons, and ſome of
the rights of men.

Other nations, provinces, and even cities,
obtained alſo charters of a ſimilar nature, but
leſs celebrated, and not ſo ſtrenuouſly defended.
They are the origin of thoſe declarations of *Declarations*
rights, regarded at preſent by every enlightened *of Rights*
mind as the baſis of liberty, and of which the
ancients neither had nor could have an idea,
becauſe their inſtitutions were ſullied by do-

meſtic

Justitia est, constans et perpetua voluntas Jus Suum cuique tribuendi.

The Decalo que, the gospel, even the Institutes of Justinian are all ancient, and yet support these rights.

meſtic ſlavery, becauſe with them the right of citizenſhip was hereditary, or conferred by voluntary adoption, and becauſe they never arrived at the knowledge of rights which are inherent in the ſpecies, and belong with a ſtrict equality to all mankind.

In France, England, and other great nations, the people appeared deſirous of reſuming their true rights ; but blinded by the ſenſe of oppreſſion, rather than enlightened by reaſon, the only fruit of its efforts were outrages, that were ſoon expiated by acts of vengeance more barbarous, and particularly more unjuſt, and pillages accompanied with greater miſery than either.

Wickliffe

In England the principles of Wickliffe, the reformer, had given riſe to one of theſe commotions, carried on under the direction of ſome of his diſciples, and which afforded a preſage of attempts, more ſyſtematic and better combined, that would be made by the people under other reformers, and in a more enlightened age.

The diſcovery of a manuſcript of the Juſtinian code produced the revival of the ſtudy of juriſprudence, as well as of legiſlation, and

ſerved

ferved to render thefe lefs barbarous even
among the people who knew how to derive
profit from the difcovery, without treating the
code as of facred obligation.

The commerce of Pifa, Genoa, Florence, *com meru*
Venice, fome cities of Belgia, and free towns
of Germany, embraced the Mediterranean,
the Baltic, and the coafts of the European
ocean. The precious commodities of the Le-
vant were fought by the merchants of thofe
places in the ports of Egypt, and at the extremities of the Black Sea.

Polity, legiflation, national economy, were *Polity not*
not yet converted into fciences; the principles *unders food*
of them were neither enquired after, invefti- *then nor*
gated, nor developed; but as the mind be- *now 179 &*
gan to be enlightened by experience, obfervations were collected tending to lead thereto,
and men became verfed in the interefts that
muft caufe the want of them to be felt.

Ariftotle was only known at firft by a tran- *Aristotle*
flation of his works made from the Arabic.
His philofophy, perfecuted at the beginning,
foon gained footing in all the fchools. I introduced there no new light, but it gave more
regularity, more method to that art of reafoning

soning which theological difputes had called into exiftence. This fcholaftic difcipline did not lead to the difcovery of truth ; it did not even ferve for the difcuffion and accurate valuation of its proofs, but it whetted the minds of men ; and the tafte for fubtle diftinctions, the neceffity of continually dividing and fubdividing ideas, of feizing their niceft fhades, and expreffing them in new words, the apparatus which was in the firft inftance employed to embarrafs one's enemy in a difpute, or to efcape from his toils, was the original fource of that philofophical analyfis to which we have fince been fo highly indebted for our intellectual progrefs.

Ina lysis

To thefe difciplinarians we are indebted for the greater accuracy that may have been obtained refpecting the Supreme Being and his attributes ; refpecting the diftinction between the firft caufe, and the univerfe which it is fuppofed to govern ; refpecting the farther diftinction between mind and matter ; refpecting the different fenfes that may be affixed to the word *liberty* ; refpecting the meaning of the word *creation* ; refpecting the manner of diftinguifhing from each other the different operations

upreme being.

of

of the human mind, and of claffing the ideas
it forms of objects and their properties.

But this method could not fail to retard in
the fchools the advancement of the natural *Natural Sci*
fciences. Accordingly the whole picture of *ences*.
thefe fciences at this period will be found
merely to comprehend a few anatomical re- *Anatomy*
fearches; fome obfcure productions of chy- *Chymiftry*
miftry, employed in the difcovery of the
grand fecret alone; a flight application to
geometry and algebra, that fell fhort of the *Geometry*
difcoveries of the Arabians, and did not even *Algebra*
extend to a complete underftanding of the
work of the ancients; and laftly, fome aftro-
nomical ftudies and calculations, confined to
the formation and improvement of tables, and *Tables*
depraved by an abfurd mixture of aftrology. *Aftrology*
Meanwhile the mechanical arts began to ap- *Mechanics*
proach the degree of perfection which they
had preferved in Afia. In the fouthern countries of Europe the culture of filk was intro- *Silk*
duced; windmills as well as paper-mills were *Windmills*
eftablifhed; and the art of meafuring time *Paper-mills*
furpaffed the bounds which it had acquired *Dials Glaffes*
either among the Ancients or the Arabians. *Watches*

In fhort, two important difcoveries characterife this epoch. The property poffeffed

by

met by the loadftone, of pointing always to the
fame quarter of the heavens, a property known
to the Chinefe, and employed by them in
fteering their veffels, was alfo obferved in
pafs Europe. The compafs came into ufe, an inftrument which gave activity to commerce,
improved the art of navigation, fuggefted the
idea of voyages to which we have fince owed
the knowledge of a new world, and enabled
man to take a furvey of the whole extent of
the globe on which he is placed. A chymift,
by mixing an inflammable matter with falt-
vder petre, difcovered the fecret of that powder
which has produced fo unexpected a revolution in the art of war. Notwithftanding the
terrible effect of fire-arms, in difperfing an
army, they have rendered war lefs murderous, and its combatants lefs brutal. Military
expeditions are more expenfive; wealth can
balance force; even the moft warlike people
feel the neceffity of providing and fecuring
the means of combating, by the acquifition of
the riches of commerce and the arts. Polifhed
nations have no longer any thing to apprehend from the blind courage of barbarian
tribes. Great conquefts, and the revolutions
which follow, are become almoft impoffible.

3   That

That fuperiority which an armour of iron, *Armour*
which the art of conducting a horfe almoft
invulnerable from his accoutrements, of ma-
naging the lance, the club, or the fword, gave
the nobility over the people, is completely
done away ; and the removal of this impediment to the liberty and real equality of mankind, is the refult of an invention, that, at the
firft glance, feemed to threaten the total extirpation of the human race.

In Italy, the language arrived almoft at its *Italy*
perfection about the fourteenth century. The
ftyle of Dante is often grand, precife, ener- *Dante*
getic. Boccace is graceful, fimple, and ele- *Boccace*
gant. The ingenious and tender Petrarch has *Petrarch*
not yet become obfolete. In this country,
whofe happy climate nearly refembles that of
Greece, the models of antiquity were ftudied ;
attempts were made to transfufe into the new
lang ome of their beauties, and to pro-
d eauties of a fimilar ftamp. Al-
t productions gave reafon to hope
that, rofed by the view of ancient monuments, infpired by thofe mute but eloquent
leffons, genius was about, for the fecond time, *Genius*
to embellifh the exiftence of man, and provide *is ftill*
for his ufofis

and the Prophet. Inspiration is his fyftem
as much as ⅟₇ of a Jew or Christian. The
Inspiration of Genius. Oh Vanity of Genius.
what Mischiefs have you not done?

for him thofe pure pleafures, the enjoyment of which is free to all, and becomes greater in proportion as it is participated.

The reft of Europe followed at an humble diftance; but a tafte for letters and poetry began at leaft to give a polifh to languages that were ftill in a ftate almoft of barbarity.

Language polifhed

The fame motives which had roufed the minds of men from their long lethargy, muft alfo have directed their exertions. Reafon could not be appealed to for the decifion of queftions, of which oppofite interefts had compelled the difcuffion. Religion, far from acknowledging its power, boafted of having fubjected and humbled it. Politics confidered as juft what had been confecrated by compact, by conftant practice, and ancient cuftoms.

Religion

Politicks

Sufpicion it fhould

No <u>doubt</u> was entertained that the rights of man were written in the book of nature, and that to confult any other would be to depart from and to violate them. Meanwhile it was only in the facred books, in refpected authors, in the bulls of popes, in the refcripts of kings, in regifters of old ufages, and in the annals of the church, that maxims or examples were fought from which to infer thofe rights. The bufinefs was never to examine the intrinfic

merits

merits of a principle, but to interpret, to appreciate, to fupport or to annul by other texts thofe upon which it might be founded. A propofition was not adopted becaufe it was true, but becaufe it was written in this or that book, and had been embraced in fuch a country and fuch an age.

Thus the authority of men was every where *Authority* fubftituted for that of reafon : books were *Books* much more ftudied than nature, and the opinions of antiquity obtained the preference over the phenomena of the univerfe. This bondage of the mind, in which men had not then the advantage of enlightened criticifm, was ftill more detrimental to the progrefs of the human fpecies, by corrupting the method of ftudy, than by its immediate effects. And the ancients were yet too far from being equalled, to think of correcting or furpaffing them.

Manners preferved, during this epoch, their corruption and ferocity ; religious intolerance *Intolerance* was even more active ; and civil difcords, and *discords* the inceffant wars of a crowd of petty fove- *Petty wars* reigns, fucceeded the invafions of the barbarians, and the peft, ftill more fatal, of fanguinary

nary

Deadly Feuds nary feuds. The gallantry indeed of the min-
Gallantry ftrels and the troubadours, the inftitution of
Chivalry orders of chivalry, profeffing generofity and
franknefs, devoting themfelves to the maintenance of religion, the relief of the oppreffed, and the fervice of the fair, were calculated to infufe into manners more mildnefs,
decorum, and dignity. But the change, confined to courts and caftles, reached not to the
bulk of the people. There refulted from it a
little more equality among the nobles, lefs
perfidy and cruelty in their relations with
each other; but their contempt for the people, the infolence of their tyranny, their au-
Robberies dacious robberies, continued the fame; and
nations, oppreffed as before, were as before
ignorant, barbarous and corrupt.

Chivalry   This poetical and military gallantry, this
of chivalry, derived in great meafure from the
Arabians Arabians, whofe natural generofity long re-
in Spain fifted in Spain fuperftition and defpotifm, had
doubtlefs their ufe: they diffufed the feeds
of humanity, which were deftined in happier
periods to exhibit their fruit; and it was the
general character of this epoch, that it difpofed the human mind for the revolution
which

which the difcovery of printing could not *Printing*
but introduce, and prepared the foil which
the following ages were to cover with fo rich
and fo abundant an harveft.

N   EIGHTH

EIGHTH EPOCH.

From the Invention of Printing, to the Period when the Sciences and Philosophy threw off the Yoke of Authority.

THOSE who have reflected but fuperficially upon the march of the human mind in the difcovery, whether of the truths of fcience, or of the proceffes of the arts, muft be afto-nifhed that fo long a period fhould elapfe be-tween the knowledge of the art of taking im-preffions of drawings, and the difcovery of that of printing characters.

Some engravers of plates had doubtlefs con-ceived this idea of the application of their art ; but they were more ftruck with the difficulty of executing it, than with the advantages of fuccefs : and it is fortunate that they did not comprehend it in all its extent ; fince priefts and kings would infallibly have united to ftifle, from its birth, the enemy that was to unmafk their hypocrify, and hurl them from their thrones.

The

The prefs multiplies indefinitely, and at a *The Prefs.* fmall expence, copies of any work. Thofe who can read are hence enabled to furnifh themfelves with books fuitable to their tafte and their wants; and this facility of exercifing the talent of reading, has increafed and propagated the defire of learning it.

Thefe multiplied copies, fpreading themfelves with greater rapidity, facts and difcoveries not only acquire a more extenfive publicity, but acquire it alfo in a fhorter fpace of time. Knowledge has become the object of an active and univerfal commerce.

Printers were obliged to feek manufcripts, as we feek at prefent works of extraordinary genius. What was read before by a few individuals only, might now be perufed by a whole people, and ftrike almoft at the fame inftant every man that underftood the fame language.

The means are acquired of addreffing remote and difperfed nations. A new fpecies of tribune is eftablifhed, from which are communicated impreffions lefs lively, but at the fame time more folid and profound; from which is exercifed over the paffions an empire *The Empire of the Prefs, over the Paffions, in the hands of Marat and others was more tyrannical than the Govt of Cæsar Borgia.*

lefs

lefs tyrannical, but over reafon a power more
certain and durable ; where all the advantage
is on the fide of truth, fince what the art may
lofe in point of feduction, is more than coun-
terbalanced by the illumination it conveys. A
public opinion is formed, powerful by the
number of thofe who fhare in it, energetic, becaufe the motives that determine it act upon
all minds at once, though at confiderable diftances from each other. A tribunal is erected
in favour of reafon and juftice, independent
of all human power, from the penetration of
which it is difficult to conceal any thing, from
whofe verdict there is no efcape.

New inventions, the hiftory of the firft fteps
in the road to a difcovery, the labours that
prepare the way for it, the views that fuggeft
the idea or give rife merely to the wifh of purfuing it, thefe, communicating themfelves with
celerity, furnifh every individual with the
united means which the efforts of all have
been able to create, and genius appears to
have more than doubled its powers.

Every new error is refifted from its birth:
frequently attacked before it has diffeminated
itfelf, it has not time to take root in the mind.
it by the Arfs in the laft ten years Thofe
in hundred before. 1798.

Thofe which, imbibed from infancy, are iden-
tified in a manner with the reafon of every individual, and by the influence of hope or of
terror endeared to the exiftence of weak underftandings, have been fhaken, from this circumftance alone, that it is now impoffible to
prevent their difcuffion, impoffible to conceal
that they are capable of being examined and
rejected, impoffible they fhould withftand the
progrefs of truths which, daily acquiring new
light, muft conclude at laft with difplaying all
the abfurdity of fuch errors.

It is to the prefs we owe the poffibility of,
fpreading thofe publications which the emer-
gency of the moment, or the tranfient fluctu-
ations of opinion, may require, and of interefting thereby in any queftion, treated in a
fingle point of view, whole communities of
men reading and underftanding the fame language.

All thofe means which render the progrefs
of the human mind more eafy, more rapid,
more certain, are alfo the benefits of the prefs.
Without the inftrumentality of this art, fuch
books could not have been multiplied as are
adapted to every clafs of readers, and every de-

gree

gree of inftruction, To the prefs we owe thofe
continued difcuffions which alone can enlighten doubtful queftions, and fix upon an
immoveable bafis, truths too abftract, too fub-
tile, too remote from the prejudices of the
people, or the common opinion of the learned,
not to be foon forgotten and loft. To the prefs
Elements we owe thofe books purely elementary, dic-
Dictionaries tionaries, works in which are collected, with
Abridgment all their details, a multitude of facts, obfervations, and experiments, in which all their
proofs are developed, all their difficulties inveftigated. To the prefs we owe thofe valu-
Compilations able compilations, containing fometimes all
that has been difcovered, written, thought,
upon a particular branch of fcience, and fome-
Magazines times the refult of the annual labours of all the
literati of a country. To the prefs we owe
Tables thofe tables, thofe catalogues, thofe pictures
of every kind, of which fome exhibit a view
of inductions which the mind could only have
acquired by the moft tedious operations;
others prefent at will the fact, the difcovery,
the number, the method, the object which we
are defirous of afcertaining; while others again
furnifh, in a more commodious form, and a

2   more

more arranged order, the materials from which
genius may fafhion and derive new truths.

To thefe benefits we fhall have occafion to
add others, when we proceed to analyfe the
effects that have arifen from the fubftitution
of the vernacular tongue of each country, in
the room of the almoft exclufive application,
which had preceded, fo far as relates to the
fciences, of one language, the common medium of communication between the learned
of all nations.

In fhort, is it not the prefs that has freed *Oh. that*
the inftruction of the people from every poli- *had.*
tical and religious chain ? In vain might either
defpotifm invade our fchools; in vain might
it attempt, by rigid inftitutions, invariably to
fix what truths fhall be preferved in them,
what errors inculcated on the mind; in vain
might chairs, confecrated to the moral inftruction of the people, and the tuition of
youth in philofophy and the fciences, be
obliged to deliver no doctrines but fuch as are
favourable to this double tyranny; the prefs
can diffufe at the fame time a pure and independent light. That inftruction which is to
be acquired from books in filence and folitude,

N 4   can

can never be universally corrupted: a single corner of the earth free to commit their leaves to the press, would be a sufficient security. How amidst that variety of productions, amidst that multitude of existing copies of the same book, amidst impressions continually renewed, will it be possible to shut so closely all the doors of truth, as to leave no opening, no crack or crevice by which it may enter? If it was difficult even when the business was to destroy a few copies only of a manuscript, to prevent for ever its revival, when it was sufficient to proscribe a truth, or opinion, for a certain number of years to devote it to eternal oblivion, is not this difficulty now rendered impossible, when it would require a vigilance incessantly occupied, and an activity that should never slumber? And even should success attend the suppression of those too palpable truths, that wound directly the interests of inquisitors, how are others to be prevented from penetrating and spreading, which include those proscribed truths without suffering them to be perceived, which prepare the way, and must one day infallibly lead to them? Could it be done without obliging the

Ask Barras and Co. 1798. ask Napoleon in 1811.

per-

perfonages in queftion to throw off that mafk
of hypocrify, the fall of which would prove no
lefs fatal than truth itfelf to the reign of error ?
We fhall accordingly fee reafon triumphing
over thefe vain efforts : we fhall fee her in
this war, a war continually reviving, and frequently cruel, fuccefsful alike againft violence
and ftratagem ; braving the flames, and refifting feduction ; crufhing in turn, under its
mighty hand, both the fanatical hypocrify
which requires for its dogmas a fincere adoration, and the political hypocrify imploring on
its knees that it may be allowed to enjoy in
peace the profit of errors, in which, if you
will take its word, it is no lefs advantageous
to the people than to itfelf, that they fhould
for ever be plunged.

The invention of the art of printing nearly
coincides with two other events, of which one
has exercifed an immediate influence on the
progrefs of knowledge, while the influence of
the other on the deftiny of the whole human
fpecies can never ceafe but with the fpecies
itfelf.

I refer to the taking of Conftantinople by
the Turks, and the difcovery both of the new
world,

America.

Cape

Greeks fly to Italy.

world, and of the route which has opened to Europe a direct communication with the eaftern parts of Africa and Afia.

The Greek literati, flying from the fovereignty of the Tartars, fought an afylum in Italy. They acquired the ability of reading, in their original language, the poets, orators, hiftorians, philofophers, and antiquarians of Greece. They firft` furnifhed manufcripts, and foon after editions of the works of thofe authors. The veneration of the ftudious was no longer confined to what they agreed in calling the doctrine of Ariftotle. They ftudied this doctrine in his own writings. They ventured to inveftigate and oppofe it. They contrafted him with Plato: and it was advancing a ftep towards throwing off the yoke, to acknowledge in themfelves the right of choofing a mafter.

Ariftotle

Plato

Euclid

The perufal of Euclid, Archimedes, Diophantus, and Ariftotle's philofophical book upon animals, rekindled the genius of natural philofophy and of geometry; while the antichriftian opinions of philofophers awakened ideas that were almoft extinct of the ancient prerogatives of human reafon.

Intrepid

Intrepid individuals, inftigated by the love *Lacepede* of glory and a paffion for difcoveries, had extended for Europe the bounds of the uni-verfe, had exhibited a new heaven, and opened to its view an unknown earth. Gama *Gama* had penetrated into India, after having pur-fued with indefatigable patience the immenfe extent of the African coafts ; while Columbus, *Columbus* configning him to the waves of the Atlantic ocean, had reached that country, hitherto un-known, extending from the weft of Europe to the eaft of Afia.

If this paffion, whofe reftlefs activity, em-bracing at that period every object, gave pro-mife of advantages highly important to the progrefs of the human fpecies, if a noble cu-riofity had animated the heroes of navigation, a mean and cruel avarice, a ftupid and brutal fanaticifm governed the kings and robbers who were to reap the profits of their labour. The unfortunate beings who inhabited thefe new countries were not treated as men, becaufe they were not chriftians. This prejudice, more degrading to the tyrants than the vic-tims, ftifled all fenfe of remorfe, and aban-doned, without controul, to their inextinguifh-
able

able thirſt for gold and for blood, thoſe greedy
and unfeeling men that Europe diſgorged from
her boſom. The bones of five millions of
human beings have covered the wretched
countries to which the Spaniards and Portu-
gueze tranſported their avarice, their ſuperſtition, and their fury. Theſe bones will
plead to everlaſting ages againſt the doctrine
of the political utility of religions, which is
ſtill able to find its apologiſts in the world.

It is in this epoch only of the progreſs of
the human mind, that man has arrived at the
knowledge of the globe which he inhabits;
that he has been able to ſtudy, in all its countries, the ſpecies to which he belongs, modified by the continued influence of natural
cauſes, or of ſocial inſtitutions; that he has
had an opportunity of obſerving the productions of the earth, or of the ſea, in all tempera-
tures and climates. And accordingly, among
the happy conſequences of the diſcoveries in
queſtion, may be included the reſources of
every kind which thoſe productions afford to
mankind, and which, ſo far from being exhauſted, men have yet no idea of their extent; the truths which the knowledge of
thoſe

thofe objects may have added to the fciences, or the long received errors that may thereby have been deftroyed ; the commercial activity that has given new life to induftry and navigation, and, by a neceffary chain of connection, to all the arts and all the fciences : and laftly, the force that free nations have acquired from this activity by which to refift tyrants, and fubjected nations to break their chains, and free themfelves at leaft from feodal defpotifm. But thefe advantages will never expiate what the difcoveries have coft to fuffering humanity, till the moment when Europe, abjuring the fordid and oppreffive fyftem of commercial monopoly, fhall acknowledge that *Monopoly* men of other climates, equals and brothers by the will of nature, have never been formed to nourifh the pride and avarice of a few privileged nations ; till, better informed refpecting its true interefts, it fhall invite all the people of the earth to participate in its independence, its liberty, and its illumination. Unfortunately, we have yet to learn whether this revolution will be the honourable fruit of the advancement of philofophy, or only, as we have hitherio feen, the fhameful confequence

fequence of national jealoufy, and the enormous exceffes of tyranny.

Till the prefent epoch the crimes of the
priefthood had efcaped with impunity. The
cries of oppreffed humanity, of violated reafon,
had been ftifled in flames and in blood. The
fpirit which dictated thofe cries was not extinct : but the filence occafioned by the operation of terror emboldened the priefthood to
farther outrages. At laft, the fcandal of farm-
ing to the monks the privilege of felling in
taverns and public places the expiation of fins,
occafioned a new explofion. Luther, holding
in one hand the facred books, expofed with
the other the right which the Pope had arro-
gated to himfelf of abfolving crimes and felling
pardons ; the infolent defpotifm which he
exercifed over the bifhops, for a long time
his equals ; the fraternal fupper of the primitive chriftians, converted, under the name of
mafs, into a fpecies of magical incantation and
an object of commerce ; priefts condemned
to the crime of irrevocable celibacy; the fame
cruel and fcandalous law extended to the
monks and nuns with w' ich pontifical ambition had inundated and polluted the church ;

all

all the fecrets of the laity confignèd, by means
of confeffion, to the intrigues and the paffions *confefsion.*
of priefts ; God himfelf, in fhort, fcarcely
retaining a feeble fhare in the adorations beftowed in profufion upon bread, men, bones
and ftatues.

Luther announced to the aftonifhed multitude, that thefe difgufting inftitutions formed
no part of chriftianity, but on the contrary
were its corruption and fhame; and that, to
be faithful to the religion of Jefus, it was
firft of all neceffary to abjure that of his priefts.
He employed equally the arms of logic and
erudition, and the no lefs powerful weapon of
ridicule. He wrote at once in German and
in Latin. It was no longer as in the days of
the Abigenfes, or of John Hufs, whofe doc- *John Hufs.*
trine, unknown beyond the walls of their
churches, was fo eafily calumniated. The
German books of the new apoftles penetrated
at the fame time into every village of the empire, while their Latin productions roufed all
Europe from the fhameful fleep into which
fuperftition had plunged it. Thofe whofe
reafon had outftripped the reformers, but
whom fear had retained in filence; thofe who

were

were tormented with fecret doubts, but which they trembled to avow even to their confciences; thofe who, more fimple, were unacquainted with all the extent of theological abfurdities; who, having never reflected upon queftions of controverfy, were aftonifhed to learn that they had the power of chufing between different opinions; entered eagerly into thefe difcuffions, upon which they conceived depended at once their temporal interefts and their eternal felicity.

All the chriftian part of Europe, from Sweden to Italy, and from Hungary to Spain, was in an inftant covered with the partifans of the new doctrines; and the reformation would have delivered from the yoke of Rome all the nations that inhabited it, if the miftaken policy of certain princes had not relieved that very facerdotal fceptre which had fo frequently fallen upon the heads of kings.

This policy, which their fucceffors unhappily have yet not abjured, was to ruin their ftates by feeking to add to them, and to meafure their power by the extent of their territory, rather than by the number of their fubjects.

Thus,

Thus, Charles the fifth and Francis the firſt, *Charles*
while contending for Italy, facrificed to the *Francis*.
intereſt of keeping well with the Pope, that
fuperior intereſt of profiting by the advantages offered by the reformatioń to every
country that ſhould have the wiſdom to
adopt it.

Perceiving that the princes of the empire
were favourable to opinions calculated to augment their power and their wealth, the empe- *Emperor.*
ror became the partifan and fupporter of the
old abufes, actuated by the hope that a religious war would furnifh an opportunity of
invading their ſtates, and deſtroying their independence ; while Francis imagined that, by *Francis*
burning the proteſtants, and protecting at the *burned and*
fame time their leaders in Germany, he ſhould *protected*
preferve the friendſhip of the Pope, without *Protestants.*
lofing his valuable allies.

But this was not their only motive. Def- *Instinct of*
potifm has alfo its inſtinct ; and that inſtinct *Despots.*
fuggeſted to thefe kings, that men, after fubjecting religious prejudices to the examination
of reafon, would foon extend their enquiries
to prejudices of another fort ; that, enlightened
upon the ufurpations of popes, they might

O ＊ wiſh

wifh at laft to be equally enlightened upon thofe of princes ; and that the reform of ecclefiaftical abufes, beneficial as it was to royal power, might involve the reform of abufes, ftill more oppreffive, upon which that power was founded. Accordingly, no king of any confiderable nation favoured voluntarily the party of the reformers. Henry the eighth, terrified at the pontifical anathema, joined in the perfecution againft them. Edward and Elizabeth, unable to embrace popery without pronouncing themfelves ufurpers, eftablifhed in England the faith and worfhip that approached neareft to it. The proteftant monarchs of Great Britain have indeed uniformly favoured the catholic religion, whenever it has ceafed to threaten them with a pretender to the crown.

In Sweden and Denmark, the eftablifhment of the religion of Luther was confidered by their kings only as a neceffary precaution to fecure the expulfion of the catholic tyrant, to whofe defpotifm they fucceeded ; and in the Pruffian monarchy, founded by a philofophical prince, we already perceive his fucceffor unable to difguife his fecret attachment to this religion, fo dear to the hearts of fovereigns.

Reli-

Religious intolerance was common to every *Intolerance* fect, and communicated itself to all the governments. The papifts perfecuted the re-
formed communions; while thefe, pronouncing
anathemas againft each other, joined at the
fame time againft the anti-trinitarians, who,
more confiftent in their conduct, had tried
every doctrine, if not by the touchftone of
reafon, at leaft by that of an enlightened criticifm, and who did not fee the neceffity of
freeing themfelves from one fpecies of abfurdity, to fall into others equally difgufting.

This intolerance ferved the caufe of popery.
For a long time there had exifted in Europe,
and efpecially in Italy, a clafs of men who, re-. *Atheist :*
jecting every kind of fuperftition, indifferent *Italy*
alike to all modes of worfhip, governed only
by reafon, regarded religion as of human invention, at which one might laugh in fecret,
but towards which prudence and policy dictated an outward refpect.

This free-thinking affumed afterwards fuperior courage; and, while in the fchools the
philofophy of Ariftotle, imperfectly underftood, had been employed to improve the fubtleties of theology, and render ingenious what

would naturally have borne the features of abfurdity, fome men of learning eftablifhed upon his true doctrine a fyftem deftructive of every religious idea, in which the human foul was confidered only as a faculty that vanifhed with life, and in which no other providence, no other ruler of the world was admitted than the neceffary laws of nature. *Platonists* This fyftem was combated by the Platonifts, whofe fentiments, refembling what has fince been called by the name of deifm, were more *Deifts,* terrifying ftill to facerdotal orthodoxy.

But the operation of punifhment foon put a ftop to this impolitic boldnefs. Italy and France were polluted with the blood of thofe martyrs to the freedom of thought. All fects, all governments, every fpecies of authority, inimical as they were to each other in every point elfe, feemed to be of accord in granting no quarter to the exercife of reafon. It was neceffary to cover it with a veil, which, hiding it from the obfervation of tyrants, might ftill permit it to be feen by the eye of philofophy.

Accordingly the moft timid caution was obferved refpecting this fecret doctrine, which

had

had never failed of numerous adherents. It had particularly been propagated among the heads of governments, as well as among thofe of the church ; and, about the period of the reformation, the principles of religious Ma-chiavelifm became the only creed of princes, of minifters, and of pontiffs. Thefe opinions had even corrupted philofophy. What code of morals indeed was to be expected from a fyftem, of which one of the principles is, that it is neceffary to fupport the morality of the people by falfe pretences ; that men of enlightened minds have a right to deceive them, provided they impofe only ufeful truths, and. to retain them in chains from which they have themfelves contrived to efcape ?

If the <u>natural equality</u> of mankind, the principal bafis of its rights, be the foundation of all genuine morality, what could it hope from a philofophy, of which an open contempt of this equality and thefe rights is a diftinguifhing feature ? This fame philofophy has contributed no doubt to the advancement of reafon, whofe reign it filently prepared ; but fo long as it was the only philofophy, its fole effect was to fubftitute hypocrify, in the

the place of fanaticifm, and to corrupt, at the fame time that it raifed above prejudices, thofe who prefided in the deftiny of ftates.

Philofophers truly enlightened, ftrangers to ambition, who contented themfelves with undeceiving men gradually and with caution, but without fuffering themfelves at the fame time to confirm them in their errors, thefe philofophers would naturally have been inclined to embrace the reformation; but, deterred by the intolerance that every where difplayed itfelf, the majority were of opinion that they ought not to expofe themfelves to the inconveniences of a change, when, by fo doing, they would ftill be fubjected to fimilar reftraint. As they muft have continued to fhew a refpect for abfurdities which they had already rejected, they faw no mighty advantage in having the number fomewhat diminifhed; they were fearful alfo of expofing themfelves, by their abjuration, to the appearance of a voluntary hypocrify : and thus, by perfevering in their attachment to the old religion, they ftrengthened it with the authority of their reputation.

The

The fpirit which animated the reformers
did not introduce a real freedom of fentiment. Each religion, in the country in which
it prevailed, had no indulgence but for certain opinions. Meanwhile, as the different
creeds were oppofed to each other, few opinions exifted that had not been attacked or
fupported in fome part of Europe. The new
communions had befide been obliged to relax
a little from their dogmatical rigour. They
could not, without the groffeft contradiction,
confine the right of examination within the
pale of their own church, fince upon this right
was founded the legitimacy of their feparation. If they refufed to reftore to reafon its
full liberty, they at leaft confented that its prifon fhould be lefs confined : the chains were
not broken, but they were rendered lefs bur-
thenfome and more permanent. In fhort, in
thofe countries where a fingle religion had
found it impracticable to opprefs all the
others, there was eftablifhed what the infolence of the ruling fect called by the name of
toleration, that is, a permiffion, granted by
fome men to other men, to believe what their
reafon adopts, to do what their confcience

dictates

dictates to them, to pay to their common God the homage they may think beft calculated to pleafe him : and in thefe countries the tolerated doctrines might then be vindicated with more or lefs freedom.

We thus fee making its appearance in Europe a fort of freedom of thought, not for men, but for chriftians : and, if we except France, for chriftians only does it any where exift to this day.

But this intolerance obliged human reafon to feek the recovery of rights too long forgotten, or which rather had never been properly known and underftood.

Afhamed at feeing the people oppreffed, in the very fanctuary of their confcience, by kings, the fuperftitious or political flaves of the priefthood, fome generous individuals dared at length to inveftigate the foundations of their power ; and they revealed this grand truth to the world : that liberty is a bleffing which cannot be alienated ; that no title, no convention in favour of tyranny, can bind a nation to a particular family ; that magiftrates, whatever may be their appellation, their functions, or their power, are the agents, not the

mafters,

masters, of the people ; that the people have
the right of withdrawing an authority originating in themselves alone, whenever that
authority shall be abused, or shall cease to be
thought useful to the interests of the community : and lastly, that they have the right to
punish, as well as to cashier their servants.

Such are the opinions which Althusius and
Languet, and afterwards Needham and Har-
rington, boldly professed, and investigated tho-
roughly.

From deference to the age in which they
lived, they too often build upon texts, authorities, and examples ; and their opinions appear to have been the result of the strength
of their minds, and dignity of their characters,
rather than of an accurate analysis of the true
principles of social order.

Meanwhile other philosophers, more timid,
contented themselves with establishing, between the people and kings, an exact reciprocity of duties and rights, and a mutual
obligation to preserve inviolate settled conventions. An hereditary magistrate might indeed be deposed or punished, but it was
only upon his having infringed this sacred

contract,

contract, which was not the lefs binding on his family. This doctrine, which facrificed natural right, by bringing every thing under pofitive inftitution, was fupported both by civilians and divines. It was favourable to powerful men, and to the projects of the ambitious, as it ftruck rather at the individual who might be invefted with fovereignty, than at fovereignty itfelf. For this reafon it was almoft generally embraced by reformifts, and adopted as a principle in political diffentions and revolutions.

Hiftory exhibits few fteps of actual progrefs towards liberty during this epoch; but we fee more order and efficacy in governments, and in nations a ftronger and particularly a more juft fenfe of their rights. Laws are better combined; they appear lefs frequently to be the immature and fhapelefs production of circumftances and caprice; they are the offspring of men of learning, if they cannot be faid as yet to be the children of philofophy.

The popular commotions and revolutions which agitated England, France, and the republics of Italy, attracted the notice of phiofophers

lofophers to that branch of politics which confifts in obferving and predicting the effects
that the conftitution, laws and eftablifhments
of a country are likely to produce upon the
liberty of the people, and the profperity,
ftrength, independence, and form of government of the ftate. Some, in imitation of
Plato, as More, for inftance, and Hobbes, *Moore littér*
deduced from general pofitions the plan of an
entire fyftem of focial order, and exhibited
the model towards which it was neceffary in
practice continually to approach. Others,
like Machiavel, fought, in a profound invefti- *Machiavel*
gation of hiftorical facts, the rules by which
were to be obtained the future maftery of
nations.

The fcience of political economy did not, *Political*
in this epoch, exift. Princes eftimated not the *Economy.*
number of men, but of foldiers, in the ftate ;
finance was the mere art of plundering the
people, without driving them to the defpera-
tion that fhould end in revolt; and governments paid no other attention to commerce
but that of loading it with taxes, of reftricting it by privileges, or of difputing for
its monopoly.

The

The nations of Europe, occupied by the common interefts that fhould unite, or the oppofite ones that they conceived ought to divide them, felt the neceffity of obferving certain rules of conduct which, independently of treaties, were to operate in their pacific intercourfe ; while other rules, refpected even in the midft of war, were calculated to foften its ferocity, to diminifh its ravages, and to prevent at leaft unproductive and unneceffary calamities. I refer to the fcience of the law of nations : but thefe laws unfortunately were fought, not in reafon and nature, the only authorities that independent nations may acknowledge, but in eftablifhed ufages and the opinions of antiquity. The rights of humanity, juftice towards individuals, were lefs confulted, in this bufinefs, than the ambition, the pride, and the avarice of governments.

In this epoch we do not obferve moralifts interrogating the heart of man, analyfing his faculties and his feelings, thereby to difcover his nature, and the origin, law and fanction of his duties. On the contrary, we fee them employing all the fubtlety of the fchools to difcover, refpecting actions the lawfulnefs of

which

which is uncertain, the precife limit where innocence ends, and fin is to begin ; to afcertain what authority has the proper degree of weight to juftify the practice of any of thefe dubious fort of actions ; to affift them in claffing fins methodically, fometimes into genus and fpecies, and fometimes according to the refpective heinoufnefs of their nature ; and laftly, to mark thofe in particular of which the commiffion of one only is fufficient to merit eternal damnation.

The fcience of morals, it is apparent, could *Morality.* not at that time have being, fince priefts alone enjoyed the privilege of being its interpreters and judges. Meanwhile, as a fkilful mechanic, by ftudying an uncouth machine, frequently derives from it the idea of a new one, lefs imperfect and truly ufeful ; fo did thefe very fubtleties lead to the difcovery, or affift in afcertaining the degree of moral turpitude of actions or their motives, the order and limits of our duties, as well as the principles that fhould determine our choice whenever thefe duties fhall appear to clafh.

The reformation, by deftroying, in the *Reformati* countries in which it was embraced, confeffion,

feffion, indulgences, and monks, refined the principles of morality, and rendered even manners lefs corrupt. It freed them from facerdotal expiations, that dangerous encouragement to vice, and from religious celibacy, the bane of every virtue, becaufe the enemy of the domeftic virtues.

Celibacy

This epoch, more than all the reft, was blotted and disfigured with acts of atrocious cruelty. It was the epoch of religious maffacres, holy wars, and the depopulation of the new world. There we fee eftablifhed the flavery of ancient periods, but a flavery more barbarous, more productive of crimes againft nature ; and that mercantile avidity, trafficking with the blood of men, felling them like other commodities, having firft purchafed them by treafon, robbery, or murder, and dragging them from one hemifphere to be devoted in another, amidft humiliation and outrages, to the tedious punifhment of a lingering, a cruel, but infallible deftruction.

flavery

At the fame time hypocrify covers Europe with executions at the ftake, and affaffinations. The monfter, fanaticifm, maddened by the

Perfecutions

4   **wounds**

wounds it has received, appears to redouble its fury, and haftens to burn its victims in heaps, fearful that reafon might be approaching to deliver them from its hands.

Meanwhile we may obferve fome of thofe mild but intrepid virtues making their appearance which are the honour and confolation of humanity. Hiftory furnifhes names which may be pronounced without a blufh. A few *who are* unfullied and mighty minds, uniting fuperior *thefe*, talents to the dignity of their characters, relieve, here and there, thefe fcenes of perfidy, of corruption, and of carnage. The picture of the human race is ftill too dreary for the philofopher to contemplate it without extreme mortification; but he no longer defpairs, fince the dawn of brighter hopes is exhibited to his view.

The march of the fciences is rapid and *Algebra* brilliant. The Algebraic language becomes generalized, fimplified and perfected, or rather it is now only that it was truly formed. The firft foundations of the general theory of equations are laid, the nature of the folutions which they give is afcertained, and thofe of the third and fourth degree are refolved.

The

ogarithms. The ingenious invention of logarithms, as abridging the operations of arithmetic, facilitates the application of calculation to the various objects of nature and art, and thus extends the fphere of all thofe fciences in which a numerical procefs is one of the means of comparing the refults of an hypothefis or theory with the actual phenomena, and thus arriving at a diftinct knowledge of the laws of nature. In mathematics, in particular, the mere length and complication of the numerical procefs practically confidered, bring us, upon certain occafions, to a term beyond which neither time, opportunity, nor even the ftretch of our faculties, can carry us ; this term, had it not been for the happy intervention of logarithms, would have alfo been the term beyond which fcience could never pafs, or the efforts of the proudeft genius proceed.

Galileo The law of the defcent of bodies was difcovered by Galileo, from which he had the ingenuity to deduce the theory of motion uniformly accelerated, and to calculate the curve defcribed by a body impelled into the air with a given velocity, and animated by a force conftantly acting upon it in parallel directions.

Coper-

Copernicus revived the true fyftem of the *Copernicus*
world, fo long buried in oblivion, deftroyed,
by the theory of apparent motions, what the
fenfes had found fo much difficulty in recon-
ciling, and oppofed the extreme fimplicity of
the real motions refulting from this fyftem,
to the complication, bordering upon abfurdity, of the Ptolemean hypothefis. The motions of the planets were better underftood;
and by the genius of Kepler were difcovered *Kepler*
the forms of their orbits, and the eternal laws
by which thofe orbits perform their evolu-
tions.

Galileo, applying to aftronomy the recent
difcovery of telefcopes, which he carried to *Telescopes*
greater perfection, opened to the view of mankind a new firmament. The fpots which he
obferved on the difk of the fun led him to
the knowledge of its rotation, of which he
afcertained the precife period, and the laws by
which it was performed. He demonftrated
the phafes of Venus, and difcovered the four
fatellites that furround and accompany Jupiter
in his immenfe orbit.

He alfo furnifhed an accurate mode of meafuring time, by the vibrations of a pendu- *Pendulum*
lum.

P   Thus

Galileo Thus man owes to Galileo the firſt mathematical theory of a motion that is not at once
uniform and rectilinear, as well as one of the
mechanical laws of nature ; while to Kepler
he is indebted for the acquiſition of one of
thoſe empirical laws, the diſcovery of which
has the double advantage of leading to the
knowledge of the mechanical law of which
they expreſs the reſult, and of ſupplying ſuch
degrees of this knowledge as man finds himſelf yet incapable of attaining.

Circulation of Blood. The diſcovery of the weight of the air, and
of the circulation of the blood, diſtinguiſh the
progreſs of experimental philoſophy, born in
the ſchool of Galileo, and of anatomy, already
too far advanced not to form a ſcience diſtinct
from that of medicine.

Natural History Chymiſtry Medicine Surgery Natural hiſtory, and chymiſtry, in ſpite of
its chimerical hopes and its enigmatical lan-
guage, as well as medicine and ſurgery, aſto-
niſh us by the rapidity of their progreſs,
though we are frequently mortified at the ſight
of the monſtrous prejudices which theſe
ſciences ſtill retain.

Gesner Agricola Without mentioning the works of Geſner
and Agricola, containing ſuch a fund of real
information, with ſo ſlight a mixture of
ſcientific

fcientific or popular errors, we obferve Ber- *Bernard de*
nard de Paliffi fometimes difplaying to us the *Paliffi*
quarries from which we derive the materials
of our edifices ; fometimes maffes of ftone
that compofe our mountains, formed from the
fkeletons of fea animals, and authentic monuments of the ancient revolutions of the globe ;
and fometimes explaining how the waters,
raifed from the fea by evaporation, reftored
to the earth by rain, ftopped by beds of clay,
affembled in fnow upon the hills, fupply
the eternal ftreams of rivers, brooks, and
fountains : while John Rei difcovered thofe *John Rei*
combinations of air with metallic fubftances,
which gave birth to the brilliant theories by
which, within a few years, the bounds of chymiftry have been fo much extended.

In Italy the arts of epic poetry, painting *Poetry*
and fculpture, arrived at a perfection unknown *Painting*
to the ancients. In France, Corneille evinced *Sculpture*
that the dramatic art was about to acquire a *Corneille*
ftill nobler elevation ; for whatever fuperiority
the enthufiaftical admirers of antiquity may
fuppofe, perhaps with juftice, the chefs-
d'œuvres of its firft geniufes to poffefs, it is by

no means difficult, by comparing their works with the productions of France and of Italy, for a rational enquirer to perceive the real progrefs which the art itfelf has attained in the hands of the moderns.

Languages The Italian language was completely formed, and in thofe of other nations we fee the marks of their ancient barbarifm continually difappearing.

Metaphysics Men began to feel the utility of metaphy-
Grammar fics and grammar, and of acquiring the art of analyfing and explaining philofophically both the rules and the proceffes eftablifhed by cuftom in the compofition of words and phrafes.

Conteft between We every where perceive, during this epoch, reafon and authority ftriving for the
Reafon and maftery, a conteft that prepared and gave
Authority. promife of the triumph of the former.

Criticifm This alfo was the period aufpicious to the birth of that fpirit of criticifm which alone can render erudition truly productive. It was ftill neceffary to examine what had been done by the ancients; but men were aware that, however they might admire, they were entitled to judge them. Reafon, which fome-

2   times

times fupported itfelf upon authority, and
againſt which authority had been fo frequently
employed, was defirous of appreciating the value of the affiftance fhe might derive therefrom,
as well as the motive of the facrifice that
was demanded of her. Thofe who affumed
authority for the bafis of their opinions, and
the guide of their conduct, felt how important
it was that they fhould be fure of the ftrength
of their arms, and not expofe themfelves to
the danger of having them broken to pieces
upon the firft attack of reafon.

The habit of writing only in Latin upon *Latin*
the fciences, philofophy, jurifprudence, and
even hiftory, with a few exceptions, gradually yielded to the practice of employing
the common language of the refpective country. And here we may examine what influence upon the progrefs of the human mind
was produced by this change, which rendered the fciences more popular, but diminifhed the facility with which the learned
were able to follow them in their route ;
which caufed a book to be read by more individuals of inferior information in a particular
country, but by fewer enlightened minds

P 3   through

through Europe in general; which fuperfeded the neceffity of learning Latin in a great
number of men defirous of inftruction, without
having the leifure or the means of founding
the depths of erudition, but at the fame time
obliged the philofopher to confume more time
in acquiring a knowledge of different languages.

We may fhow that, as it was impoffible to
make the Latin a vulgar tongue common to
all Europe, the continuance of the cuftom of
writing in it upon the fciences would have
been attended with a tranfient advantage only
to thofe who ftudied them; that the exiftence
of a fort of fcientific language among the
learned of all nations, while the people of
each individual nation fpoke a different one,
would have divided men into two claffes,
would have perpetuated in the people prejudices and errors, would have placed an infurmountable impediment to true equality, to
an equal ufe of the fame reafon, to an equal
knowledge of neceffary truths; and thus by
ftopping the progrefs of the mafs of mankind, would have ended at laft, as in the Eaft;
by putting a period to the advancement of the
fciences themfelves.

For

For a long time there had been no inftruction but in churches and cloifters.

The univerfities were ftill under the domination of the priefts, 'Compelled to refign to
the civil authority a part of their influence,
they retained it without the fmalleft defalca-
tion, fo far as related to the early inftruction
of youth, that inftruction which is equally
fought in all profeffions, and among all claffes
of mankind. Thus they poffeffed themfelves
of the foft and flexible mind of the child, of
the boy, and directed at their pleafure the firft
unfinifhed thoughts of man. To the fecular
power they left the fuperintendence of thofe
ftudies which had for their object jurifprudence, medicine, fcientifical analyfis, literature and the humanities, the fchools of which
were lefs numerous, and received no pupils
who were not already broken to the facerdotal yoke.

In reformed countries the clergy loft this
influence. The common inftruction, however,
though dependent on the government, did not
ceafe to be directed by a theological fpirit ;
but it was no longer confined to members of
the priefthood. It ftill corrupted the minds

of

of men by religious prejudices, but it did not bend them to the yoke of facerdotal authority; it ftill made fanatics, vifionaries, fophifts, but it no longer formed flaves for fuperftition.

Meanwhile education, being every where fubjugated, had corrupted every where the general underftanding, by clogging the reafon of children with the weight of the religious prejudices of their country, and by ftifling in youth, deftined to a fuperior courfe of inftruction, the fpirit of liberty by means of political prejudices.

Left to himfelf, every man not only found between him and truth a clofe and terrible phalanx of the errors of his country and age, but the moft dangerous of thofe errors were in a manner already rendered perfonal to him. Before he could diffipate the errors of another, it was neceffary he fhould begin with afcertaining his own; before he combated the difficulties oppofed by nature to the difcovery of truth, his underftanding, fo to fpeak, was obliged to undergo a thorough repair. Inftruction at this period conveyed fome knowledge; but to render it ufeful, the operation of refining muft take place, to feparate it from
the

the drofs in which fuperftition and tyranny
together had contrived to bury it.

We may fhow what obftacles, more or lefs
powerful, thefe vices of education, thofe religious and contradictory creeds, that influence of the different forms of government,
oppofed to the progrefs of the human mind.
It will be feen that this progrefs was by fo
much the flower and unequal, in proportion
as the objects of fpeculative enquiry inti-
mately affected the ftate of politics and religion; that philofophy, in its moft general
fenfe, as well as metaphyfics, the truths of
which were in direct hoftility to every kind
of fuperftition, were more obftinately retarded
than political enquiry itfelf, the improvement
of which was only dangerous to the authority
of kings and ariftocratic affemblies; and that
the fame obfervation will equally apply to the
fcience of material nature.

We may farther develope the other fources
of this inequality, as they may be traced in
the objects of which each fcience treats, and
the methods to which it has recourfe.

In the fame manner the fources of inequality and counteraction, which operate refpecting

ing the very fame fcience in different countries, are alfo the joint effect of political and
natural caufes. We may enquire, in this
inequality, what it is that is to be afcribed to
the different modes of religion, to the form of
government, to the wealth of any nation, to
its political importance, to its perfonal character, to its geographical fituation, to the
events and viciffitudes it has experienced, in
fine, to the accident which has produced in
the midft of it any of thofe extraordinary men,
whofe influence, while it extends over the
whole human race, exercifes itfelf with a double energy in a more reftrained fphere.

We may diftinguifh the progrefs of each
fcience as it is in itfelf, which has no other
limit than the number of truths it includes
within its fphere, and the progrefs of a nation in each fcience, a progrefs which is regulated firft by the number of men who are
acquainted with its leading and moft important truths, and next by the number and nature of the truths fo known.

In fine, we are now come to that point of
civilization, at which the people derive a profit
from intellectual knowledge, not only by the
fervices

fervices it reaps from men uncommonly inftructed, but by means of having made of intellectual knowledge a fort of patrimony, and
employing it directly and in its proper
form to refift error, to anticipate or fupply
their wants, to relieve themfelves from the
ills of life, or to take off the poignancy of thefe
ills by the intervention of additional pleafure.

The hiftory of the perfecutions to which
the champions of liberty were expofed, during
this epoch, ought not to be forgotten. Thefe
perfecutions will be found to extend from the
truths of philofophy and politics to thofe of
medicine, natural hiftory and aftronomy. In
the eighth century an ignorant pope had perfecuted a deacon for contending that the earth
was round, in oppofition to the opinion of the
rhetorical Saint Auftin. In the feventeenth,
the ignorance of another pope, much more
inexcufeable, delivered Galileo into the hands
of the inquifition, accufed of having proved
the diurnal and annual motion of the earth.
The greateft genius that modern Italy has
given to the fciences, overwhelmed with age
and infirmities, was obliged to purchafe his
releafe from punifhment and from prifon, by
asking

afking pardon of God for having taught men better to underſtand his works, and to admire him in the ſimplicity of the eternal laws by which he governs the univerſe.

Meanwhile, ſo great was the abſurdity of the theologians, that, in condeſcenſion to human underſtanding, they granted a permiſſion to maintain the motion of the earth, at the ſame time that they infiſted that it ſhould be only in the way of an hypotheſis, and that the faith ſhould receive no injury. The aſtronomers, on the other hand, did the exact oppoſite of this ; they treated the motion of the earth as a reality, and ſpoke of its immoveablenefs with a deference only hypothetical.

The tranſition from the epoch we have been conſidering to that which follows, has been diſtinguiſhed by three extraordinary perſonages, Bacon, Galileo, and Deſcartes. Bacon has revealed the true method of ſtudying nature, by employing the three inſtruments with which ſhe has furniſhed us for the diſcovery of her ſecrets, obſervation, experiment and calculation. He was defirous that the philoſopher, placed in the midſt of the uni‑
verſe,

Bacon.

verfe, fhould, as a firft and neceffary ftep in his
career, renounce every creed he had received,
and even every notion he had formed, in order to create, as it were, for himfelf, a new underftanding, in which no idea fhould be admitted but what was precife, no opinion but
what was juft, no truth of which the degree of
certainty or probability had not been fcrupu-
loufly weighed. But Bacon, though poffefs-
ing in a moft eminent degree the genius of
philofophy, added not thereto the genius of
the fciences ; and thefe methods for the difcovery of truth, of which he furnifhed no
example, were admired by the learned, but
produced no change in the march of the
fciences.

Galileo had enriched them with the moft *Galileo.*
ufeful and brilliant difcoveries ; he had taught
by his own example the means of arriving
at the knowledge of the laws of nature in a
way fure and productive, in which men were
not obliged to facrifice the hope of fuccefs to
the fear of being mifled. He founded the
firft fchool in which the fciences have been
taught without a mixture of fuperftition, prejudice, or authority ; in which every other

means

means than experiment and calculation have been rigoroufly profcribcd : but confining him-felf exclufively to the mathematical and phyfi-cal fciences, he was unable to communicate to the general mind that impulfion which it feemed to want.

This honour was referved for the daring and ingenious Defcartes. Endowed with a mafter genius for the fciences, he joined example to precept, in exhibiting the method of finding and afcertaining truth. This me-thod he applied to the difcovery of the laws of dioptrics, of the collifion of bodies, and finally of a new branch of mathematical fci-ence, calculated to extend and enlarge the bounds of all the other branches.

He wifhed to extend his method to every objeét of human intelligence ; God, man, the univerfe, were in turn the fubject of his me-ditations. If, in the phyfical fciences, his march be lefs fure than that of Galileo, if his philofophy be lefs wary than that of Bacon, if he may be accufed of not having fufficiently availed himfelf of the leffons of the one, and the example of the other, to diftruft his ima-gination, to interrogate nature by experi-ment

ment alone, to have no faith but in calculation, to obſerve the univerſe, inſtead of conſtructing it, to ſtudy man, inſtead of truſting
to vague conjectures for a knowledge of his
nature; yet the very boldneſs of his errors
was inſtrumental to the progreſs of the human ſpecies. He gave activity to minds
which the circumſpection of his rivals could
not awake from their lethargy. He called
upon men to throw off the yoke of authority,
to acknowledge no influence but what reaſon
ſhould avow : and he was obeyed, becauſe
he ſubjected by his daring, and faſcinated by
his enthuſiaſm.

The human mind was not yet free, but it
knew that it was formed to be free. Thoſe
who perſiſted in the deſire of retaining it in
its fetters, or who attempted to forge new
ones, were under the neceſſity of proving that
they ought to be impoſed or retained, and it
requires little penetration to foreſee that from
that period they would ſoon be broken in
pieces.

NINTH

NINTH EPOCH.

From the Time of Defcartes, to the Formation
of the French Republic.

WE have feen human reafon forming
itfelf flowly by the natural progrefs of civilization ; fuperftition ufurping dominion over
it, thereby to corrupt it, and defpotifm degrading and ftupifying the mental faculties
by the operation of fear, and actual infliction
of calamity.

One nation only efcaped for a while this
double influence. In that happy land, where
liberty had kindled the torch of genius, the
human mind, freed from the trammels of infancy, advanced towards truth with a firm
and undaunted ftep. But conqueft foon introduced tyranny, fure to be followed by fuperftition, its infeparable companion, and the
whole race of man was re-plunged into darknefs, deftined, from appearance, to be eternal. The dawn, however, at length was obferved

ferved to peep ; the eyes, long condemned to
obfcurity, opened and fhut their lids, inuring
themfelves gradually till they could gaze at
the light, and genius dared once again to fhine
forth upon the globe, from which, by fanaticifm and barbarity, it fo long had been ba-
nifhed.

We have feen reafon revolting at, and
fhaking off part of its chains, and by the continual acquifition of new ftrength preparing
and haftening the epoch of its liberty.

We have now to run through the period in
which it compleated its emancipation ; in
which, fubjected ftill to a degree of bondage,
it throws off, one by one, the remainder of its
fetters ; in which, free at length to purfue its
courfe, it can no longer be ftopped but by
thofe obftacles the occurrence of which is inevitable upon every new progrefs, as being
the refult of the conformation of the mind
itfelf, or of the connection which nature has
eftablifhed between our means of difcovering
truth, and the obftacles fhe oppofes to our
efforts.

Religious intolerance had obliged feven
of the Belgic provinces to throw off the yoke

Q   of

of Spain, and to form themfelves into a federal republic. The fame caufe had revived in
England a fpirit of liberty, which, tired of long
and fanguinary commotions, fat down at laft
contented with a conftitution, admired for a
while by philofophers, but having at prefent
no other fupport than national fuperftition and
political hypocrify.

Jpciurrui.

To facerdotal perfecution is it likewife to
be afcribed that the Swedes had the fortitude
to regain a portion of their rights.

Meanwhile, amidft the commotions occafioned by theological contefts, France, Spain,
Hungary and Bohemia faw the feeble remains
of their liberty, or of what, at leaft, bore the
femblance of liberty, totally vanifh from their
fight.

Even in countries faid to be free, it is in vain
to look for that freedom which violates none
of the natural rights of man, and which fecures their indefeafible poffeffion and uncontrouled exercife. On the contrary, the liberty
exifting there, founded upon a pofitive right
unequally fhared, confers upon an individual prerogatives greater or lefs according to
the town which he inhabits, the clafs in which

he

2

he is born, the fortune he poſſeſſes, or the trade he may exerciſe ; and a conciſe picture of theſe fantaſtical diſtinctions in different nations, will furniſh the beſt anſwer to thoſe men who are ſtill diſpoſed to vindicate the advantage and neceſſity of them.

In theſe countries, however, civil and perſonal liberty are guarantied by the laws. If man be not all that he ought to be, ſtill the dignity of his nature is not totally degraded ; ſome of his rights are at leaſt acknowledged ; it can no longer be ſaid of him that he is a ſlave, but only that he does not yet know how to become truly free.

In nations among whom, during the ſame period, liberty may have incurred loſſes more or leſs real, ſo reſtricted were the political rights enjoyed by the generality of the people, that the annihilation of the ariſtocracy, almoſt deſpotic, under which they had groaned, ſeems to have been more than a compenſation. They have loſt the title of citizen, which inequality had nearly rendered illuſory ; but the quality of man has been more reſpected, and royal deſpotiſm has ſaved them *True.* from a ſtate of feodal oppreſſion, an oppreſ-

ſion

fion fo much the more painful and humiliating, as the number and prefence of the tyrants are continually reviving the fentiment
of it.

In nations partially free the laws muft neceffarily have improved, becaufe the interefts
of thofe who hold therein the reins of power,
are not in all cafes at variance with the general interefts of the people ; and they muft
nearly true alfo have improved in defpotic ftates, either
becaufe the intereft of the public profperity is
fometimes confounded with that of the defpot, or becaufe, feeking to deftroy the remains of authority in the nobles or the clergy,
the defpot himfelf thereby communicates to
the laws a fpirit of equality, of which the motive indeed was the eftablifhment of an equality of flavery, but which has often been attended with falutary confequences.

We may here minutely explain the caufes
which have produced in Europe that fpecies of
defpotifm, of which neither the ages that preceded, nor the other quarters of the world,
have furnifhed an example; a defpotifm almoft abfolute, but which, reftrained by opinion, influenced by the ftate of knowledge,
and

and tempered in a manner by its own intereft, has frequently contributed to the progrefs of wealth, induftry, inftruction, and fometimes even to that of civil liberty.

The manners of men were meliorated by the mere decay of thofe prejudices which had kept alive their ferocity, by the influence of commerce and induftry, the natural ene-mies of diforder and violence, from which wealth takes its flight, by the fear and terror occafioned by the recollection, ftill recent, of the barbarities of the preceding period, by a more general diffufion of the philofophical ideas of juftice and equality, and laftly, by the flow but fure effect of the progrefs of mental illumination.

Religious intolerance ftill furvived ; but it was merely in the way of precaution, as a homage to the prejudices of the people, or as a fafeguard againft their inconftancy. It had loft its fierceft features. Executions at the ftake, feldom reforted to, were replaced by other modes of directing religious opinions, which, if they frequently proved more arbi-trary, were however lefs barbarous, till at length perfecution appeared only at inter-

Q 3   vals,

vals, and refulted chiefly from the inveteracy
of former habit, or from temporary weaknefs
and complaifance.

In every nation, and upon every fubject,
the policy of government followed the fteps
not only of opinion, but even of philofophy;
it was however flowly, and with a fort of
reluctance : and we fhall always find that, in
proportion as there exifts a confiderable diftance between the point at which men of
profound meditation arrive in the fcience of
politics and morals, and that attained by the
generality of thinking men, whofe fentiments,
when imbibed by the multitude, form what
is called the public opinion, fo thofe who
direct the affairs of a nation, whatever may
be its form of government, are uniformly
feen below the level of this opinion; they
walk in its path, they purfue its courfe ; but
it is with fo fluggifh a pace, that, fo far from
outftripping, they never come up with it,
and are always behind by a confiderable number of years, and by a portion, no lefs confiderable, of truths.

And now we arrive at the period when
philofophy, the moft general and obvious
effects

effects of which we have before remarked,
obtained an influence on the thinking clafs of
men, and thefe on the people and their governments, that, ceafing any longer to be gradual, produced a revolution in the entire mafs
of certain nations, and gave thereby a fecure
pledge of the general revolution one day to
follow. that fhall embrace·the whole human
fpecies.

After ages of error, after wandering in all
the mazes of vague and defective theories,
writers upon politics and the law of nations
at length arrived at the knowledge of the
true rights of man, which they deduced from
this fimple principle : that *he is a being endowed
with fenfation, capable of reafoning upon and
underftanding his interefts, and of acquiring
moral ideas.*

They faw that the maintenance of his rights
was the only object of political union, and
that the perfection of the focial art confifted
in preferving them with the moft entire
equality, and in their fulleft extent. They
perceived that the means of fecuring the
rights of the individual, confifting of general
rules to be laid down in every community,

the

the power of choosing these means, and determining these rules, could vest only in the
majority of the community ; and that for this
reason, as it is impossible for any individual
in this choice to follow the dictates of his
own understanding, without subjecting that
of others, the will of the majority is the
only principle which can be followed by all,
without infringing upon the common equality.

Each individual may enter into a previous
engagement to comply with the will of the
majority, which by this engagement becomes
unanimity ; he can however bind nobody
but himself, nor can he bind himself except
so far as the majority shall not violate his individual rights, after having recognised them.

Such are at once the rights of the majority
over individuals, and the limits of these rights ;
such is the origin of that unanimity, which
renders the engagement of the majority binding upon all ; a bond that ceases to operate
when, by the change of individuals, this species of unanimity ceases to exist. There are
objects, no doubt, upon which the majority
would pronounce perhaps oftener in favour
of

of error and mifchief, than in favour of truth
and happinefs; ftill the majority, and the
majority only, can decide what are the objects which cannot properly be referred to its
own decifion; it can alone determine as to
the individuals whofe judgement it refolves
to prefer to its own, and the method which
thefe individuals are to purfue in the exercife
of their judgement; in fine, it has alfo an indifpenfible authority of pronouncing whether
the decifions of its officers have or have not
wounded the rights of all,

From thefe fimple principles men difcovered the folly of former notions refpecting
the validity of contracts between a people and *compact*
its magiftrates, which it was fuppofed could *fpurned.*
only be annulled by mutual confent, or by a
violation of the conditions by one of the parties; as well as of another opinion, lefs fervile, but equally abfurd, that would chain
a people for ever to the provifions of a con- *conftituti*
ftitution when once eftablifhed, as if the right *fpurned.*
of changing it were not the fecurity of every
other right, as if human inftitutions, neceffarily defective, and capable of improvement
as we become enlightened, were to be condemned

demned to an eternal monotony. Accordingly
the governors of nations faw themfelves obliged
to renounce that falfe and fubtle policy, which,
forgetting that all men derive from nature an
equality of rights, would fometimes meafure
the extent of thofe which it might think proper to grant by the fize of territory, the
temperature of the climate, the national character, the wealth of the people, the ftate of
commerce and induftry ; and fometimes cede
them in unequal portions among the different
claffes of fociety, according to their birth, their
fortune, or their profeffion, thereby creating
contrary interefts and jarring powers, in order afterwards to apply correctives, which,
but for thefe inftitutions, would not be wanted,
and which, after all, are inadequate to the
end.

It was now no longer practicable to divide
mankind into two fpecies, one deftined to govern, the other to obey, one to deceive, the
other to be dupes : the doctrine was obliged
univerfally to be acknowledged, that all have
an equal right to be enlightened refpecting
their interefts, to fhare in the acquifition of
truth, and that no political authorities ap-
pointed

[Handwritten marginalia, left margin:]
Here are prs
found Truths
of Philosophy
and Politicks
delivered in
the Slang of
Party News
papers.
His great
Model of Infidelity Bolingbroke however
in his Patriot King, thinks, that a few
Ethereal Spirits are ordained by God to do all
the good and all the Evil in Society, All the re
are Dutch Travellers. How shall we decide, when
such great Doctors as Bolingbroke and Tonkin et

[handwritten at top:] ...disagree. No authority has a Right to retain the People in Ignorance. Agreed. But twenty four Million and an half in France will retain themselves in Ignorance and if left to themselves will soon extinguish the remaining ... soon extinguish ... The Pen and Ink Men as Aristocrats, ... Oligarchs, Orleans and Tyrants.

pointed by the people for the benefit of the
people, can be entitled to retain them in ignorance and darknefs.

Thefe principles, which were vindicated
by the generous Sydney, at the expence of
his blood, and to which Locke gave the authority of his name, were afterwards developed with greater force, precifion, and extent by Rouffeau, whofe glory it is to have
placed them among thofe truths henceforth
impoffible to be forgotten or difputed.

Man is fubject to wants, and he has faculties to provide for them; and from the application of thefe faculties, differently modified and diftributed, a mafs of wealth is derived, deftined to fupply the wants of the
community. But what are the principles by
which the formation or allotment, the prefervation or confumption, the increafe or di-
minution of this wealth is governed? What
are the laws of that equilibrium between the
wants and refources of men which is continually tending to eftablifh itfelf; and from
which refults, on the one hand, a greater facility of providing for thofe wants, and of confequence an adequate portion of general felicity,

city, when wealth increafes, till it has reached
its higheft degree of advancement ; and on the
other, as wealth diminifhes, greater difficulties, and of confequence proportionate mifery and wretchednefs, till abftinence or depopulation fhall have again reftored the balance ? How, in this aftonifhing multiplicity
of labours and their produce, of wants and
refources ; in this alarming, this terrible complication of interefts, which connects the fub-
fiftence and well-being of an obfcure individual with the general fyftem of focial exiftence, which renders him dependent on all
the accidents of nature and every political
event, and extends in a manner to the whole
globe his faculty of experiencing privations
or enjoyments ; how is it that, in this feeming chaos, we ftill perceive, by a general law
of the moral world, the efforts of each individual for himfelf conducing to the good of
the whole, and, notwithftanding the open
conflict of inimical interefts, the public welfare requiring that each fhould underftand
his own intereft, and be able to purfue it
freely and uncontrouled ?

Hence it appears to be one of the rights of
man,

man that he fhould employ his faculties, difpofe of his wealth, and provide for his wants in whatever manner he fhall think beſt. The general intereſt of the fociety, fo far from reſtraining him in this refpect, forbids, on the contrary, every fuch attempt ; and in this department of public adminiftration, the care of fecuring to every man the rights which he derives from nature, is the only found policy, the only controul which the general will can exercife over the individuals of the community.

· But this principle acknowledged, there are ſtill duties incumbent upon the adminiftrators of the general will, the fovereign authority. It is for this authority to eſtabliſh the regulations which are deſtined to afcertain, in exchanges of every kind, the weight, the bulk, the length, and quantity of things to be exchanged. It is for this authority to ordain a common ſtandard of valuation, that may apply to all commodities and facilitate the calculation of their valuations and comparifon, and which, bearing itfelf an intrinfic value, may be employed in all cafes as the medium of exchange ;

a regu-

a regulation without which commerce, reftrained to the mere operations of barter, cannot acquire the neceffary activity.

The growth of every year prefents us with
a fupererogatory value, which is deftined neither to remunerate the labour of which this
growth is the fruit, nor to fupply the ftock
which is to fecure an equal and more abundant growth in time to come. The poffeffor
of this fupererogatory value does not owe it
immediately to his labour, and poffeffes it independently of the daily and indifpenfible ufe
of his faculties for the fupply of his wants.
This fupererogatory growth is therefore the
ftock to which the fovereign authority may
have recourfe, without injuring the rights of
any, to fupply the expences which are requifite for the fecurity of the ftate, its intrinfic
tranquillity, the prefervation of the rights of
all, the exercife of the authorities inftituted
for the eftablifhment or adminiftration of law,
in fine, of the maintenance through all its
branches of the public profperity.

There are certain operations, eftablifhments, and inftitutions, beneficial to the community at large, which it is the office of the
commu-

community to introduce, direct, and fuper-
intend, and which are calculated to fupply
the defects of perfonal inclination, and to
parry the ftruggle of oppofite interefts, whether
for the improvement of agriculture, induftry,
and commerce, or to prevent or diminifh the
evils entailed on our nature, or thofe which
accident is continually accumulating upon us.

Till the commencement of the epoch we
are now confidering, and even for fome time
after, thefe objects had been abandoned to
chance, to the rapacity of governments, to
the artifices of pretenders, or to the prejudices and partial interefts of the powerful
claffes of fociety; but a difciple of Defcartes,
the illuftrious and unfortunate John de Witt, *De Witt.*
perceived how neceffary it was that political
economy, like every other fcience, fhould be
governed by the principles of philofophy,
and fubjected to the rules of a rigid calculation.

It made however little progrefs, till the peace
of Utrecht promifed to Europe a durable
tranquillity. From this period, neglected as
it had hitherto been, it became a fubject of
almoft general attention; and by Stuart, Smith, *Stuart*
and particularly by the French economifts, *Smith and*
French Economists. it

it was fuddenly elevated, at leaft as to precifion and purity of principles, to a degree of perfection, not to have been expected after the long and total indifference which had prevailed upon the fubject.

Metaphyfics. The caufe however of fo unparalleled a progrefs is chiefly to be found in the advancement of that branch of philofophy comprehended in the term metaphyfics, taking the word in its moft extenfive fignification.

Defcartes had reftored this branch of phylofophy to the dominion of reafon. He perceived the propriety of deducing it from thofe fimple and evident truths which are revealed to us by an inveftigation of the operations of the mind. But fcarcely had he difcovered this principle than his eager imagination led him to depart from it, and philofophy appeared for a time to have refumed its independence only to become the prey of new errors.

Locke. At length Locke made himfelf mafter of the proper clew. He fhewed that a precife and accurate analyfis of ideas, reducing them to ideas earlier in their origin or more fimple in their ftructure, was the only means to avoid

the

the being loft in a chaos of notions incomplete, incoherent, and undetermined, diforderly becaufe fuggefted by accident, and afterwards entertained without reflecting on their nature.

He proved by this analyfis, that the whole circle of our ideas refults merely from the operations of our intellect upon the fenfations we have received, or more accurately fpeaking, are compounded of fenfations offering themfelves fimultaneoufly to the memory, and after fuch a manner, that the attention is fixed and the perception bounded to a particular branch or view of the fenfations themfelves.

He fhewed that by taking one fingle word to reprefent one fingle idea, properly analifed and defined, we are enabled to recal conftantly the fame idea, that is, the fame fimultaneous refult of certain fimple ideas, and of confequence can introduce this idea into a train of reafoning without rifk of mifleading ourfelves.

On the contrary, if our words do not reprefent fixed and definite ideas, they will at different times fuggeft different ideas to the mind and become the moft fruitful fource of error.

R   In

In fine, Locke was the firſt who ventured to preſcribe the limits of the human underſtanding, or rather to determine the nature of the truths it can afcertain and the objeſts it can embrace.

It was not long before this method was adopted by philoſophers in general, in treating of morals and politics, by which a degree of certainty was given to thoſe ſciences little inferior to that which obtained in the natural ſciences, admitting only of ſuch concluſions as could be proved, ſeparating theſe from doubtful notions, and content to remain ignorant of whatever is out of the reach of human comprehenſion.

In the ſame manner, by analiſing the faculty of experiencing pain and pleaſure, men arrived at the origin of their notions of morality, and the foundation of thoſe general principles which form the neceſſary and immutable laws of juſtice ; and confequently difcovered the proper motives of conferming their conduſt to thoſe laws, which, being deduced from the nature of our feeling, may not improperly be called our moral conſtitution.

The ſame ſyſtem became, in a manner, a general inſtrument of acquiring knowledge.

It

It was employed to afcertain the truths of natural philofophy, to try the facts of hiftory,
and to give laws to tafte. In a word, the
procefs of the human mind in every fpecies of
enquiry was regulated by this principle; and
it is this lateft effort of fcience which has
placed an everlafting barrier between the human race and the old miftakes of its infancy,
that will for ever preferve us from a relapfe
into former ignorance, fince it has prepared
the means of undermining not only our prefent errors, but all thofe by which they may
be replaced, and which will fucceed each other
only to poffefs a feeble and temporary influence.

In Germany, however, a man of a vaft and *Leibnitz.*
profound genius laid the foundations of a new
theory. His bold and ardent mind difdained
to reft on the fuppofitions of a modeft phifo-
phy, which left in doubt thofe great queftions of fpiritual exiftence, the immortality of
the foul, the free will of man and of God,
and the exiftence of vice and mifery in a
world framed by a being whofe infinite wifdom and goodnefs might be fuppofed to ba-
nifh them from his creation. Leibnitz cut

the

Atoms.

the knot which a timid fyftem had in vain attempted to unloofe. He fuppofed the univerfe to be compofed of atoms, which were fimple, eternal, and equal in their nature. He contended that the relative fituation of each of thefe atoms, with refpect to every other, occafioned the qualities diftinguifhing it from all others; the human foul, and the minuteft particle of a mafs of ftone, being each of them equally one of thefe atoms, differing only in confequence of the refpective places they occupy in the order of the univerfe.

He maintained that, of all the poffible combinations which could be formed of thefe atoms, an infinitely wife being had preferred, and could not but prefer, the moft perfect; and that if, in that which exifts, we are afflicted with the prefence of vice and mifery, ftill there is no other poffible combination that would not be productive of greater evils.

Such was the nature of this theory, which, fupported by the countrymen of Leibnitz, retarded in that part of the world the progrefs of philofophy. Meanwhile there ftarted up in England an entire fect, who embraced with zeal,

zeal, and defended with eloquence, the fcheme
of optimifm : but, lefs acute and profound *Optimism*
than Leibnitz, who founded his fyftem upon
the fuppofition of its being impoffible, from
his very nature, that an all-wife being fhould
plan any other univerfe than that which was
beft, they endeavoured to difcover in the
terraqueous part of the world the proofs of
this perfection, and lofing thereby the advantages which attach to this fyftem, confidered
generally and in the abftract, they frequently
fell into abfurd and ridiculous reafonings.

Meanwhile, in Scotland, other philofo- *Hutchins*
phers, not perceiving that the analyfis of the
developement of our actual faculties led to a
principle which gave to the morality of our
actions a bafis fufficiently folid and pure, attributed to the human foul a new faculty, *Conscience*
diftinct from thofe of fenfation and reafon,
though at the fame time combining itfelf
with them ; of the exiftence of which they
could advance no other proof, than that it
was impoffible to form a confiftent theory
without it. In the hiftory of thefe opinions
it will be feen, that, while they have proved
injurious to the progrefs of philofophy itfelf,

they

they have tended to give a more rapid and extenfive fpread to ideas truly fcientific, connected with philofophy.

Hitherto we have exhibited the ftate of philofophy only among men by whom it has in a manner been ftudied, inveftigated, and perfected. It remains to mark its .influence on the general opinion, and to fhow, that, while it arrived at the certain and infallible means of difcovering and recognifing truth, reafon at the fame time detected the delufions into which it had fo often been led by a refpect for authority or a mifguided imagination, and undermined thofe prejudices in the mafs of individuals which had fo long been the fcourge, at once corrupting and inflicting calamity upon the human fpecies.

The period at length arrived when men no longer feared openly to avow the right, fo long withheld, and even unknown, of fubjecting every opinion to the teft of reafon, or, in other words, of employing, in their fearch after truth, the only means they poffefs for its difcovery. Every man learned, with a degree of pride and exultation, that nature had not condemned him to fee with

the

(247)

the eyes and to conform his judgement to the caprice of another. The fuperftitions of antiquity accordingly difappeared; and the debafement of reafon to the fhrine of fuper-natural faith, was as rarely to be found in <u>fociety</u> as in the circles of metaphyfics and philofophy.

A clafs of men fpeedily made their appear-ance in Europe, whofe object was lefs to dif-cover and inveftigate truth, than to deffemi-nate it; who, purfuing prejudice through all the haunts and afylums in which the clergy, the fchools, governments, and privileged cor-porations had placed and protected it, made it their glory rather to eradicate popular er-rors, than add to the ftores of human know-ledge; thus aiding indirectly the progrefs of mankind, but in a way neither lefs arduous, nor lefs beneficial.

In England, Collins and Bolingbroke, and in France, Bayle, Fontenelle, Montefquieu, and the refpective difciples of thefe celebrated men, combated on the fide of truth with all the weapons that learning, wit and genius were able to furnifh; affuming every fhape, employing every tone, from the fublime and

R 4   pathetic

(248)

pathetic to pleafantry and fatire, from the moft laboured inveftigation to an interefting romance or a fugitive effay : accommodating truth to thofe eyes that were too weak to bear its effulgence; artfully careffing prejudice, the more eafily to ftrangle it ; never aiming a direct blow at errors, never attacking more than one at a time, nor even that one in all its fortreffes ; fometimes foothing the enemies of reafon, by pretending to require in religion but a partial toleration, in politics but a limited freedom ; fiding with defpotifm, when their hoftilities were directed againft the priefthood, and with priefts, when their object was to unmafk the defpot ; fapping the principle of both thefe pefts of human happinefs, ftriking at the root of both thefe baneful trees, while apparently wifhing for the reform only of glaring abufes and feemingly confining themfelves to lopping off the exuberant branches ; fometimes reprefenting to the partifans of liberty, that fuperftition, which covers defpotifm as with a coat of mail, is the firft victim which ought to be facrificed, the firft chain that ought to be broken ; and fometimes denouncing it to tyrants as the true

enemy

enemy of their power, and alarming them with
recitals of its hypocritical confpiracies and its
fanguinary vengeance. Thefe writers, mean- *How did*
while, were uniform in their vindication of free- *they tolerate*
dom of thinking and freedom of writing, as pri- *this fredom*
vileges upon which depended the falvation of *when they*
mankind. They declaimed, without ceffa- *poffeffed pow*
tion or wearinefs, againft the crimes both of *er?*
fanatics and tyrants, expofing every feature of
feverity, of cruelty, of oppreffion, whether in
religion, in adminiftration, in manners, or in
laws ; commanding kings, foldiers, magiftrates and priefts, in the name of truth and of
nature, to refpect the blood of mankind ; call- *How did*
ing upon them, with energy, to anfwer for the *thefe Writers*
lives ftill profufely facrificed in the field of bat- *respect the*
tle or by the infliction of punifhments, or elfe *Blood, of them*
to correct this inhuman policy, this murderous *they obtained*
infenfibility ; and laftly, in every place, and *Power in*
upon every occafion, rallying the friends of *1792,3,4,5*
mankind with the cry of *reafon, toleration,* *&c.?*
and humanity !
Such was this new philofophy. Accordingly
to thofe numerous claffes that exift by prejudice, that live upon error, and that, but for
the credulity of the people, would be power-
                                            lefs

This is to true.

lefs and extinct, it became a common object of deteftation. It was every where received, and every where perfecuted, having kings, priefts, nobles and magiftrates among the number of its friends as well as of its ene-mies. Its leaders, however, had almoft al-ways the art to elude the purfuits of ven-geance, while they expofed themfelves to hatred ; and to fcreen themfelves from perfe-cution, while at the fame time they fufficiently difcovered themfelves not to lofe the laurels of their glory.

This is very true.

It frequently happened that a government rewarded them with one hand, and with the other paid their enemies for calumniating them ; profcribed them, yet was proud that fortune had honoured its dominions with their birth ; punifhed their opinions, and at the fame time would have been afhamed not to be fuppofed a convert thereto.

Thefe opinions were fhortly embraced by every enlightened mind. By fome they were openly avowed, by others concealed under an hypocrify more or lefs apparent, according to the timidity or firmnefs of their charac-ters, and accordingly as they were influenced

by

by the contending interests of their profeffion
or their vanity. At length the pride of
ranging on the fide of erudition became pre-
dominant, and fentiments were profeffed
with the flighteft caution, which, in the ages
that preceded, had been concealed by the
moft profound diffimulation.

Look to the different countries of Europe
into which, from the prevalence of the French
language, become almoft univerfal, it was impoffible for the inquifitorial fpirit of governments and priefts to prevent this philofophy
from penetrating, and we fhall fee how rapid
was its progrefs. Meanwhile we cannot over-
look how artfully tyranny and fuperftition
employed againft it all the arguments invented to prove the weaknefs and fallibility
of human judgement, all the motives which
the knowledge of man had been able to fuggeft for miftrufting his fenfes, for doubting
and fcrutinizing his reafon ; thus converting
fcepticifin itfelf into an inftrument by which
to aid the caufe of credulity.

This admirable fyftem, fo fimple in its
principles, which confiders an unreftricted
freedom as the fureft encouragement to commerce

onomists

merce and induſtry, which would free the people from the deſtructive peſtilence, the humiliating yoke of thoſe taxes apportioned with ſo great inequality, levied with ſo improvident an expence, and often attended with circumſtances of ſuch atrocious barbarity, by ſubſtituting in their room a mode of contribution at once equal and juſt, and of which the burthen would ſcarcely be felt; this theory, which connects the power and wealth of a ſtate with the happineſs of individuals, and a reſpect for their rights, which unites by the bond of a common felicity the different claſſes into which ſocieties naturally divide themſelves; this benevolent idea of a fraternity of the whole human race, of which no national intereſt ſhall ever more intervene to diſturb the harmony; theſe principles, ſo atractive from the generous ſpirit that pervades them, as well as from their ſimplicity and comprehenſion, were propagated with enthuſiaſm by the French economiſts.

The ſucceſs of theſe writers was leſs rapid and leſs general than that of the philoſophers; they had to combat prejudices more refined, errors more ſubtle. Frequently they

were

were obliged to enlighten before they could undeceive, and to inſtruct good ſenſe before they could venture to appeal to it as their judge.

If, however, to the whole of their doctrine they gained but a ſmall number of converts; if the general nature and inflexibility of their principles were diſcouraging to the minds of many; if they injured their cauſe by affecting an obſcure and dogmatical ſtyle, by too much poſtponing the intereſts of political freedom to the freedom of commerce, and by infiſting too magiſterially upon certain branches of their ſyſtem, which they had not ſufficiently inveſtigated; they neverthelefs ſucceeded in rendering odious and contemptible that daſtardly, that baſe and corrupt policy, which places the proſperity of a nation in the ſubjection and impoveriſhment of its neighbours, in the narrow views of a code of prohibitions, and in the petty calculations of a tyrannical revenue.

But the new truths with which genius had enriched philoſophy and the ſcience of political economy, adopted in a greater or leſs degree by men of enlightened underſtandings, extended ſtill farther their ſalutary influence.

The

The art of printing had been applied to fo many fubjects, books had fo rapidly increafed, they were fo admirably adapted to every tafte, every degree of information, and every fituation of life, they afforded fo eafy and frequently fo delightful an inftruction, they had opened fo many doors to truth, which it was impoffible ever to clofe again, that there was no longer a clafs or profeffion of mankind from whom the light of knowledge could abfolutely be excluded. Accordingly, though there ftill remained a multitude of individuals condemned to a forced or voluntary ignorance, yet was the barrier between the enlightened and unenlightened portion of mankind nearly effaced, and an infenfible gradation occupied the fpace which feparates the two extremes of genius and ftupidity.

Thus there prevailed a general knowledge of the natural rights of man ; the opinion even that thefe rights are inalienable and imprefcriptible ; a decided partiality for freedom of thinking and writing ; for the enfranchifement of induftry and commerce ; for the melioration of the condition of the people ; for the repeal of penal ftatutes againft religious nonconformifts ; for the abolition of torture

and

and barbarous punifhments; the defire of a
milder fyftem of criminal legiflation; of a
jurifprudence that fhould give to innocence a
complete fecurity; of a civil code more fimple, as well as more conformable to reafon and
juftice; indifference as to fyftems of religion,
confidered at length as the offspring of fuperftition, or ranked in the number of political
inventions; hatred of hypocrify and fanaticifm; contempt for prejudices; and laftly, a
zeal for the propagation of truth. Thefe
principles, paffing by degrees from the writings
of philofophers into every clafs of fociety whofe
inftruction was not confined to the catechifm
and the fcriptures, became the common creed,
the fymbol and type of all men who were not
idiots on the one hand, or, on the other, af-
fertors of the policy of Machiavelifm. In
fome countries thefe fentiments formed fo
nearly the general opinion, that the mafs even
of the people feemed ready to obey their dictates and act from their impulfe.

The love of mankind, that is to fay, that
active compaffion which interefts itfelf in all
the afflictions of the human race, and regards
with horror whatever, in public inftitutions,

in

in the acts of government, or the purfuits of
individuals, adds to the inevitable misfor-
tunes of nature, was the neceffary refult of thefe
principles. It breathed in every work, it
prevailed in every converfation, and its be-
nign effects were already vifible even in the
laws and adminiftration of countries fubject
to defpotifm.

The philofophers of different nations em-
bracing, in their meditations, the entire interefts of man, without diftinction of country,
of colour, or of fect, formed, notwithftand-
ing the difference of their fpeculative opinions, a firm and united phalanx againft every
defcription of error, every fpecies of tyranny.
Animated by the fentiment of univerfal philanthropy, they declaimed equally againft injuftice, whether exifting in a foreign country,
or exercifed by their own country againft a
foreign nation. They impeached in Europe
the avidity which ftained the fhores of America, Africa, and Afia with cruelty and crimes.
The philofophers of France and England glo-
ried in affuming the appellation, and fulfilling
the duties, of *friends* to thofe very negroes
whom their ignorant oppreffors difdained to
rank

rank in the clafs of men. The French writers
beftowed the tribute of their praife on the toleration granted in Ruffia and Sweden, while
Beccaria refuted in Italy the barbarous maxims
of Gallic jurifprudence. The French alfo
endeavoured to open the eyes of England refpecting her commercial prejudices, and her
fuperftitious reverence for the errors of her
conftitution; while the virtuous Howard re-
monftrated at the fame time with the French
upon the cool barbarity which facrificed fo
many human victims in their prifons and
hofpitals.

Neither the violence nor the corrupt arts
of government, neither the intolerance of
priefts, nor even the prejudices of the people
themfelves, poffeffed any longer the fatal
power of fuppreffing the voice of truth; and
nothing remained to fcreen the enemies of
reafon, or the oppreffors of liberty, from the
fentence which was about to be pronounced
upon them by the unanimous fuffrage of Europe.

While the fabric of prejudice was thus tot-
tering to its foundations, a fatal blow was
given to it by a doctrine, of which Turgot,

S   Price,

Price, and Prieftley were the firft and moft illuftrious advocates : it was the doctrine of the infinite perfectibility of the human mind. The confideration of this opinion will fall under the tenth divifion of our work, where it will be developed with fufficient minutenefs. But we fhall embrace this opportunity of expofing the origin and progrefs of a falfe fyftem of philofophy, to the overthrow of which the doctrine of the perfectibility of man is become fo neceffary.

The fophiftical doctrine to which I allude, derived its origin from the pride of fome men, and the felfifhnefs of others. Its real, though concealed object, was to give duration to ignorance, and to prolong the reign of prejudice. The adherents of this doctrine, who have been numerous, fometimes attempted to delude the reafon by brilliant paradoxes, or to feduce it by the fpecious charms of an univerfal pyrrhonifm. Sometimes they affumed the boldnefs peremptorily to declare, that the advancement of knowledge threatened the moft fatal confequences to human happinefs and liberty ; at other times they declaimed, with pompous enthu-

fiafm

fiafm, in favour of an imaginary wifdom and fublimity, that difdained the cold progrefs of analyfis, and the tardy mechanical path of experience. Upon one occafion, they were accuftomed to fpeak of philofophy and the abftrufe fciences as theories too fubtle for the inveftigation of the human underftanding, urged as we are by daily wants, and fub-jected to the moft fudden viciffitudes; at ano-ther, they treated them as a mafs of blind and idle conjectures, the falfe eftimation of which was fure to difappear from the mind of a man habituated to life and experience. Inceffantly did they lament the decay and decrepitude of knowledge, in the midft of its moft brilliant progrefs; the rapid degradation of the human fpecies, at the moment that men were ready to affert their rights and truft to their own underftandings; an approaching æra of bar-barifm, darknefs and flavery, when evidence was fo perpetually accumulating, that the re-vival of fuch an æra was no longer to be feared. They feemed humbled by the ad-vances of their fpecies, either becaufe they could not boaft of having contributed to them, or becaufe they faw themfelves menaced with

a fpeedy

a fpeedy termination of their influence or importance. In the meanwhile, a certain number of intellectual mountebanks, more fkilful
than thofe who defperately endeavoured to
prop the edifice of declining fuperftition, attempted, out of the wreck of fuperftition, to
erect a new religious creed which fhould no
longer demand of our reafon any more than
a fort of formal fubmiffion, and which indulged us with a perfect liberty of confcience,
provided we would admit fome flight frag-
ment of incomprehenfibility into our fyftem.
A fecond clafs of thefe mountebanks affayed
to revive, by means of fecret affociations, the
forgotten myfteries of a fort of oriental theurgy.
The errors of the people they left undifturbed:
upon their own difciples they entailed new
dogmas and new terrors, and ventured to
hope, by a procefs of cunning, to reftore the
ancient tyranny of the facerdotal princes of
India and Egypt. In the mean time, philofophy, leaning upon the pillar which fcience
had prepared, fmiled at their efforts, and faw
one attempt vanifh after another, as the waves
retire from the foot of an immoveable rock.

By comparing the difpofition of the public
mind,

mind, which I have already fketched, with
the prevailing fyftems of government, we
fhall perceive, without difficulty, that an important revolution was inevitable, and that
there were two ways only in which it could
take place : either the people themfelves would
eftablifh a fyftem of policy upon thofe principles of nature and reafon, which philofophy
had rendered fo dear to their hearts ; or government might haften to fuperfede this event,
by reforming its vices, and governing its conduct by the public opinion. One of thefe revolutions would be more fpeedy, more radi-
cal, but alfo more tempeftuous ; the other
lefs rapid, lefs complete, but more tranquil :
in the one, liberty and happinefs would be
purchafed at the expence of tranfient evils;
in the other, thefe evils would be avoided ;
but a part of the enjoyments neceffary to a
ftate of perfect freedom, would be retarded in
its progrefs, perhaps, for a confiderable period, though it would be impoffible in the end
that it fhould not arrive.

The corruption and ignorance of the
rulers of nations have preferred, it feems,
the former of thefe modes ; and the fudden

triumph

triumph of reafon and liberty has avenged the human race.

The fimple dictates of good fenfe had taught the inhabitants of the Britifh colonies, that men born on the American fide of the Atlantic ocean had received from nature the fame rights as others born under the meridian of Greenwich, and that a difference of fixty-fix degrees of longitude could have no power of changing them. They underftood, more perfectly perhaps than Europeans, what were the rights common to all the individuals of the human race ; and among thefe they included the right of not paying any tax to which they had not confented. But the Britifh Government, pretending to believe that God had created America, as well as Afia, for the gratification and good pleafure of the inhabitants of London, refolved to hold in bondage a fubject nation, fituated acrofs the feas at the diftance of three thoufand miles, intending to make her the inftrument in due time of enflaving the mother country itfelf. Accordingly, it commanded the fervile reprefentatives of the people of England to violate the rights of America, by fubjecting her to a com-

compulfory taxation. This injuftice, fhe conceived, authorifed her to diffolve every tie of
connection, and fhe declared her independence.

Then was obferved, for the firft time, the *But, if this*
example of a great people throwing off at once *learn sole it*
every fpecies of chains, and peaceably framing *followed it to*
for itfelf the form of government and the laws *clofely by*
which it judged would be moft conducive to *Europe an*
its happinefs; and as, from its geographical *nations, the*
pofition, and its former political ftate, it was *will repuly*
obliged to become a federal nation, thirteen *as Strong.*
republican conftitutions were feen to grow up *was done.*
in its bofom, having for their bafis a folemn
recognition of the natural rights of man, and
for their firft object the prefervation of thofe
rights through every department of the union.

If we examine the nature of thefe conftitu- *I got*
tions, we fhall difcover in what refpect they
were indebted to the progrefs of the political *I fool*
fciences, and what was the portion of error,
refulting from the prejudices of education,
which formed its way into them : why, for
inftance, the fimplicity of thefe conftitutions
is disfigured by the fyftem of a balance of *Is it poffible*
powers; and why an identity of interefts, *that a Philoso-*
pher, who

S 4   rather *underftood*

*uman Nature, had read History, and knew any
Thing of Government, free or arbitrary: Should have written
this? what is his Idea of an identity of Interests? and an Equality of Rights. Is an Equality of Rights, any where more explicitly afferted
than in the american Constitution*

rather than an equality of rights, is adopted as
their principle. It is manifeſt that this principle of identity of intereſts, when made the
rule of political rights, is not only a violation
of ſuch rights, with reſpeȼt to thoſe who are
denied an equal ſhare in the exerciſe of them,
but that it ceaſes to exiſt the very inſtant it
becomes an aȼtual inequality. We inſiſt the
rather upon this, as it is the only dangerous
error remaining, the only error reſpeȼting
which men of enlightened minds want ſtill to
be undeceived. At the ſame time, however,
we ſee realized in theſe republics an idea, at
that time almoſt new even in theory; I mean
Now indeed, the neceſſity of eſtabliſhing by law a regular
But France and peaceable mode of reforming the conſti-
and America tutions themſelves, and of placing this buſi-
too, have found
it difficult to neſs in other hands than thoſe entruſted with
practise. the legiſlative power.

Meanwhile, in conſequence of America
declaring herſelf independent of the Britiſh
governmemt, a war enſued between the two
enlightened nations, in which one contended
for the natural rights of mankind, the other
for that impious doȼtrine which ſubjeȼts theſe
rights to preſcription, to political intereſts,

and

and written conventions. The great caufe at
iffue was tried, during this war, in the tribunal of opinion, and, as it were, before the
affembled nations of mankind. The rights
of men were freely inveftigated, and ftre-
nuoufly fupported, in writings which circu-
lated from the banks of the Neva to thofe of
the Guadalquivir. Thefe difcuffions penetrated into the moft enflaved countries, into
the moft diftant and retired hamlets. The
fimple inhabitants were aftonifhed to hear of
rights belonging to them : they enquired into
the nature and importance of thofe rights ;
they found that other men were in arms, to
re-conquer or to defend them.

In this ftate of things it could not be long
before the tranfatlantic revolution muft find
its imitators in the European quarter of the
world. And if there exifted a country in
which, from attachment to their caufe, the
writings and principles of the Americans
were more widely diffeminated than in any
other part of Europe ; a country at once the
moft enlightened, and the leaft free ; in which
philofophers had foared to the fublimeft pitch
of intellectual attainment, and the government

was

was funk in the deepeſt and moſt intolerable
ignorance; where the ſpirit of the laws was
ſo far below the general ſpirit and illumination, that national pride and inveterate prejudice were alike aſhamed of vindicating the old
inſtitutions : if, I ſay, there exiſted ſuch a
country, were not the people of that country
deſtined, by the very nature of things, to
give the firſt impulſe to this revolution, expected by the friends of humanity with ſuch
eager impatience, ſuch ardent hope? Accordingly it was to commence with France.

How have these friends been disapointed.

The impolicy and unſkilfulneſs of the French
government haſtened the event. It was guided
by the hand of philoſophy, and the popular
force deſtroyed the obſtacles that otherwiſe
might have arreſted its progreſs.

.Sans Guloti is now des troyed. Mirabeau and them, Lostroy'd itself. Danton

It was more complete, more entire than
that of America, and of conſequence was attended with greater convulſions in the inte-
rior of the nation, becauſe the Americans, ſa-
tisfied with the code of civil and criminal legiſlation which they had derived from England, having no corrupt ſyſtem of finance to
reform, no feodal tyrannies, no hereditary
diſtinctions, no privileges of rich and powerful

ful corporations, no fyftem of religious intolerance to deftroy, had only to direct their
attention to the eftablifhment of new powers
to be fubftituted in the place of thofe hitherto
exercifed over them by the Britifh government. In thefe innovations there was nothing that extended to the mafs of the people,
nothing that altered the fubfifting relations
formed between individuals : whereas the
French revolution, for reafons exactly the reverfe, had to embrace the whole economy of
fociety, to change every focial relation, to
penetrate to the fmalleft link of the political
chain, even to thofe individuals, who, living
in peace upon their property, or by their induftry, were equally unconnected with public
commotions, whether by their opinions and
their occupations, or by the interefts of fortune, of ambition, or of glory.

The Americans, as they appeared only to
combat againft the tyrannical prejudices of the
mother country, had for allies the rival powers
of England; while other nations, jealous of
the wealth, and difgufted at the pride of that
country, aided, by their fecret afpirations, the
triumph of juftice : thus all Europe leagued,

as

as it were, againſt the oppreſſor. The French,
on the contrary, attacked at once the deſpotiſm of kings, the political inequality of conſtitutions partially free, the pride and prerogatives of nobility, the domination, intolerance,
and rapacity of prieſts, and the enormity of
feodal claims, ſtill reſpected in almoſt every
nation in Europe ; and accordingly the powers
we have mentioned, united in favour of tyranny ; and there appeared on the ſide of
the Gallic revolution the voice only of ſome
enlightened ſages, and the timid wiſhes of
certain oppreſſed nations : ſuccours, meanwhile, of which all the artifices of calumny
have been employed to deprive it.

It would be eaſy to ſhow how much more

pure, accurate, and profound, are the principles upon which the conſtitution and laws
of France have been formed, than thoſe which
directed the Americans, and how much more
completely the authors have withdrawn themſelves from the influence of a variety of prejudices; that the great baſis of policy, · the
equality of rights, has never been ſuperſeded
by that fictitious identity of intereſts, which
has ſo often been made its feeble and hypocritical

tical fubftitute ; that the limits prefcribed to
political power have been put in the place of
that fpecious balance which has fo long been
admired ; that we were the firft to dare, in a
great nation neceffarily difperfed, and which
cannot perfonally be affembled but in broken
and numerous parcels, to maintain in the
people their rights of fovereignty, the right
of obeying no laws but thofe which, though
originating in a reprefentative authority, fhall
have received their laft fanction from the nation itfelf, laws which, if they be found injurious to its rights or interefts, the nation is
always organized to reform by a regular act of
its fovereign will.

From the time when the genius of Defcartes impreffed on the minds of men
that general impulfe, which is the firft principle of a revolution in the deftiny of the
human fpecies, to the happy period of entire
focial liberty, in which man has not been
able to regain his natural independence till
after having paffed through a long feries of
ages of misfortune and flavery, the view of
the progrefs of mathematical and phyfical
fcience prefents to us an immenfe horizon, of
which

which it is neceffary to diftribute and affort the feveral parts, whether we may be defirous of fully comprehending the whole, or of obferving their mutual relations.

The application of algebra to geometry not only became the fruitful fource of difcoveries in both fciences, but they prove, from this ftriking example, how much the method of computation of magnitudes in general may be extended to all queftions, the object of which confifts in meafure and extenfion. Defcartes firft announced the truth, that they would be employed with equal fuccefs hereafter upon all objects fufceptible of precife valuation ; and this great difcovery, by fhewing for the firft time the ultimate purpofe of thefe fciences, that is to fay, the ftrict calculation of every fpecies of truth, afforded the hope of attaining this point, at the fame time that it exhibited the means.

This difcovery was foon fucceeded by that of a new method of computing, which teaches us to find the ratios of the fucceffive increments or decrements of a variable quantity, or to deduce the quantity itfelf when this ratio is given ; whether the increments be fuppofed

pofed of finite magnitude, or their ratio be
fought for the inftant only of their vanifh-
ment ; a method which, being extended to
all the combinations of variable magnitudes,
and to all the hypothefes of their variations,
leads to a determination, with regard to all
things precifely menfurable, of the ratios of
their elements, or of the things themfelves,
from the knowledge of thofe proportions
which they mutually have, provided the ratios of their elements only be given.

We are indebted to Newton and Leibnitz
for the invention of thefe methods ; but the
labours of the geometers of the preceding age
prepared the way for this difcovery. The
progrefs of thefe fciences, which has been uninterrupted for more than a century, is the
work, and eftablifhes the reputation, of a number of men of genius. They prefent to the
eyes of the philofopher, who is able to obferve them, even though he may not follow
their fteps, a ftriking monument of the force
of the human mind.

When we explain the formation and principles of algebraic language, which alone is
accurate and truly analytic ; the nature of the
technical

3

technical proceſſes of this ſcience ; and the compariſon of theſe proceſſes with the natural operations of the human mind, we may prove that, if this method be not itſelf a peculiar inſtrument in the ſcience of quantity, it certainly includes the principles of an univerſal inſtrument applicable to all poſſible combinations of ideas.

Rational mechanics ſoon became a vaſt and profound ſcience. The true laws of the colliſion of bodies, reſpecting which Deſcartes was deceived, were at length known.

Huyghens Huyghens diſcovered the laws of circular motions ; and at the ſame time he gives a method of determining the radius of curvature for every point of a given curve. By uniting both theories, Newton invented the theory of curve-lined motions, and applied it *Kepler* to thoſe laws according to which Kepler had diſcovered that the planets deſcribe their elliptical orbits.

A planet, ſuppoſed to be projected into ſpace at a given inſtant, with a given velocity and direction, will deſcribe round the ſun an ellipſis, by virtue of a force directed to that ſtar, and proportional to the inverſe ratio of

I   the

the fquares of the diftances. The fame force retains the fatellites in their orbits round the primary planets: it pervades the whole fyftem of heavenly bodies, and acts reciprocally between all their component parts.

The regularity of the planetary ellipfes is difturbed, and the calculation precifely explains the very flighteft degrees of thefe perturbations. It is equally applicable to the comets, and determines their orbits with fuch precifion, as to foretel their return. The peculiar motion obferved in the axes of rotation of the earth and the moon, affords additional proof of the exiftence of this univerfal force. Laftly, it is the caufe of the weight of terreftrial bodies, in which effect it appears to be invariable, becaufe we have no means of obferving its action at diftances from the centre, which are fufficiently remote from each other.

Thus we fee man has at laft become acquainted, for the firft time, with one of the phyfical laws of the univerfe. Hitherto it *law of the univerfe.* ftands unparalleled, as does the glory of him who difcovered it.

An hundred years of labour and inveftiga-

T   tion

tion have confirmed this law, to which all the celeftial phenomena are fubjected, with an accuracy which may be faid to be miraculous. Every time in which an apparent deviation has prefented itfelf, the tranfient uncertainty has foon become a fubject of new triumph to the fcience.

The philofopher is, in almoft every inftance, compelled to have recourfe to the works of a man of genius for the fecret clue which led him to difcovery; but here intereft, infpired by admiration, has difcovered and preferved anecdotes of the greateft value, fince they permit us to follow Newton ftep by ftep. They ferve to fhew how much the happy combinations of external events, or chance, unite with the efforts of genius in producing a great difcovery, and how eafily combinations of a lefs favourable nature might have retarded them, or referved them for other hands.

But Newton did more, perhaps, in favour of the progrefs of the human mind, than merely difcovering this general law of nature; he taught men to admit in natural philofophy no other theories but fuch as are precife, and fufceptible of calculation; which give

an

an account not only of the exiftence of a
phenomenon, but its quantity and extent.
Neverthelefs he was accufed of reviving the
occult qualities of the ancients, becaufe he
had confined himfelf to refer the general caufe
of celeftial appearances to a fimple fact, of
which obfervation proved the inconteftable
reality; and this accufation is itfelf a proof
how much the methods of the fciences ftill
require to be enlightened by philofophy.

A great number of problems in ftatics and *ftatics*
dynamics had been fucceffively propofed and *dynamics*
refolved, when Alembert difcovered a general *Alembert*
principle adequate to the determination of the
motions of any number of points acted on by
any forces, and connected by conditions. He
foon extended the fame principle to finite bodies of a determinate figure; to thofe which,
from elafticity or flexibility, are capable of
changing their figure, but according to certain laws and preferving certain relations between their parts; and laftly to fluids themfelves, whether they preferve the fame den-
fity, or exift in a ftate of expanfibility. A
new calculation was neceffary to refolve thefe
laft queftions; the means did not efcape him,

T 2   and

and mechanics at prefent form a fcience of pure calculation.

Thefe difcoveries belong to the mathematical fciences; but the nature of the law of univerfal gravitation, or of thefe principles of mechanics, and the confequences which may thence be drawn and applied to the eternal order of the univerfe, belong to philofophy. We learn that all bodies are fubject to neceffary laws, which tend of themfelves to produce or maintain an equilibrium, which caufes or preferves the regularity of their motions.

He fhould have allowed an Equilibrium in Politicks.

The knowledge of thofe laws which govern the celeftial phenomena, the difcoveries of that mathematical analyfis which leads to the moft precife methods of calculating the appearances, the very unexpected degree of perfection to which optical and goniometrical inftruments have been brought, the precifion of machines for meafuring time, the more general tafte for the fciences, which unites itfelf with the intereft of governments, to multiply the number of aftronomers and obfervations; all thefe caufes unite to fecure the progrefs of aftronomy.

The

The heavens are enriched for the man of *Astronomy.*
fcience with new ftars, and he applies his
knowledge to determine and foretel with accuracy their pofition and movements. Natural philofophy, gradually delivered from the
vague explanations of Defcartes, in the fame
manner as it before was difembarraffed from
the abfurdities of the fchools, is now nothing
more than the art of interrogating nature by
experiment, for the purpofe of afterwards
deducing more general facts by computation.

The weight of the air is known and meafured : it is known that the tranfmiffion of
light is not inftantaneous ; its velocity is determined, with the effects which muft refult from
that velocity, as to the apparent pofition of
the celeftial bodies ; and the decompofition of
the folar rays into others of different refrangi-
bility and colour. The rainbow is explained,
and the methods of caufing its colours to be
produced or to difappear are fubjected to calculation. Electricity, formerly confidered as
the property of certain fubftances only, is
now known to be one of the moft general
phenomena in the univerfe. The caufe of
thunder is no longer a fecret ; Franklin has *Franklin*

taught

taught the artiſt to change its courſe, and direct it at pleaſure. New inſtruments are employed to meaſure the variations of weight
and humidity in the atmoſphere, and the temperature of all bodies. A new ſcience, under
the name of meteorology, teaches us to know,
and ſometimes to foretel, the atmoſpheric appearances of which it will hereafter diſcloſe to
us the unknown laws.

While we preſent a ſketch of theſe diſcoveries, we may remark how much the methods which have directed philoſophers in
their reſearches are ſimplified and brought to
perfection; how greatly the art of making
experiments, and of conſtructing inſtruments,
has ſucceſſively become more accurate; ſo
that philoſophy is not only enriched every
day with new truths, but the truths already
known have been more exactly aſcertained;
ſo that not only an immenſe maſs of new
facts have been obſerved and analyſed, but the
whole has been ſubmitted in detail to methods
of greater ſtrictneſs.

*Natural Philo-
ophy* Natural philoſophy has been obliged to
combat with the prejudices of the ſchools, and
the attraction of general hypotheſes, ſo ſe-
ducing

ducing to indolence. Other obftacles retarded the progrefs of chemiftry. It was *Chemiftry,*
imagined that this fcience ought to afford the
fecret of making gold, and that of rendering
man immortal.

The effect of great interefts, is to render
man fuperftitious. It was not fuppofed that
fuch promifes, which flatter the two ftrongeft
paffions of vulgar minds, and befides roufe
that of acquiring glory, could be accomplifhed
by ordinary means ; and every thing which
credulity or folly could ever invent of extravagance, feemed to unite in the minds of che-
mifts.

But thefe chimeras gradually gave place to
the mechanical philofophy of Defcartes, which
in its turn gave place to a chemiftry truly experimental. The obfervation of thofe facts
which accompany the mutual compofition and
decompofition of bodies, the refearch into the
laws of thefe operations, with the analyfis of
fubftances into elements of greater fimplicity,
acquire a degree of precifion and ftrictnefs
ever increafing.

But to thefe advances of chemiftry we muft
add others, which embrace the whole fyftem

of

of the fcience, and rather by extending the
methods than immediately increafing the mafs
of truths, foretel and prepare a revolution of
the happieft kind. Such has been the difcovery of new means of confining and examining
thofe elaftic fluids, which formerly were fuf-
fered to efcape ; a difcovery which, by per-
mitting us to operate upon an entire clafs
of new principles, and upon thofe already
known, reduced to a ftate which efcaped our
refearches, and by adding an element the
more to almoft every combination, has
changed, as it were, the whole fyftem of
chemiftry. Such has been the formation of
a language, in which the names denoting
fubftances fometimes exprefs the refemblance
or differences of thofe which have a common
element, and fometimes the clafs to which
they belong. To thefe advantages we may
add the ufe of a fcientific method, wherein
thefe fubftances are reprefented by characters
analytically combined, and moreover capable
of expreffing the moft common operations and
the general laws of affinity. And, again,
this fcience is enriched by the ufe of all the
means and all the inftruments which philofophers

phers have applied to compute with the ut-
moft rigor the refults of experiment; and
laftly, by the application of the mathematics to
the phenomena of chryftalization, and to the
laws according to which the elements of certain bodies effect in their combination regular
and conftant forms.

Men who long had poffeffed no other
knowledge than that of explaining by fuperftitious or philofophical reveries the formation of the earth, before they endeavoured to
become acquainted with its parts, have at laft
perceived the neceffity of ftudying with the
moft fcrupulous attention the furface of
the ground, the internal parts of the earth
into which neceffity has urged men to penetrate, the fubftances there found, their fortuitous or regular diftribution, and the difpofition of the maffes they have formed by their
union. They have learned to afcertain the
effects of the flow and long-continued action of
the waters of the fea, of rivers, and the effect of
volcanic fires; to diftinguifh thofe parts of the
furface and exterior cruft of the globe, of
which the inequalities, difpofition, and frequently the materials themfelves, are the work

of

of thefe agents ; from the other portion of the
furface, formed for the moft part of heteroge-
neous fubftances, bearing the marks of more
ancient revolutions by agents with which we
are yet unacquainted.

Minerals, vegetables, and animals are divided into various fpecies, of which the individuals differ by infenfible variations fcarcely
conftant, or produced by caufes purely local.
Many of thefe fpecies refemble each other
by a greater or lefs number of common qualities, which ferve to eftablifh fucceffive divi-
fions regularly more and more extended. Na-
turalifts have invented methods of claffing the
objects of fcience from determinate characters
eafily afcertained, the only means of avoiding
confufion in the midft of this numberlefs
multitude of individuals. Thefe methods are,
indeed, a real language, wherein each object
is denoted by fome of its moft conftant qualities, which, when known, are applicable to
the difcovery of the name which the article
may bear in common language. Thefe general languages, when well compofed, likewife
indicate, in each clafs of natural objects, the
truly effential qualities which by their union
caufe

caufe a more or lefs perfect refemblance in the
reft of their properties.

We have formerly feen the effects of that
pride which magnifies in the eyes of men the
objects of an exclufive ftudy, and knowledge
painfully acquired, which attaches to thefe
methods an exaggerated degree of importance,
and miftakes for fcience itfelf that which is
nothing more than the dictionary and grammar of its real language. And fo likewife,
by a contrary excefs, we have feen philofophers falfely degrade thefe fame methods, and
confound them with arbitrary nomenclatures,
as futile and laborious compilations.

The chemical analyfis of the fubftances in
the three great kingdoms of nature ; the defcription of their external form ; the expofition of their phyfical qualities and ufual properties ; the hiftory of the developement of
organized bodies, animals, or plants ; their nu-
trition and reproduction ; the details of their
organization ; the anatomy of their various
parts ; the functions of each ; the hiftory of
the manners of animals, and their induftry to
procure food, defence, and habitation, or to
feize their prey, or efcape from their enemies ;
the

the focieties of family or fpecies which are
formed amongft them ; that great mafs of
truth to which we are led by meditating on
the immenfe chain of organifed beings ; the
relation which fucceffive years produce from
brute matter at the moft feeble degree of organization, from organifed matter to that which
affords the firft indications of fenfibility and
fpontaneous motion ; and from this ftation to
that of man himfelf ; the relation of all thefe
beings with him, whether relative to his wants,
the analogies which bring him nearer to them,
or the differences by which he is feparated :
fuch is the fketch prefented to the mind by
atural modern natural hiftory.

iftory. The phyfical man is himfelf the objeɗ of a
natomy feparate fcience, anatomy, which, in its general acceptation, includes phyfiology. This
fcience, which a fuperftitious refpeɗ for the
dead had retarded, has taken advantage of the
general difappearance of prejudice, and has
happily oppofed the intereft of the prefervation of man, which has fecured it the patro-
nage of men of eminence. Its progrefs has
been fuch, that it feems in fome fort to be at
a ftand, in the expeɗation of more perfeɗ
inftru-

inftruments and new methods. It is nearly
reduced to feek, in the comparative anatomy
of the parts of animals and man, in the organs
common to the different fpecies, and the manner in which they exercife fimilar functions,
thofe truths which the direct obfervation of
the human frame appears to refule. Almoft
every thing which the eye of the obferver,
afflifted by the microfcope, has been able to difcover, is already afcertained. Anatomy appears to ftand in need of experiments, fo ufeful to the progrefs of other fciences ; but the
nature of its object deprives it of this means,
fo evidently neceffary to its perfection.

The circulation of the blood was long fince *Circulation of*
known ; but the difpofition of the veffels *the Blood.*
which conveyed the chyle to mix with it,
and repair its loffes ; the exiftence of a gaftric *Gaftric Flui.*
fluid which difpofes the elements to the decompofition neceffary to feparate from organifed matter, that portion which is proper to
become affimilated with the living fluids; the
changes undergone by the various parts and
organs in the interval between conception and
birth, and afterwards during the different
ages of life ; the diftinction between the parts
poffeffing

poſſeſſing ſenſibility and thoſe in which irri-
tability only reſides, a property diſcovered by
Haller, and common to almoſt every organic
ſubſtance : theſe facts are the whole of what
phyſiology has been enabled to diſcover, by
indubitable obſervations, during this brilliant
epoch ; and theſe important truths may ſerve
as an apology for the numerous explanations,
mechanical, chemical, and organical, which
have ſucceeded each other, and loaded this
ſcience with hypotheſes deſtructive to its progreſs, and dangerous when uſed as the ground
of medical practice.

To the outline of the ſciences we may add
that of the arts, which, being founded upon
them, have advanced with greater certainty,
and broken the ſhackles of cuſtom and common practice, which heretofore impeded their
progreſs.

We may ſhew the influence which the progreſs of mechanics, of aſtronomy, of optics,
and of the art of meaſuring time, has exerciſed on the art of conſtructing, moving, and
directing veſſels at ſea. We may ſhew how
greatly an increaſe of the number of obſervers,
and a greater degree of accuracy in the aſtro-
nomical

2

nomical determinations of pofitions, and in topographical methods, have at laft produced an acquaintance with the furface of the globe, of which fo little was known at the end of the laft century.

How greatly the mechanic arts, properly fo called, have given perfection to the proceffes of art in conftructing inftruments and machines in the practice of trade, and thefe laft have no lefs added force to rational mechanifm and philofophy. Thefe arts are alfo greatly indebted to the employment of firft movers already known, with lefs of expence and lofs, as well as to the invention of new principles of motion.

We have beheld architecture extend its *Architecture* refearches into the fcience of equilibriums and the theory of fluids, for the means of giving the moft commodious and leaft expenfive form to arches, without fear of altering their folidity; and to oppofe againft the effort of water a refiftance computed with greater certainty; to direct the courfe of that fluid, and to employ it in canals with greater fkill and fuccefs.

We have beheld the arts dependent on
chemiftry

chemiftry enriched with new procefles; the ancient methods have been fimplified, and cleared
from ufelefs or noxious fubftances, and from
abfurd or imperfect practices introduced from
former rude trials ; means have been invented
to avert thofe frequently terrible dangers to
which workmen were expofed. Thus it is
that the application of fcience has fecured to
us more of riches and enjoyment, with much
lefs of painful facrifice or of regret.

In the mean time, chemiftry, botany, and
natural hiftory, have very much enlightened
the economical arts, and the culture of vegetables deftined to fupply our wants; fuch as the
art of fupporting, multiplying, and preferving
domeftic animals ; the bringing their races to
perfection, and meliorating their products ;
the art of preparing and preferving the productions of the earth, or thofe articles which
are of animal product.

Surgery and pharmacy have become almoft
new arts, from the period when anatomy and
chemiftry have offered them more enlightened
and more certain direction.

The art of medicine, for in its practice it
muft be confidered as an art, is by this means
deli-

delivered at leaft of its falfe theories, its pedantic jargon, its deftructive courfe of practice,
and the fervile fubmiffion to the anthority of
men, or the doctrine of colleges ; it is taught
to depend only on experience. The means
of this art have become multiplied, and their
combination and application better known ;
and though it may be admitted that in fome
parts its progrefs is merely of a negative kind,.
that is to fay, in the deftruction of dangerous
practices and hurtful prejudices, yet the new
methods of ftudying chemical medicine, and
of combining obfervations, give us reafon to
expect more real and certain advances.

We may endeavour more efpecially to trace
that practice of genius in the fciences which
at one time defcends from an abftract and profound theory to learned and delicate applications ; at another, fimplifying its means, and
proportioning them to its wants, concludes by
fpreading its advantages through the moft ordinary practices ; and at others again being
rouzed by the wants of this fame courfe of
art, it plunges into the moft remote fpecula-
tions, in fearch of refources which the ordinary ftate of our knowledge muft have refufed.

U   We

We may remark that thofe declamations which are made againft the utility of theories, even in the moft fimple arts, have never fhewn any thing but the ignorance of the declaimers. We may prove that it is not to the profundity of thefe theories, but, on the contrary, to their imperfection, that we ought to attribute the inutility or unhappy effects of fo many ufelefs applications.

Thefe obfervations will lead us to one general truth, that in all the arts the refults of theory are neceffarily modified in practice; that certain fources of inaccuracy exift, which are really inevitable, of which our aim fhould be to render the effect infenfible, without indulging the chimerical hope of removing them; that a great number of data relative to our wants, , our means, our time, and our expences, which are neceffarily overlooked in the theory, muft enter into the relative problem of immediate and real practice; and that, laftly, by introducing thefe requifites with that fkill which truly conftitutes the genius of the practical man, we may at the fame time go beyond the narrow limits wherein prejudice againft theory threatens to detain

the

the arts, and prevent thofe errors into which an improper ufe of theory might lead us.

Thofe fciences which are remote from each other, cannot be extended without bringing them nearer, and forming points of contact between them:

An expofition of the progrefs of each fcience is fufficient to fhew, that in feveral the intermediate application of numbers has been ufeful, as, in almoft all, it has been employed to give a greater degree of precifion to experiments and obfervations; and that the fciences are indebted to mechanics, which has fupplied them with more perfect and more accurate inftruments. How much have the difcovery of microfcopes, and of meteorological inftruments, contributed to the perfection of natural hiftory. How greatly is this fcience indebted to chemiftry, which, alone, has been fufficient to lead to a more profound knowledge of the objects it confiders, by difplaying their moft intimate nature, and moft effential properties——by fhewing their compofition and elements; while natural hiftory offers to chemiftry fo many operations to execute, fuch a numerous fet of combina-

tions

tions formed by nature, the true elements of
which require to be feparated, and fometimes
difcovered, by an imitation of the natural
proceffes: and, laftly, how great is the mutual affiftance afforded to each other by chemiftry and natural philofophy; and how
greatly have anatomy and natural hiftory
been already benefited by thefe fciences.

But we have yet expofed no more than a
fmall portion of the advantages which have
been received, or may be expected, from
thefe applications.

Many geometers have given us general
methods of deducing, from obfervations of
the empiric laws of phenomena, methods
which extend to all the fciences; becaufe
they are in all cafes capable of affording us
the knowledge of the law of the fucceffive
values of the fame quantity, for a feries of
inftants or pofitions; or that law according
to which they are diftributed, or which is
followed by the various properties and values
of a fimilar quality among a given number
of objects.

Applications have already proved, that
the fcience of combination may be fuccefsfully

fully employed to difpofe obfervations, in
fuch a manner, that their relations, refults,
and fum may with more facility be feen.

The ufes of the calculation of probabilities
foretel how much they may be applied to
advance the progrefs of other fciences; in
one cafe, to determine the probability of extraordinary facts, and to fhew whether they
ought to be rejected, or whether, on the
contrary, they ought to be verified; or in
calculating the probability of the return of
thofe facts which often prefent themfelves in
the practice of the arts, and are not connected together in an order, yet confidered
as a general law. Such, for example, in
medicine, is the falutary effect of certain remedies, and the fuccefs of certain preferva-
tives. Thefe applications likewife fhew us
how great is the probability that a feries of
phenomena fhould refult from the intention
of a thinking being; whether this being
depends on other co-exiftent, or antecedent
phenomena; and how much ought to be
attributed to the neceffary and unknown
caufe denominated chance, a word the fenfe *Chance,*
of which can only be known with precifion
by ftudying this method of computing.

U 3   The

The fciences have likewife taught us to afcertain the feveral degrees of certainty to which we may hope to attain ; the probability according to which we can adopt an opinion, and make it the bafis of our reafonings, without injuring the rights of found argument, and the rules of our conduct— without deficiency in prudence, or offence to juftice. They fhew what are the advantages or difadvantages of various forms of election, and modes of decifion dependant on the plurality of voices ; the different degrees of probability which may refult from fuch proceedings ; the method which public intereft requires to be followed, according to the nature of each queftion ; the means of obtaining it nearly with certainty, when the decifion is not abfolutely neceffary, or when the inconveniences of two conclufions being unequal, neither of them can become legitimate until beneath this probability ; or the affurance beforehand of moft frequently obtaining this fame probability, when, on the contrary, a decifion is neceffary to be made, and the moft feeble preponderance of probability is fufficient to produce a rule of practice.

Among

Among the number of thefe applications we may likewife ftate, an examination of the probability of facts for the ufe of fuch as have not the power, or means, to fupport their conclufions upon their own obfervations; a probability which refults either from the authority of witneffes, or the connection of thofe facts with others immediately obferved.

How greatly have inquiries into the duration of human life, and the influence in this refpect of fex, temperature, climate, profeffion, government, and habitudes of life; on the mortality which refults from different difeafes; the changes which population experiences; the extent of the action of different caufes which produce thefe changes; the manner of its diftribution in each country, according to the age, fex, and occupation :—how greatly ufeful have thefe refearches been to the phyfical knowledge of man, to medicine, and to public economy.

How extenfively have computations of this nature been applied for the eftablifhment of annuities, tontines, accumulating funds, benefit focieties, and chambers of affurance of every kind,

U 4

Is

Is not the application of numbers alfo neceffary to that part of the public economy
which includes the theory of public meafures,
of coin, of banks and financial operations,
and laftly, that of taxation, as eftablifhed by
law, and its real diftribution, which fo frequently differs, in its effects on all the parts
of the focial fyftem.

What a number of important queftions in
this fame fcience are there, which could not
have been properly refolved without the
knowledge acquired in natural hiftory, agriculture, and the philofophy of vegetables,
which influence the mechanical or chemical
arts.

In a word, fuch has been the general progrefs of the fciences, that it may be faid
there is not one which can be confidered as
to the whole extent of its principles and detail, without our being obliged to borrow the
affiftance of all the others.

In prefenting this fketch both of the new
facts which have enriched the fciences ref-
pectively, and the advantages derived in each
from the application of theories, or methods,
which feem to belong more particularly to
another

another department of knowledge, we may
endeavour to afcertain what is the nature and
the limits of thofe truths to which obfervation, experience, or meditation, may lead us
in each fcience; we may likewife inveſtigate
what it is precifely that conſtitutes that talent
of invention which is the firſt faculty of the *Invention*
human mind, and is known by the name
of genius; by what operations the under- *genius.*
ſtanding may attain the difcoveries it purfues,
or fometimes be led to others not fought, or
even poſſible to have been foretold; we may
ſhew how far the methods which lead to
difcovery may be exhauſted, fo that fcience
may, in a certain refpect, be at a ſtand, till
new methods are invented to afford an additional inſtrument to genius, or to facilitate
the ufe of thofe which cannot be employed
without too great a confumption of time and
fatigue.

If we confine ourfelves to exhibit the advantages deduced from the fciences in their immediate ufe or application to the arts, whether
for the welfare of individuals or the profperity
of nations, we ſhall have ſhewn only a fmall
part of the benefits they afford. The moſt
important

4

important perhaps is, that prejudice has been destroyed, and the human underftanding in fome fort rectified; after having been forced into a wrong direction by abfurd objects of belief, tranfmitted from generation to generation, taught at the misjudging period of infancy, and enforced with the terrors of fuperftition and the dread of tyranny.

All the errors in politics and in morals are founded upon philofophical miftakes, which, themfelves, are connected with phyfical errors. There does not exift any religious fyftem, or fupernatural extravagance, which is not founded on an ignorance of the laws of nature. The inventors and defenders of thefe abfurdities could not forefee the fucceffive progrefs of the human mind. Being perfuaded that the men of their time knew every thing, they would ever know, and would always believe that in which they then had fixed their faith; they confidently built their reveries upon the general opinions of their own country and their own age.

The progrefs of natural knowledge is yet more deftructive of thefe errors, becaufe it frequently deftroys them without feeming to

attack

attack them, by attaching to thofe who obftinately defend them the degrading ridicule of
ignorance.

At the fame time, the juft habit of reafoning on the objeft of thefe fciences, the precife ideas which their methods afford, and
the means of afcertaining or proving the
truth, muft naturally lead us to compare the
fentiment which forces us to adhere to opinions founded on thefe real motives of credi-
bility, and that which attaches us to our habitual prejudices, or forces us to yield to authority. This comparifon is fufficient to
teach us to miftruft thefe laft opinions, to
fhew that they were not really believed, even
when that belief was the moft earneftly and
the moft fincerely profeffed. When this
difcovery is once made, their deftruction becomes much more fpeedy and certain.

Laftly, this progrefs of the phyfical fciences,
which the paffions and intereft do not inter-
fere to difturb; wherein it is not thought
that birth, profeffion, or appointment have
given a right to judge what the individual is
not in a fituation to underftand; this more
certain progrefs cannot be obferved, unlefs
enlightened

enlightened men fhall fearch in the other
fciences to bring them continually together.
This progrefs at every ftep exhibits the model
they ought to follow; according to which
they may form a judgment of their own efforts, afcertain the falfe fteps they may have
taken, preferve themfelves from pyrrhonifm
as well as credulity, and from a blind miftruft
or too extenfive fubmiffion to the authorities
even of men of reputation and knowledge.

The metaphyfical analyfis would, no doubt,
lead to the fame refults, but it would have
afforded only abftract principles.   In this
method, the fame abftract principles being
put into action, are enlightened by example
and fortified by fuccefs.

Until the prefent epoch, the fciences have
been the patrimony only of a few; but they
are already become common, and the moment approaches in which their elements,
their principles, and their moft fimple practice, will become really popular.   Then it
will be feen how truly univerfal their utility
will be in their application to the arts, and
their influence on the general rectitude of
the mind.

We

We may trace the progrefs of European *Education*.
nations in the inftruction of children, or of
men; a progrefs hitherto feeble, if we attend
merely to the philofophical fyftem of this
inftruction, which, in moft parts, is ftill confined, to the prejudices of the fchools; but
very rapid if we confider the extent and nature of the objects taught, which no longer
comprehending any points of knowledge but
fuch as are real, includes the elements of
almoft all the fciences; while men of all
defcriptions find in dictionaries, abridgments,
and journals the information they require,
though not always of the pureft kind. We
may examine the degree of utility refulting
from oral inftruction in the fciences, added
to that which is immediately received by
books and ftudy; whether any advantage has
refulted from the labour of compilation having become a real trade, a means of fubfift-
ence, which has multiplied the number of
inferior works, but has likewife multiplied
the means of acquiring common knowledge
to men of fmall information. We may mark
the influence which learned focieties have *Academ*
exercifed on the progrefs of the human
mind,

mind, a barrier which will long be ufeful to oppofe againft ignorant pretenders and falfe knowledge: and laftly, we may exhibit the hiftory of the encouragements given by go-vernments to that progrefs, and the obftacles which have often been oppofed to it in the fame country and at the fame period. We may fhew what prejudices or principles of Machiavelifm have directed them in this op-pofition to the advances of man towards truth; what views of interefted policy, or even public good, have directed them when they have appeared, on the contrary, to be defirous of accelerating and protecting them.

Fine Arts The picture of the fine arts offers to our view refults of no lefs brilliancy. *Mufic* Mufic is become, in a certain refpect, a new art; while the fcience of combination, and the ap-plication of numbers to the vibrations of fo-norous bodies, and the ofcillations of the air, have enlightened its theory. The arts of *Defign* defign, which formerly paffed from Italy to Flanders, Spain, and France, elevated them-felves in this laft country to the fame degree that Italy carried them in the preceding epocha; where they have been fupported

with

with more reputation than in Italy itſelf.
The art of our painters is that of Raphael *Painters*
and Carrachi. All the means of the art being preſerved in the ſchools, are ſo far from
being loſt, that they have become more extended. Neverthelefs, it muſt be admitted, *The Mythol*
that too long a time has elapſed without *gy of the Greeks*
producing a genius which may be compared *and the Trade*
to them, to admit of this long ſterility being *gy of chriſtian*
attributed to chance. It is not becauſe the *Rome have*
means of art are exhauſted that great ſuccefs is *been the great*
really become difficult; it is not that nature *encouraged*
has refuſed us organs equally perfeą with *and rewarded*
thoſe of the Italians of the ſixth age; it is *of Painters*
merely to the changes of politics and man- *Italia curious an*
ners that we ought to attribute, not the de- *Architects.*
cay of the art, but the mediocrity of its productions.

Literary productions cultivated in Italy, *French*
with lefs of ſuccefs, but without having de- *Language.*
generated, have made ſuch progreſs in the
French language, as has acquired it the honour of becoming, in ſome ſort, the univerſal language of Europe.

The tragic art, in the hands of Corneille, *Tragedy*
Racine, and Voltaire, has been raiſed, by

ſucceſſive

fucceffive progrefs, to a perfection before unknown. The comic art is indebted to Mo-
liere for having fpeedily arrived to an elevation not yet attained by any other people.

Comedy

In England, from the commencement of the
fame epoch, and in a ftill later time in Germany, language has been rendered more perfect. The art of poetry, as well as that of
profe writing, have been fubjected, though
with lefs docility than in France, to the univerfal rules of reafon and nature, which
ought to direct them. Thefe rules are equally
true for all languages and all people, though
the number of men has hitherto been few
who have fucceeded in arriving at the knowledge of them, and rifing to the juft and
pure tafte which refults from that knowledge.
Thefe rules prefided over the compofitions of
Sophocles and Virgil, as well as thofe of Pope
and Voltaire; they taught the Greeks and
Romans, as well as the French, to be ftruck
with the fame beauties, and fhocked at the
fame faults. We may alfo inveftigate what
it is in each nation that has favoured or retarded the progrefs of thefe arts; by what
caufes the different kinds of poetry, or works

England

German

in

in profe, have attained in the different countries a degree of perfection fo unequal; and
how far thefe univerfal rules may, without
offending their own fundamental principles,
be modified by the manners and opinions of
the people who are to poffefs their productions, and even by the nature of the ufes to
which their different fpecies are defigned.
Thus, for example, a tragedy daily recited
before a fmall number of fpectators, in a
theatre of confined extent, cannot follow the
fame practical rules as a tragedy exhibited on
an immenfe theatre, in the folemn feftivals
to which a whole people was invited. We
may attempt to fhew, that the rules of tafte
poffefs the fame generality and the fame conftancy, though they are fufceptible of the
fame modifications as the other laws of the
moral and phyfical univerfe, when it is neceffary to apply them to the immediate practice of a common art.

We may fhew how far the art of print- *Printing*
ing, by multiplying and diffeminating even
thofe works which are defigned to be publicly read or recited, tranfmit them to a
number of readers incomparably greater than

X   that

that of the auditors. We may fhew how moft of the important decifions by numerous affemblies, having been determined from the previous inftruction their members had received by writing, there muft have refulted in the art of perfuafion among the ancients and among the moderns, differences in the rules, analogous to the effect intended to be produced and the means employed; and how, laftly, in the different fpecies of knowledge, even with the ancients, certain works were for perufal only—fuch as thofe of hiftory or philofophy. The facility which the invention of printing affords, to enter into a more entenfive detail and more accurate developement, muft have likewife influenced the fame rules.

The progrefs of philofophy and the fciences have extended and favoured thofe of letters, and thefe in their turn have ferved to render the ftudy of the fciences more eafy, and philofophy itfelf more popular. They have lent mutual affiftance to each other, in fpite of the efforts of ignorance and folly to difunite and render them inimical. Erudition, which a refpect for human authority

and

(307)

and ancient things feemed to have deftined
to fupport the caufe of hurtful prejudices;
this erudition has, neverthelefs, affifted in
deftroying them, becaufe the fciences and
philofophy have enlightened it with a more
legitimate criticifm. It already knew the
method of weighing authorities, and comparing them with each other, but it has at
length fubmitted them to the tribunal of reafon; it had rejected the prodigies, abfurd *Miracles;*
tales, and facts contrary to probability; but, *he means,*
by attacking the teftimony upon which they *no doubt.*
were fupported, men have learned to reject *Testimony*
them, in fpite of the force of thefe witneffes, *of Moses Ma*
that they might give way to that evidence *them and John*
which the phyfical or moral improbability of *It does not*
extraordinary facts might carry with them. *appear that*
Hence it is feen that all the intellectual *Mark and Luke*
occupations of men, however differing in *were Eye Witness*
the·· object, their method, or the qualities *Jes.*
of mind which they require, have concurred
in the progrefs of human reafon. It is the
fame with the entire fyftem of the labours
of men as with a well-compofed work; of
which the parts, though methodically diftinct,
muft, neverthelefs, be clofely connected to

X 2   form

form one fingle whole, and tend to one fingle
object.

While we thus take a general view of the
human fpecies, we may prove that the difcovery of true methods in all the fciences;
the extent of the theories they include; their
application to all the objects of nature, and
all the wants of man; the lines of communication eftablifhed between them; the great
number of thofe who cultivate them; and,
laftly, the multiplication of printing preffes,
are fufficient to affure us, that none of them
will hereafter defcend below the point to
which it has been carried. We may fhew
that the principles of philofophy, the maxims
of liberty, the knowledge of the true rights
of man, and his real intereft, are fpread over
too many nations, and in each of thofe nations direct the opinions of too great a number of enlightened men, for them ever to fall
again into oblivion.

A pleasing hope.

What fear can be entertained when we
find that the two languages the moft univerfally extended, are, likewife, the languages
of two people who poffefs the moft extended liberty; who have beft known its principles. So that no confederacy of tyrants,

nor

English and of French,

nor any poffible combination of policy, can prevent the rights of reafon, as well as thofe of liberty, from being openly defended in both languages.

But if it be true, as every profpect affures us, that the human race fhall not again re-lapfe into its ancient barbarity; if every thing ought to affure us againft that pufil-lanimous and corrupt fyftem which condemns man to eternal ofcillations between truth and falfhood, liberty and fervitude, we muft, at the fame time, perceive that the light of information is fpread over a fmall part only of our globe; and the number of thofe who poffefs real inftruction, feems to vanifh in the comparifon with the mafs of men con-figned over to ignorance and prejudice. We behold vaft countries groaning under flavery, and prefenting nations, in one place, de-graded by the vices of civilization, fo corrupt as to impede the progrefs of man; and in others, ftill vegetating in the infancy of its early age. We perceive that the exertions of thefe laft ages have done much for the progrefs of the human mind, but little for the perfection of the human fpecies; much

X 3   for

for the glory of man, fomewhat for his liberty, but fcarcely any thing yet for his happinefs. In a few directions, our eyes are
ftruck with a dazzling light ; but thick darknefs ftill covers an immenfe horizon. The
mind of the philofopher repofes with fatis-
faction upon a fmall number of objects, but
the fpectacle of the ftupidity, the flavery,
the extravagance, and the barbarity of man,
afflicts him ftill more ftrongly. The friend
'of humanity cannot receive unmixed pleafure
but by abandoning himfelf to the endearing
hope of the future.

Such are the objects which ought to enter
into an hiftorical fketch of the progrefs of
the human mind. We may endeavour, while
we hold them forward, to fhew more efpecially the influence of this progrefs upon the
opinions and the welfare of the general mafs
of different nations, at the different epochas
of their political exiftence ; to fhew what
truths they have known, what errors have
been deftroyed, what virtuous habits contracted, what new developement of their faculties has eftablifhed a happier proportion
between their powers and their wants : And,

unde

under an oppofite point of view, what may
be the prejudices to which they have been
enflaved ; what religious or political fuperftitions have been introduced ; by what vices,
of ignorance or defpotifm, they have been
corrupted ; and to what miferies, violence or
their own degradation have fubjected them.

Hitherto, political hiftory, as well as that *Political His-*
of philofophy and the fciences, has been *tory.*
merely the hiftory of a few men. That
which forms in truth the human fpecies, the *History only*
mafs of families, which fubfift almoft en- *preserves th*
tirely upon their labour, has been forgotten ; *Memory of th*
and even among that clafs of men who, de- *Few. i.e. the*
voted to public profeffions, act not for them- *Aristocrat*
felves but for fociety ; whofe occupation it is *or rather the*
to inftruct, to govern, to defend, and to *Oligarchs.*
comfort other men, the chiefs only have fixed
the attention of hiftorians,

It is enough for the hiftory of individuals
that facts be collected, but the hiftory of a
mafs of men can be founded only on obfervations ; and, in order to felect them, and to
feize the effential traits, it is requifite the
hiftorian fhould poffefs confiderable information, and no lefs of philofophy, to make a
proper ufe of them.

X 4   Again,

Again, thefe obfervations relate to common things, which ftrike the eyes of all, and which every one is capable himfelf of knowing when he thinks proper to attend to them. Hence the greater part have been collected by travellers and foreigners, becaufe things very trivial in the place where they exift, have become an object of curiofity to ftrangers. Now it unfortunately happens, that thefe travellers are almoft always inaccurate obfervers; they fee objects with too much rapidity, through the medium of the prejudices of their own country, and not unfrequently by the eyes of the men of the country they run through : their conferences are held with fuch men as accident has connected them with; and the anfwer is, in almoft every cafe, dictated by intereft, party fpirit, national pride, or ill-humour.

It is not alone, therefore, to the bafenefs of hiftorians, as has been juftly urged againft thofe of monarchies, that we are to attribute the want of monuments from which we may trace this moft important part of the hiftory of men.

The defect cannot be fupplied but very imperfectly by a knowledge of the laws, the

I   practical

practical principles of government and public economy, or by that of religion and general prejudices.

In fact, the law as written, and the law as executed; the principles of thofe who govern, and the manner in which their action is modified by the genius of thofe who are governed; the inftitution fuch as it has flowed from the men who formed it, and fuch as it becomes when realized by practice; the religion of books, and that of the people; the apparent univerfality of prejudice, and the real reception which it obtains, may differ to fuch a degree, that the effects fhall abfolutely ceafe to correfpond to thefe public and known caufes.

To this part of the hiftory of the human fpecies, which is the moft obfcure, the moft neglected, and for which facts offer us fo few materials, it is that we fhould more particularly attend in this outline; and whether an account be rendered of a new difcovery, an important theory, a new fyftem of laws, or a political revolution, the problem to be determined will confift in afcertaining what effects ought to have arifen from the will of

the

the moſt numerous portion of each ſociety. This is the true object of philoſophy; becauſe all the intermediate effects of theſe ſame càuſes can be conſidered only as means of acting, at leaſt upon this portion, which truly conſtitutes the maſs of the human race.

It is by arriving at this laſt link of the chain, that the obſervation of paſt events, as well as the knowledge acquired by meditation, become truly uſeful. It is by arriving at this term, that men learn to appreciate their real titles to reputation, or to enjoy, with a well-grounded pleaſure, the progreſs of their reaſon. Hence, alone, it is, that they can judge of the true improvement of the human ſpecies.

The notion of referring every thing to this latter point, is dictated by juſtice and by reaſon ; but it may be ſuppoſed to be without foundation. The ſuppoſition, neverthelefs, is not true ; and it will be enough if we prove it in this place by two ſtriking examples.

The poſſeſſion of the moſt common objects of conſumption, however abundantly they may now ſatisfy the wants of man ; of thoſe objects which the ground produces in conſe-

quence

quence of human effort, is due to the continued exertions of induftry, affifted by the
light of the fciences; and thence it follows,
from hiftory, that this poffeffion attaches itfelf to the gain of the battle of Salamis,
without which the darknefs of oriental defpotifm threatened to cover the whole of the
earth. And, again, the accurate obfervation of
the longitude, which preferves navigators from
fhipwreck, is indebted to a theory which, by
a chain of truths, goes as far back as to difcoveries made in the fchool of Plato, though
buried for twenty centuries in perfect inutility,

TENTH

TENTH EPOCH.

Future Progress of Mankind.

IF man can predict, almoſt with certainty, thoſe appearances of which he underſtands the laws; if, even when the laws are unknown to him, experience of the paſt enables him to foreſee, with conſiderable probability, future appearances; why ſhould we ſuppoſe it a chimerical undertaking to delineate, with ſome degree of truth, the picture of the future deſtiny of mankind from the reſults of its hiſtory? The only foundation of faith in the natural ſciences is the principle, that the general laws, known or unknown, which regulate the phenomena of the univerſe, are regular and conſtant; and why ſhould this principle, applicable to the other operations of nature, be leſs true when applied to the developement of the intellectual and moral faculties of man? In ſhort, as opinions formed from experience, relative to the ſame claſs of objects, are the only rule by which men of ſoundeſt underſtanding

ſtanding are governed in their conduct, why~~why indeed~~ ?
ſhould the philoſopher be proſcribed from
ſupporting his conjectures upon a ſimilar baſis,
provided he attribute to them no greater
certainty than the number, the conſiſtency,
and the accuracy of actual obſervations ſhall
authoriſe ?

Our hopes, as to the future condition of
the human ſpecies, may be reduced to three
points : the deſtruction of inequality between *hope Up.*
different nations ; the progreſs of equality in *is not quite*
one and the ſame nation ; and laſtly, the *hope Up.*
real improvement of man.

Will not every nation one day arrive at the
ſtate of civilization attained by thoſe people
who are moſt enlightened, moſt free, moſt
exempt from prejudices, as the French, for *Oroh dolor !*
inſtance, and the Anglo-Americans ? Will not
the ſlavery of countries ſubjected to kings, the
barbarity of African tribes, and the ignorance
of ſavages gradually vaniſh ? Is there upon the
face of the globe a ſingle ſpot the inhabitants
of which are condemned by nature never to
enjoy liberty, never to exerciſe their reaſon ? *Not that I know of.*

Does the difference of knowledge, of
means, and of wealth, obſervable hitherto in
all

all civilized nations, between the claſſes into which the people conſtituting thoſe nations are divided; does that inequality, which the earlieſt progreſs of ſociety has augmented, or, to ſpeak more properly, produced, belong to civilization itſelf, or to the imperfections of the ſocial order ? Muſt it not continually weaken, in order to give place to that actual equality, the chief end of the ſocial art, which, diminiſhing even the effects of the natural difference of the faculties, leaves no other inequality ſubſiſting but what is uſeful to the intereſt of all, becauſe it will favour civilization, inſtruction, and induſtry, without drawing after it either dependence, humiliation or poverty ? In a word, will not men be continually verging towards that ſtate, in which all will poſſeſs the requiſite knowledge for conducting themſelves in the common affairs of life by their own reaſon, and of maintaining that reaſon uncontaminated by prejudices ; in which they will underſtand their rights, and exerciſe them according to their opinion and their conſcience ; in which all will be able, by the developement of their faculties, to procure the certain means of providing for their wants ; laſtly,

laftly, in which folly and wretchednefs
will be accidents, happening only now and
then, and not the habitual lot of a confiderable portion of fociety?

·In fine, may it not be expected that the
human race will be meliorated by new difcoveries in the fciences and the arts, and, as an
unavoidable confequence, in the means of
individual and general profperity ; by farther
progrefs in the principles of conduct, and in
moral practice ; and laftly, by the real improvement of our faculties, moral, intellectual
and phyfical, which may be the refult either
of the improvement of the inftruments which
increafe the power and direct the exercife of
thofe faculties, or of the improvement of our
natural organization itfelf?

In examining he three queftions we have
enumerated, we fhall find the ftrongeft reafons to believe, from paft experience, from
obfervation of the progrefs which the fciences
and civilization have hitherto made, and from
the analyfis of the march of the human underftanding, and the developement of its faculties, that nature has fixed no limits to our
hopes.

If

If we take a furvey of the exifting ftate of
the globe, we fhall perceive, in the firft place,
that in Europe the principles of the French
conftitution are thofe of every enlightened
mind. We fhall perceive that they are too
widely diffeminated, and too openly profeffed,
for the efforts of tyrants and priefts to prevent them from penetrating by degrees into
the miferable cottages of their flaves, where
they will foon revive thofe embers of
good fenfe, and roufe that filent indignation
which the habit of fuffering and terror have
failed totally to extinguifh in the minds of the
oppreffed.

If we next look at the different nations, we
fhall obferve in each, particular obftacles op-
pofing, or certain difpofitions favouring this
revolution. We fhall diftinguifh fome in
which it will be effected, perhaps flowly, by
the wifdom of the refpective governments;
and others in which, rendered violent by refiftance, the governments themfelves will
neceffarily be involved in its terrible and
rapid motions.

Can it be fuppofed that either the wifdom
or the fenfelefs feuds of European nations,
co-operating

co-operating with the flow but certain effects
of the progrefs of their colonies, will not
fhortly produce the independence of the entire new world ; and that then, European population, lending its aid, will fail to civilize
or caufe to difappear, even without conqueft,
thofe favage nations ftill occupying there immenfe tracts of country ?

Run through the hiftory of our projects
and eftablifhments in Africa or in Afia, and
you will fee our monopolies, our treachery,
our fanguinary contempt for men of a different complexion or a different creed, and
the profelyting fury or the intrigues of our
priefts, deftroying that fentiment of refpect
and benevolence which the fuperiority of our
information and the advantages of our commerce had at firft obtained.

But the period is doubtlefs approaching,
when, no longer exhibiting to the view of
thefe people corruptors only or tyrants, we
fhall become to them inftruments of benefit,
and the generous champions of their redemp-
tion from bondage.

The cultivation of the fugar-cane, which
is now eftablifhing itfelf in Africa, will put

Y   an

an end to the fhameful robbery by which, for two centuries, that country has been depopulated and depraved.

Already, in Great Britain, fome friends of humanity have fet the example ; and if its Machiavelian government, forced to refpect public reafon, has not dared to oppofe this meafure, what may we not expect from the fame fpirit, when, after the reform of an abject and venal conftitution, it fhall become worthy of a humane and generous people ? Will not France be eager to imitate enterprifes which the philanthropy and the true intereft of Europe will equally have dictated ? Spices are already introduced into the French iflands, Guiana, and fome Englifh fettlements ; and we fhall foon witnefs the fall of that monopoly which the Dutch have fupported by fuch a complication of perfidy, of oppreffion, and of crimes. The people of Europe will learn in time that exclufive and chartered companies are but a tax upon the refpective nation, granted for the purpofe of placing a new inftrument in the hands of its government for the maintenance of tyranny.

Then will the inhabitants of the European
quarter

quarter of the world, satisfied with an unreftricted commerce, too enlightened as to their
own rights to fport with the rights of others,
refpect that independence which they have
hitherto violated with fuch audacity. Then will
their eftablifhments, inftead of being filled by the
creatures of power, who, availing themfelves
of a place or a privilege, haften, by rapine
and perfidy, to amafs wealth, in order to
purchafe, on their return, honours and titles,
be peopled with induftrious men, feeking in
thofe happy climates that eafe and comfort
which in their native country eluded their purfuit. There will they be retained by liberty,
ambition having loft its allurements ; and thofe
fettlements of robbers will then become colonies of citizens, by whom will be planted in
Africa and Afia the principles and example
of the freedom, reafon, and illumination of
Europe. To thofe monks alfo, who inculcate
on the natives of the countries in queftion
the moft fhameful fuperftitions only, and who
excite difguft by menacing them with a new
tyranny, will fucceed men of integrity and benevolence, anxious to fpread among thefe
people truths ufeful to their happinefs, and

to

to enlighten them upon their interefts as well as their rights : for the love of truth is alfo a paffion ; and when it fhall have at home no grofs prejudices to combat, no degrading errors to diffipate, it will naturally extend its regards, and convey its efforts to remote and foreign climes.

Thefe immenfe countries will afford ample fcope for the gratification of this paffion. In one place will be found a numerous people, who, to arrive at civilization, appear only to wait till we fhall furnifh them with the means ; and who, treated as brothers by Europeans, would inftantly become their friends and difciples. In another will be feen nations crouching under the yoke of facred defpots or ftupid conquerors, and who, for fo many ages, have looked for fome friendly hand to deliver them : while a third will exhibit either tribes nearly favage, excluded from the benefits of fuperior civilization by the feverity of their climate, which deters thofe who might otherwife be difpofed to communicate thefe benefits from making the attempt ; or elfe conquering hordes, knowing no law but force, no trade but robbery. The

advances

advances of thefe two laft claffes will be more
flow, and accompanied with more frequent
ftorms; it may even happen that, reduced in
numbers in proportion as they fee themfelves
repelled by civilized nations, they will in the
end wholly difappear, or their fcanty remains
become blended with their neighbours.

We might fhew that thefe events will be
the inevitable confequence not only of the
progrefs of Europe, but of that freedom
which the republic of France, as well as of
America, have it in their power, and feel it
to be their intereft, to reftore to the commerce of Africa and Afia; and that they muft
alfo neceffarily refult alike, whether from the
new policy of European nations, or their obftinate adherence to mercantile prejudices.

A fingle combination, a new invafion of
Afia by the Tartars, might be fufficient to
fruftrate this revolution; but it may be fhewn
that fuch combination is henceforth impoffible to be effected. Meanwhile every thing
feems to be preparing the fpeedy downfal of
the religions of the Eaft, which, partaking of
the abjectnefs of their minifters, left almoft
exclufively to the people, and, in the majo-

rity

rity of countries, confidered by powerful men as political inflitutions only, no longer threaten to retain human reafon in a ftate of hopelefs bondage, and in the eternal fhackles of infancy.

The march of thefe people will be lefs flow and more fure than ours has been, becaufe they will derive from us that light which we have been obliged to difcover, and becaufe for them to acquire the fimple truths and infallible methods which we have obtained after long wandering in the mazes of error, it will be fufficient to feize upon their developements and proofs in our difcourfes and publications. If the progrefs of the Greeks was loft upon other nations, it was for want of a communication between the people ; and to the tyrannical domination of the Romans muft the whole blame be afcribed. But, when mutual wants fhall have drawn clofer the intercourfe and ties of all mankind ; when the moft powerful nations fhall have eftabliflied into political principles equality between focieties as between individuals, and refpect for the independence of feeble ftates, as well as compaffion for ignorance and

wretched-

wretchednefs ; when to the maxims which bear heavily upon the fpring of the human faculties, thofe fhall fucceed which favour their action and energy, will there ftill be reafon to fear that the globe will contain fpaces inacceffible to knowledge, or that the pride of defpotifm will be able to oppofe barriers to truth that will long be infurmountable ?

Then will arrive the moment in which the fun will obferve in its courfe free nations only, acknowledging no other mafter than their reafon ; in which tyrants and flaves, priefts and their ftupid or hypocritical inftruments, will no longer exift but in hiftory and upon the ftage ; in which our only concern will be to lament their paft victims and dupes, and, by the recollection of their horrid enormities, to exercife a vigilant circumfpection, that we may be able inftantly to recognife and effectually to ftifle by the force of reafon, the feeds of fuperftition and tyranny, fhould they ever prefume again to make their appearance upon the earth.

In tracing the hiftory of focieties we have had occafion to remark, that there frequently exifts a confiderable diftinction between the

Y 4 rights

rights which the law acknowledges in the citizens of a ſtate, and thoſe which they really enjoy ; between the equality eſtabliſhed by political inſtitutions, and that which takes place between the individual members : and that to this diſproportion was chiefly owing the deſtruction of liberty in the ancient republics, the ſtorms which they had to encounter, and the weakneſs that ſurrendered them into the power of foreign tyrants.

Three principal cauſes may be aſſigned for theſe diſtinctions : inequality of wealth, inequality of condition between him whoſe reſources of ſubſiſtance are ſecured to himſelf and deſcendable to his family, and him whoſe reſources are annihilated with the termination of his life, or rather of that part of his life in which he is capable of labour ; and laſtly, inequality of inſtruction.

It will therefore behove us to ſhew, that theſe three kinds of real inequality muſt continually diminiſh ; but without becoming abſolutely extinct, ſince they have natural and neceſſary cauſes, which it would be abſurd as well as dangerous to think of deſtroying ; nor can we attempt even to deſtroy entirely their effects,

effects, without opening at the fame time more fruitful fources of inequality, and giving to the rights of man a more direct and more fatal blow.

It is eafy to prove that fortunes naturally tend to equality, and that their extreme difproportion either could not exift, or would quickly ceafe, if pofitive law had not introduced factitious means of amaffing and perpetuating them; if an entire freedom of commerce and induftry were brought forward to fuperfede the advantages which prohibitory laws and fifcal rights neceffarily give to the rich over the poor; if duties upon every fort of transfer and convention, if prohibitions to certain kinds, and the tedious and expenfive formalities prefcribed to other kinds; if the uncertainty and expence attending their execution had not palfied the efforts of the poor, and fwallowed up their little accumulations; if political inftitutions had not laid certain prolific fources of opulence open to a few, and fhut them againft the many; if avarice, and the other prejudices incident to an advanced age, did not prefide over marriages; in fine, if the fimplicity

city

city of our manners and the wifdom of our
inftitutions were calculated to prevent riches
from operating as the means of gratifying vanity or ambition, at the fame time that an
ill-judged aufterity, by forbidding us to render them a means of coftly pleafures, fhould
not force us to preferve the wealth that had
once been accumulated.

Let us compare, in the enlightened nations
of Europe, the actual population with the extent of territory ; let us obferve, amidft the
fpectacle of their culture and their induftry,
the way in which labour and the means of
fubfiftance are diftributed, and we fhall fee
that it will be impoffible to maintain thefe
means in the fame extent, and of confequence
to maintain the fame mafs of population, if
any confiderable number of individuals ceafe
to have, as now, nothing but their induftry,
and the pittance neceffary to fet it at work, or
to render its profit equal to the fupplying their
own wants and thofe of their family. But
neither this induftry, nor the fcanty referve
we have mentioned, can be perpetuated, except fo long as the life and health of each head
of a family is perpetuated. Their little fortune

tune therefore is at beft an annuity, but in reality with features of precarioufnefs that an annuity wants : and from hence refults a moft important difference between this clafs of fociety and the clafs of men whofe refources confift either of a landed income, or the intereft of a capital, which depends little upon perfonal induftry, and is therefore not fubject to fimilar rifks.

There exifts then a neceffary caufe of inequality, of dependence, and even of penury, which menaces without ceafing the moft numerous and active clafs of our focieties.

This inequality, however, may be in great meafure deftroyed, by fetting chance againft chance, in fecuring to him who attains old age a fupport, arifing from his favings, but augmented by thofe of other perfons, who, making a fimilar addition to a common ftock, may happen to die before they fhall have occafion to recur to it ; in procuring, by a like regulation, an equal refource for women who may lofe their hufbands, or children who may lofe their father ; laftly, in preparing for thofe youths, who arrive at an age to be capable of working for themfelves, and of giving

birth

birth to a new family, the benefit of a capital fufficient to employ their induftry, and increafed at the expence of thofe whom premature death may cut off before they arrive at that period. To the application of mathematics to the probabilities of life and the intereft of money, are we indebted for the hint of thefe means, already employed with fome degree of fuccefs, though they have not been carried to fuch extent, or employed in fuch variety of forms, as would render them truly beneficial, not merely to a few families, but to the whole mafs of fociety, which would thereby be relieved from that periodical ruin obfervable in a number of families, the everflowing fource of corruption and depravity.

Thefe eftablifhments, which may be formed in the name of the focial power, and become one of its greateft benefits, might alfo be the refult of individual affociations, which may be inftituted without danger, when the principles by which the eftablifhments ought to be organifed, fhall have become more popular, and the errors, by which a great number of fuch affociations have been deftroyed, fhall ceafe to be an objeĉt of apprehenfion.

We

We may enumerate other means of fecuring the equality in queftion, either by preventing credit from continuing to be a privilege exclufively attached to large fortunes, without at the fame time placing it upon a lefs folid foundation ; or by rendering the progrefs of induftry and the activity of commerce more independent of the exiftence of great capitalifts : and for thefe refources alfo we fhall be indebted to the fcience of calculation.

The equality of inftruction we can hope to attain, and with which we ought to be fatisfied, is that which excludes every fpecies of dependence, whether forced or voluntary. We may exhibit, in the actual ftate of human knowledge, the eafy means by which this end may be attained even for thofe who can devote to ftudy but a few years of infancy, and, in fubfequent life, only fome occafional hours of leifure. We might fhew, that by a happy choice of the fubjects to be taught, and of the mode of inculcating them, the entire mafs of a people may be inftructed in every thing neceffary for the purpofes of domeftic economy ; for the tranfaction of their affairs ; for the free developement of their induftry and their faculties ;

faculties; for the knowledge, exercife and pro-
tection of their rights; for a fenfe of their
duties, and the power of difcharging them;
for the capacity of judging both their own
actions, and the actions of others, by their own
underftanding; for the acquifition of all the
delicate or dignified fentiments that are an
honour to humanity; for freeing themfelves
from a blind confidence in thofe to whom they
may entruft the care of their interefts, and the
fecurity of their rights; for chufing and watch-
ing over them, fo as no longer to be the dupes
of thofe popular errors that torment and
way-lay the life of man with fuperftitious
fears and chimerical hopes; for defending
themfelves againft prejudices by the fole
energy of reafon; in fine, for efcaping from
the delufions of impofture, which would
fpread fnares for their fortune, their health,
their freedom of opinion and of confcience,
under the pretext of enriching, of healing, and
of faving them.

The inhabitants of the fame country being
then no longer diftinguifhed among themfelves
by the alternate ufe of a refined or a vulgar language; being equally governed by their own

under-

underftandings ; being no more confined to
the mechanical knowledge of the proceffes of
the arts, and the mere routine of a profeffion;
no more dependent in the moft trifling affairs,
and for the flighteft information, upon men
of fkill, who, by a neceffary afcendancy,
controul and govern, a real equality muft be
the refult; fince the difference of talents and
information can no longer place a barrier between men whofe fentiments, ideas, and
phrafeology are capable of being mutually
underftood, of whom the one part may defire to be inftruded, but cannot need to be
guided by the other; of whom the one part
may delegate to the other the office of a rational government, but cannot be forced to
regard them with blind and unlimited confidence.

Then it is that this fuperiority will become
an advantage even for thofe who do not par-
take of it, fince it will exift not as their
enemy, but as their friend. The natural difference of faculties between men whofe underftandings have not been cultivated, produces, even among favages, empirics and
dupes, the one fkilled in delufion, the others

eafy

eafy to be deceived : the fame difference will
doubtlefs exift among a people where inftruction fhall be truly general ; but it will be here
between men of exalted underftandings and
men of found minds, who can admire the
radiance of knowledge, without fuffering
themfelves to be dazzled by it ; between talents and genius on the one hand, and on the
other the good fenfe that knows how to appreciate and enjoy them : and fhould this
difference be even greater in the latter cafe,
comparing the force and extent of the faculties only, ftill would the effects of it not be the
lefs imperceptible in the relations of men with
each other, in whatever is interefting to their
independence or their happinefs.

The different caufes of equality we have
enumerated do not act diftinctly and apart ;
they unite, they incorporate, they fupport
one another ; and from their combined influence refults an action proportionably forcible,
fure, and conftant. If inftruction become
more equal, induftry thence acquires greater
equality, and from induftry the effect is communicated to fortunes ; and equality of fortunes neceffarily contributes to that of inftruction,

tion, while equality of nations, like that eftablifhed between individuals, have alfo a mutual operation upon each other.

In fine, inftruction, properly directed, cor-
rects the natural inequality of the faculties, inftead of ftrengthening it, in like manner as
good laws remedy the natural inequality of
the means of fubfiftance; or as, in focieties
whofe inftitutions fhall have effected this equality, liberty, though fubjected to a regular
government, will be more extenfive, more
complete, than in the independence of favage
life. Then has the focial art accomplifhed its
end, that of fecuring and extending for all
the enjoyment of the common rights which
impartial nature has bequeathed to all.

The advantages that muft refult from the
ftate of improvement, of which I have proved
we may almoft entertain the certain hope, can
have no limit but the abfolute perfection of the
human fpecies, fince, in proportion as different
kinds of equality fhall be eftablifhed as to the
various means of providing for our wants, as
to a more univerfal inftruction, and a more
entire liberty, the more real will be this equality, and the nearer will it approach towards

Z   embracing

embracing every thing truly important to the happinefs of mankind.

It is then by examining the progreffion and the laws of this perfection, that we can alone arrive at the knowledge of the extent or boundary of our hopes.

It has never yet been fuppofed, that all the facts of nature, and all the means of acquiring precifion in the computation and analyfis of thofe facts, and all the connections of objects with each other, and all the poffible combinations of ideas, can be exhaufted by the human mind. The mere relations of magnitude, the combinations, quantity and extent of this idea alone, form already a fyftem too immenfe for the mind of man ever to grafp the whole of it ; a portion, more vaft than that which he may have penetrated, will always remain unknown to him. It has, however, been imagined, that, as man can know a part only of the objects which the nature of his intelligence permits him to inveftigate, he muft at length reach the point at which, the number and complication of thofe he already knows having abforbed all his powers, farther progrefs will become abfolutely impoffible.

But,

But, in proportion as facts are multiplied, man learns to clafs them, and reduce them to more general facts, at the fame time that the inftruments and methods for obferving them, and regiftering them with exactnefs, acquire a new precifion : in proportion as relations more multifarious between a greater number of objects are difcovered, man continues to reduce them to relations of a wider denomination, to exprefs them with greater fimplicity, and to prefent them in a way which may enable a given ftrength of mind, with a given quantity of attention, to take in a greater number than before : in proportion as the underftanding embraces more complicated combinations, a fimple mode of announcing thefe combinations renders them more eafy to be treated. Hence it follows that truths, the difcovery of which was accompanied with the moft laborious efforts, and which at firft could not be comprehended but by men of the fevereft attention, will after a time be unfolded and proved in methods that are not above the efforts of an ordinary capacity. And thus fhould the methods that led to new combinations be exhaufted, fhould

Z 2   their

their applications to queſtions, ſtill unreſolved, demand exertions greater than the time or the powers of the learned can beſtow, more ge-neral methods, means more ſimple would ſoon come to their aid, and open a farther career to genius. The energy, the real ex-tent of the human intellect may remain the ſame ; but the inſtruments which it can em-ploy will be multiplied and improved ; but the language which fixes and determines the ideas will acquire more preciſion and com-paſs ; and it will not be here, as in the ſcience of mechanics, where, to increaſe the force, we muſt diminiſh the velocity ; on the con-trary the methods by which genius will ar-rive at the diſcovery of new truths, augment at once both the force and the rapidity of its operations.

In a word, theſe changes being themſelves the neceſſary conſequences of additional pro-greſs in the knowledge of truths of detail, and the cauſe which produces a demand for new reſources, producing at the ſame time the means of ſupplying them, it follows that the actual maſs of truths appertaining to the ſciences of obſervation, calculation and experiment

periment, may be perpetually augmented, and that without fuppofing the faculties of man to poffefs a force and activity, and a fcope of action greater than before.

By applying thefe general reflections to the different fciences, we might exhibit, refpecting each, examples of this progreffive improvement, which would remove all poffibility of doubt as to the certainty of the further improvement that may be expected. We might indicate particularly in thofe which prejudice confiders as neareft to being exhaufted, the marks of an almoft certain and early advance. We might illuftrate the extent, the precifion, the unity which muft be added to the fyftem comprehending all human knowledge, by a more general and philofophical application of the fcience of calculation to the individual branches of which that fyftem is compofed. We might fhew how favourable to our hopes a more univerfal inftruction would prove, by which a greater number of individuals would acquire the elementary knowledge that might infpire them with a tafte for a particular kind of ftudy; and how much thefe hopes would be further heightened

if

if this application to ſtudy were to be rendered ſtill more extenſive by a more general
eaſe of circumſtances. At preſent, in the
moſt enlightened countries, ſcarcely do one
in fifty of thoſe whom nature has bleſſed
with talents receive the neceſſary inſtruction
for the developement of them: how different
would be the proportion in the caſe we are
ſuppoſing? and, of conſequence, how different the number of men deſtined to extend
the horizon of the ſciences?

We might ſhew how much this equality
of inſtruction, joined to the national equality
we have ſuppoſed to take place, would accelerate thoſe ſciences, the advancement of
which depends upon obſervations repeated in
a greater number of inſtances, and extending
over a larger portion of territory; how much
benefit would be derived therefrom to mineralogy, botany, zoology, and the doctrine
of meteors; in ſhort, how infinite the difference between the feeble means hitherto
enjoyed by theſe ſciences, and which yet
have led to uſeful and important truths, and
the magnitude of thoſe which man would
then have it in his power to employ.

Laſtly,

Laftly, we might prove that, from the advantage of being cultivated by a greater number of perfons, even the progrefs of thofe fciences, in which difcoveries are the fruit of individual meditation, would, alfo, be confiderably advanced by means of minuter improvements, not requiring the ftrength of intellect, neceffary for inventions, but that prefent themfelves to the reflection of the leaft profound underftandings.

If we pafs to the progrefs of the arts, thofe arts particularly the theory of which depends on thefe very fame fciences, we fhall find that it can have no inferior limits; that their proceffes are fufceptible of the fame improvement, the fame fimplifications, as the fcientific methods; that inftruments, machines, looms, will add every day to the capabilities and fkill of man—will augment at once the excellence and precifion of his works, while they will diminifh the time and labour neceffary for executing them; and that then will difappear the obftacles that ftill oppofe themfelves to the progrefs in queftion, accidents which will be forefeen and prevented; and, laftly, the unhealthinefs at prefent at-

Z 4

tendant

tendant upon certain operations, habits and climates.

A fmaller portion of ground will then be made to produce a portion of provifions of higher value or greater utility; a greater quantity of enjoyment will be procured at a fmaller expence of confumption; the fame manufactured or artificial commodity will be produced at a fmaller expence of raw materials, or will be ftronger and more durable; every foil will be appropriated to productions which will fatisfy a greater number of wants with the leaft labour, and taken in the fmalleft quantities. Thus the means of health and frugality will be encreafed, together with the inftruments in the arts of production, of curing commodities and manufacturing their produce, without demanding the facrifice of one enjoyment by the confumer.

Thus, not only the fame fpecies of ground will nourifh a greater number of individuals, but each individual, with a lefs quantity of labour, will labour more fuccefsfully, and be furrounded with greater conveniences.

It may, however, be demanded, whether, amidft this improvement in induftry and happinefs,

happinefs, where the wants and faculties of
men will continually become better propor-
tioned, each fucceffive generation poffefs more
various ftores, and of confequence in each
generation the number of individuals be
greatly increafed ; it may, I fay, be demanded, whether thefe principles of improvement
and increafe may not, by their continual
operation, ultimately lead to degeneracy and.
deftruction ? Whether the number of inhabitants in the univerfe at length exceeding
the means of exiftence, there will not refult
a continual decay of happinefs and population, and a progrefs towards barbarifm, or at
leaft a fort of ofcillation between good and
evil ? Will not this ofcillation, in focieties
arrived at this epoch, be a perennial fource
of periodical calamity and diftrefs ? In
a word, do not thefe confiderations point
out the limit at which all farther improvement will become impoffible, and confequently the perfectibility of man arrive at a period
which in the immenfity of ages it may attain,
but which it can never pafs ?

There is, doubtlefs, no individual that does
not perceive how very remote from us will
be

be this period: but muſt it one day arrive?
It is equally impoſſible to pronounce on either
ſide reſpecting an event, which can only be
realized at an epoch when the human ſpecies
will neceſſarily have acquired a degree of
knowledge, of which our ſhort-ſighted underſtandings can ſcarcely form an idea. And
who ſhall preſume to foretel to what perfection the art of converting the elements of
life into ſubſtances fitted for our uſe, may,
in a progreſſion of ages, be brought?

But ſuppoſing the affirmative, ſuppoſing it
actually to take place, there would reſult
from it nothing alarming, either to the happineſs of the human race, or its indefinite
perfectibility; if we conſider, that prior to
this period the progreſs of reaſon will have
walked hand in hand with that of the ſciences; that the abſurd prejudices of ſuperſtition will have ceaſed to infuſe into morality
a harſhneſs that corrupts and degrades, inſtead of purifying and exalting it; that men
will then know, that the duties they may be
under relative to propagation will conſiſt not
in the queſtion of giving *exiſtence* to a greater
number of beings, but *happineſs*; will have for
their

their object, the general welfare of the human species; of the society in which they live; of the family to which they are attached; and not the puerile idea of encumbering the earth with ufelefs and wretched mortals. Accordingly, there might then be a limit to the poffible mafs of provifion, and of confequence to the greateft poffible population, without that premature deftruction, fo contrary to nature and to focial profperity, of a portion of the beings who may have received life, being the refult of thofe limits.

As the difcovery, or rather the accurate folution of the firft principles of metaphyfics, morals, and politics, is ftill recent; and as it has been preceded by the knowledge of a confiderable number of truths of detail, the prejudice, that they have thereby arrived at their higheft point of improvement, becomes eafily eftablifhed in the mind ; and men fuppofe that nothing remains to be done, becaufe there are no longer any grofs errors to deftroy, or fundamental truths to eftablifh.

But it requires little penetration to perceive how imperfect is ftill the developement of the intellectual and moral faculties of
man ;

man; how much farther the fphere of his duties, including therein the influence of his actions upon the welfare of his fellow-creatures and of the fociety to which he belongs, may be extended by a more fixed, a more profound and more accurate obfervation of that influence; how many queftions ftill remain to be folved, how many focial ties to be examined, before we can afcertain the precife catalogue of the individual rights of man, as well as of the rights which the focial ftate confers upon the whole community with regard to each member. Have we even afcertained with any precifion the limits of thefe rights, whether as they exift between different focieties, or in any fingle fociety, over its members, in cafes of divifion and hoftility; or, in fine, the rights of individuals, their fpontaneous unions in the cafe of a primitive formation, or their feparations when feparation becomes neceffary?

If we pafs on to the theory which ought to direct the application of thefe principles, and ferve as the bafis of the focial art, do we not fee the neceffity of acquiring an exactnefs of which firft truths, from their general nature,

ture, are not fufceptible? Are we fo far advanced as to confider juftice, or a proved and
acknowledged utility, and not vague, uncertain, and arbitrary views of pretended political advantages, as the foundation of all inftitutions of law? Among the variety, almoft
infinite, of poffible fyftems, in which the
general principles of equality and natural
rights fhould be refpected, have we yet fixed
upon the precife rules of afcertaining with
certainty thofe which beft fecure the prefervation of thefe rights, which afford the
freeft fcope for their exercife and enjoyment,
which promote moft effectually the peace and
welfare of individuals, and the ftrength, repofe, and profperity of nations?

The application of the arithmetic of combinations and probabilities to thefe fciences,
promifes an improvement by fo much the
more confiderable, as it is the only means of
giving to their refults an almoft mathematical
precifion, and of appreciating their degree of
certainty or probability. The facts upon
which thefe refults are built may, indeed,
without calculation, and by a glance only,
lead to fome general truths; teach us whether

the

the effects produced by fuch a caufe have been favourable or the reverfe : but if thefe facts have neither been counted nor eftimated; if thefe effects have not been the object of an exact admeafurement, we cannot judge of the quantity of good or evil they contain : if the good or evil nearly balance each other, nay, if the difference be not confiderable, we cannot pronounce with certainty to which fide the balance inclines. Without the ap-plication of this arithmetic, it would be al-moft impoffible to chufe, with found reafon, between two combinations propofing to them-felves the fame end, when their advantages are not diftinguifhable by any confiderable difference. In fine, without this alliance, thefe fciences would remain for ever grofs and narrow, for want of inftruments of fuf-ficient polifh to lay hold of the fubtility of truth—for want of machines fufficiently ac-curate to found the bottom of the well where it conceals its wealth.

Meanwhile this application, notwithftand-ing the happy efforts of certain geometers, is ftill, if I may fo fpeak, in its firft rudi-ments; and to the following generations muft

it

it open a fource of intelligence inexhauftible as calculation itfelf, or as the combinations, analogies, and facts that may be brought within the fphere of its operations.

There is another fpecies of progrefs, appertaining to the fciences in queftion, equally important; I mean, the improvement of their language, at prefent fo vague and fo obfcure. To this improvement muft they owe the advantage of becoming popular, even in their firft elements. Genius can triumph over thefe inaccuracies, as over other obftacles; it can recognife the features of truth, in fpite of the mafk that conceals or disfigures them. But how is the man who can devote but a few leifure moments to inftruction to do this? how is he to acquire and retain the moft fimple truths, if they be difguifed by an inaccurate language? The fewer ideas he is able to collect and combine, the more requifite it is that they be juft and precife. He has no fund of truths ftored up in his mind, by which to guard himfelf againft error; nor is his underftanding fo ftrengthened and refined by long exercife, that he can catch thofe feeble rays of light which

efcape under the obfcure and ambiguous
drefs of an imperfect and vicious phrafeology.

It will be impoffible for men to become
enlightened upon the nature and developement of their moral fentiments, upon the
principles of morality, upon the motives for conforming their conduct to thofe
principles, and upon their interefts, whether
relative to their individual or focial capacity,
without making, at the fame time, an advancement in moral practice, not lefs real
than that of the fcience itfelf. Is not a miftaken intereft the moft frequent caufe of actions contrary to the general welfare? Is
not the impetuofity of our paffions the continual refult, either of habits to which we
addict ourfelves from a falfe calculation, or
of ignorance of the means by which to refift their firft impulfe, to divert, govern,
and direct their action?

Is not the practice of reflecting upon our
conduct; of trying it by the touchftone of
reafon and confcience; of exercifing thofe
humane fentiments which blend our happinefs with that of others, the neceffary confequence

quence of the well-directed ftudy of morality, and of a greater equality in the conditions of the focial compact? Will not that confci- oufnefs of his own dignity, appertaining to the man who is free, that fyftem of educa- tion built upon a more profound knowledge of our moral conftitution, render common to almoft every man thofe principles of a ftrict and unfullied juftice, thofe habitual propen- fities of an active and enlightened benevo- lence, of a delicate and generous fenfibility, of which nature has planted the feeds in our hearts, and which wait only for the genial influence of knowledge and liberty to ex- pand and to fructify? In like manner as the mathematical and phyfical fciences tend to improve the arts that are employed for our moft fimple wants, fo is it not equally in the neceffary order of nature that the mo- ral and political fciences fhould exercife a fimilar influence upon the motives that di- rect our fentiments and our actions?

What is the object of the improvement of laws and public inftitutions, confequent upon the progrefs of thefe fciences, but to reconcile, to approximate, to blend and unite into one mafs the common intereft of each

A a   indi-

individual with the common intereſt of all? What is the end of the ſocial art, but to deſtroy the oppoſition between theſe two apparently jarring ſentiments? And will not the conſtitution and laws of that country beſt accord with the intentions of reaſon and nature where the practice of virtue ſhall be leaſt difficult, and the temptations to deviate from her paths leaſt numerous and leaſt powerful.

What vicious habit can be mentioned, what practice contrary to good faith, what crime even, the origin and firſt cauſe of which may not be traced in the legiſlation, inſtitutions, and prejudices of the country in which we obſerve ſuch habit, ſuch practice, or ſuch crime to be committed?

In ſhort, does not the well-being, the proſperity, reſulting from the progreſs that will be made by the uſeful arts, in conſequence of their being founded upon a ſound theory, reſulting, alſo, from an improved legiſlation, built upon the truths of the political ſciences, naturally diſpoſe men to humanity, to benevolence, and to juſtice? Do not all the obſervations, in fine, which we propoſed to develope in this work prove, that the moral goodneſs of man, the neceſſary conſequence

of

of his organization, is, like all his other faculties, fufceptible of an indefinite improvement? and that nature has connected, by a
chain which cannot be broken, truth, happinefs, and virtue?

Among thofe caufes of human improvement that are of moft importance to the general welfare, muft be included, the total annihilation of the prejudices which have eftablifhed between the fexes an inequality of
rights, fatal even to the party which it favours.   In vain might we fearch for motives
by which to juftify this principle, in difference of phyfical organization, of intellect, or
of moral fenfibility.   It had at firft no other
origin but abufe of ftrength, and all the attempts which have fince been made to fupport
it are idle fophifms.

And here we may obferve, how much the
abolition of the ufages authorized by this
prejudice, and of the laws which it has
dictated, would tend to augment the happinefs of families; to render common the
virtues of domeftic life, the fountain-head of
all the others; to favour inftruction, and,
efpecially, to make it truly general, either
becaufe it would be extended to both fexes

with

with greater equality, or becaufe it cannot become general, even to men, without the concurrence of the mothers of families. Would not this homage, fo long in paying, to the divinities of equity and good fenfe, put an end to a too fertile principle of injuftice, cruelty, and crime, by fuperfeding the oppofition hitherto maintained between that natural propenfity, which is, of all others, the moft imperious, and the moft difficult to fubdue, and the interefts of man, or the duties of fociety? Would it not produce, what has hitherto been a mere chimera, national manners of a nature mild and pure, formed, not by imperious privations, by hypocritical appearances, by referves impofed by the fear of fhame or religious terrors, but by habits freely contracted, infpired by nature and avowed by reafon?

The people being more enlightened, and having refumed the right of difpofing for themfelves of their blood and their treafure, will learn by degrees to regard war as the moft dreadful of all calamities, the moft terrible of all crimes. The firft wars that will be fuperfeded, will be thofe into which the ufurpers of fovereignty have hitherto drawn

their

their fubjects for the maintenance of rights
pretendedly hereditary.

Nations will know, that they cannot become conquerors without lofing their freedom; that perpetual confederations are the
only means of maintaining their independance; that their object fhould be fecurity,
and not power. By degrees commercial prejudices will die away; a falfe mercantile intereft will lofe the terrible power of imbuing
the earth with blood, and of ruining nations
under the idea of enriching them. As the
people of different countries will at laft be
drawn into clofer intimacy, by the principles
of politics and morality, as each, for its own
advantage, will invite foreigners to an equal
participation of the benefits which it may
have derived either from nature or its own
induftry, all the caufes which produce, en-
venom, and perpetuate national animofities,
will one by one difappear, and will no more
furnifh to warlike infanity either fuel or
pretext.

Inftitutions, better combined than thofe
projects of perpetual peace which have occupied the leifure and confoled the heart of
certain philofophers, will accelerate the pro-

A a 3   grefs

grefs of this fraternity of nations ; and wars, like affaffinations, will be ranked in the num-ber of thofe daring atrocities, humiliating and loathfome to nature ; and which fix up-on the country or the age whofe annals are ftained with them, an indeliable opprobrium.

In fpeaking of the fine arts in Greece, in Italy, and in France, we have obferved, that it is neceffary to diftinguifh, in their produc-tions, what really belongs to the progrefs of the art, and what is due only to the talent of the artift. And here let us enquire what progrefs may ftili be expected, whether, in confequence of the advancement of philofo-phy and the fciences, or from an additional ftore of more judicious and profound obfer-vations relative to the object, the effects and the means of thefe arts themfelves ; or, laft-ly, from the removal of the prejudices that have contracted their fphere, and that ftill retain them in the fhackles of authority, from which the fciences and philofophy have at length freed themfelves. Let us afk, whether, as has frequently been fuppofed, thefe means may be confidered as exhaufted ? or, if not exhaufted, whether, becaufe the moft fub-lime and pathetic beauties have been feized ;

the

the moſt happy ſubjects treated; the moſt
ſimple and ſtriking combinations employed;
the moſt prominent and general characters
exhibited; the moſt energetic paſſions, their
true expreſſions and genuine features deli-
neated; the moſt commanding truths, the
moſt brilliant images diſplayed; that, therefore, the arts are condemned to an eternal and
monotonous imitation of their firſt models ?

We ſhall perceive that this opinion is
merely a prejudice, derived from the habit
which exiſts among men of letters and artiſts
of appreciating the merits of men, inſtead of
giving themſelves up to the enjoyment to be
received from their works. The ſecond-hand
pleaſure which ariſes from comparing the
productions of different ages and countries,
and from contemplating the energy and ſucceſs of the efforts of genius, will perhaps be
loſt; but, in the mean time, the pleaſure
ariſing from the productions conſidered in
themſelves, and flowing from their abſolute
perfection, need not be leſs lively, though
the improvement of the author may leſs excite our aſtoniſhment. In proportion as excellent productions ſhall multiply, every ſucceſſive generation of men will direct its at-

tention

tention to thofe which are moft perfect, and
the reft will infenfibly fall into oblivion;
while the more fimple and palpable traits,
which were feized upon by thofe who firft
entered the field of invention, will not the
lefs exift for our pofterity, though they fhall
be found only in the lateft productions.

The progrefs of the fciences fecures the
progrefs of the art of inftruction, which
again accelerates in its turn that of the fciences; and this reciprocal influence, the action of which is inceffantly increafed, muft be
ranked in the number of the moft prolific
and powerful caufes of the improvement of
the human race. At prefent, a young man,
upon finifhing his ftudies and quitting our
fchools, may know more of the principles of
mathematics than Newton acquired by profound ftudy, or difcovered by the force of
his genius, and may exercife the inftrument
of calculation with a readinefs which at that
period was unknown. The fame obfervation,
with certain reftrictions, may be applied to
all the fciences. In proportion as each fhall
advance, the means of compreffing, within a
fmaller circle, the proofs of a greater number
of truths, and of facilitating their comprehenfion,

henfion, will equally advance. Thus, notwithftanding future degrees of progrefs, not
only will men of equal genius find themfelves, at the fame period of life, upon a
level with the actual ftate of fcience, but,
refpecting every generation, what may be
acquired in a given fpace of time, by the
fame ftrength of intellect and the fame degree of attention, will necefarily increafe,
and the elementary part of each fcience, that
part which every man may attain, becoming
more and more extended, will include, in a
manner more complete, the knowledge ne-
cefary for the direction of every man in the
common occurences of life, and for the free
and independant exercife of his reafon.

In the political fciences there is a defcription of truths, which, particularly in free
countries (that is, in all countries in certain generations), can only be ufeful when
generally known and avowed. Thus, the
influence of thefe fciences upon the freedom
and profperity of nations, muft, in fome
fort, be meafured by the number of thofe
truths that, in confequence of elementary inftruction, fhall pervade the general mind:
and thus, as the growing progrefs of this
ele-

elementary inftruction is connected with the neceffary progrefs of the fciences, we may expect a melioration in the doctrines of the • human race which may be regarded as indefinite, fince it can have no other limits than thofe of the two fpecies of progrefs on which it depends.

We have ftill two other means of general application to confider, and which muft influence at once both the improvement of the art of inftruction and that of the fciences. One is a more extenfive and more perfect adoption of what may be called technical methods; the other, the inftitution of an univerfal language.

By technical methods I underftand, the art of uniting a great number of objects in an arranged and fyftematic order, by which we may be enabled to perceive at a glance their bearings and connections, feize in an inftant their combinations, and form from them the more readily new combinations.

Let us develope the principles, let us examine the utility of this art, as yet in its infancy, and we fhall find that, when improved and perfected, we might derive from it, either the advantage of poffeffing within the

the narrow compafs of a picture, what it
would be often difficult for volumes to explain to us fo readily and fo well; or the
means, ftill more valuable, of prefenting ifolated facts in a difpofition and view beft
calculated to give us their general refults.
We fhall perceive how, by means of a fmall
number of thefe pictures or tables, the ufe of
which may be eafily learned, men who have
not been able to appropriate fuch ufeful details and elementary knowledge as may apply
to the purpofes of common life, may turn to
them at the fhorteft notice; and how elementary
knowledge itfelf, in all thofe fciences where this
knowledge is founded either upon a regular
code of truths or a feries of obfervations and
experiments, may hereby be facilitated.

An univerfal language is that which expreffes by figns, either the direct objects, or
thofe well-defined collections conftituted of
fimple and general ideas, which are to be
found or may be introduced equally in the
underftandings of all mankind; or, laftly,
the general relations of thefe ideas, the operations of the human mind, the operations
peculiar to any fcience, and the mode of
procefs in the arts. Thus, fuch perfons as
fhall

fhall have become mafters of thefe figns, the
method of combining and the rules for conftructing them, will underftand what is written in this language, and will read it with
fimilar facility in the language of their own
country, whatever it may happen to be.

It is apparent, that this language might
be employed to explain either the theory of
a fcience or the rules of an art; to give an
account of a new experiment or a new obfervation, the acquifition of a fcientific truth,
the invention of a method, or the difcovery
of a procefs; and that, like algebra, when
obliged to make ufe of new figns, thofe already known would afford the means of afcertaining their value.

A language like this has not the inconve-
nience of a fcientific idiom, different from the
vernacular tongue. We have before obferved,
that the ufe of fuch an idiom neceffarily di-
vides focieties into two extremely unequal
claffes; the one compofed of men, underftanding the language, and, therefore, in
poffeffion of the key to the fciences; the
other of thofe who, incapable of learning it,
find themfelves reduced almoft to an abfolute
impoffibility of acquiring knowledge. On
the

the contrary, the univerfal language we are
fuppofing, might be learned, like the language
of algebra, with the fcience itfelf; the fign
might be known at the fame inftant with the
object, the idea, or the operation which it
expreffes. He who, having attained the elements of a fcience, fhould wifh to profecute
farther his enquiries, would find in books,
not only truths that he could underftand, by
means of thofe figns, of which he already
knows the value, but the explanation of the
new figns of which he has need in order to
afcend to higher truths.

It might be fhown that the formation of
fuch a language, if confined to the expreffing
of fimple and precife propofitions, like thofe
which form the fyftem of a fcience, or the
practice of an art, would be the reverfe of
chimerical ; that its execution, even at prefent, would be extremely practicable as to a
great number of objects ; and that the chief
obftacle that would ftand in the way of extending it to others, would be the humiliating
neceffity of acknowledging how few precife
ideas, and accurately defined notions, underftood exactly in the fame fenfe by every
mind, we really poffefs.

2   It

It might be fhown that this language, improving every day, acquiring inceffantly greater extent, would be the means of giving to every object that comes within the reach of human intelligence, a rigour, and precifion, that would facilitate the knowledge of truth, and render error almoft impoffible. Then would the march of every fcience be as infallible as that of the mathematics, and the propofitions of every fyftem acquire, as far as nature will admit, geometrical demonftration and certainty.

All the caufes which contribute to the improvement of the human fpecies, all the means we have enumerated that infure its progrefs, muft, from their very nature, exercife an influence always active, and acquire an extent for ever increafing. The proofs of this have been exhibited, and from their developement in the work itfelf they will derive additional force: accordingly we may already conclude, that the perfectibility of man is indefinite. Meanwhile we have hitherto confidered him as poffeffing only the fame natural faculties, as endowed with the fame organization. How much greater would be the certainty, how much wider the compafs of our hopes, could

we

we prove that thefe natural facultics themfelves, that this very organization, are alfo fufceptible of melioration? And this is the laft quéftion we fhall examine.

The organic perfectibility or deterioration of the claffes of the vegetable, or fpecies of the animal kingdom, may be regarded as one of the general laws of nature.

This law extends itfelf to the human race ; and it cannot be doubted that the progrefs of the fanative art, that the ufe of more wholefome food and more comfortable habitations, that a mode of life which fhall develope the phyfical powers by exercife, without at the fame time impairing them by excefs ; in fine, that the deftruction of the two moft active caufes of deterioration, penury and wretchednefs on the one hand, and enormous wealth on the other, muft neceffarily tend to prolong the common duration of man's exiftence, and fecure him a more conftant health and a more robuft conftitution. It is manifeft that the improvement of the practice of medicine, become more efficacious in confequence of the progrefs of reafon and the focial order, muft in the end put a period to tranfmiffible or contagious diforders, as well to thofe general maladies refulting from climate, aliments, and the

nature

nature of certain occupations. Nor would it be difficult to prove that this hope might be extended to almoft every other malady, of which it is probable we fhall hereafter difcover the moft remote caufes. Would it even be abfurd to fuppofe this quality of melioration in the human fpecies as fufceptible of an indefinite advancement; to fuppofe that a period muft one day arrive when death will be nothing more than the effect either of extraordinary accidents, or of the flow and gradual decay of the vital powers; and that the duration of the middle fpace, of the interval between the birth of man and this decay, will itfelf have no affignable limit? Certainly man will not become immortal; but may not the diftance between the moment in which he draws his firft breath, and the common term when, in the courfe of nature, without malady, without accident, he finds it impoffible any longer to exift, be neceffarily protracted? As we are now fpeaking of a progrefs that is capable of being reprefented with precifion, by numerical quantities or by lines, we fhall embrace the opportunity of explaining the two meanings that may be affixed to the word *indefinite.*

In reality, this middle term of life, which in

in proportion as men advance upon the ocean of futurity, we have fuppofed inceffantly to increafe, may receive additions either in conformity to a law by which, though approaching continually an illimitable extent, it could never poffibly arrive at it; or a law by which, in the immenfity of ages, it may acquire a greater extent than any determinate quantity whatever that may be affigned as its limit. In the latter cafe, this duration of life is indefinite in the ftricteft fenfe of the word, fince there exift no bounds on this fide of which it muft neceffarily ftop. And in the former, it is equally indefinite to us ; if we cannot fix the term, it may for ever approach, but can never furpafs; particularly if, knowing only that it can never ftop, we are ignorant in which of the two fenfes the term indefinite is applicable to it : and this is precifely the ftate of the knowledge we have as yet acquired relative to , the perfectibility of the fpecies.

Thus, in the inftance we are confidering, we are bound to believe that the mean duration of human life will for ever increafe, unlefs its increafe be prevented by the phyfical revolutions of the fyftem : but we cannot tell what

B b   is

is the bound which the duration of human life can never exceed ; we cannot even tell, whether there be any circumftance in the laws of nature which has determined and laid down its limit.

But may not our phyfical faculties, the force, the fagacity, the acutenefs of the fenfes, be numbered among the qualities, the individual improvement of which it will be practicable to tranfmit? An attention to the different breeds of domeftic animals muft lead us to adopt the affirmative of this queftion, and a direct obfervation of the human fpecies itfelf will be found to ftrengthen the opinion.

Laftly, may we not include in the fame circle the intellectual and moral faculties? May not our parents, who tranfmit to us the advantages or defects of their conformation, and from whom we receive our features and fhape, as well as our propenfities to certain phyfical affections, tranfmit to us alfo that part of organization upon which intellect, ftrength of underftanding, energy of foul or moral fenfibility depend? Is it not probable that education, by improving thefe qualities, will at the fame time have an influence upon,

will

will modify and improve this organization itfelf? Analogy, an inveftigation of the human faculties, and even fome facts, appear to authorife thefe conjectures, and thereby to enlarge the boundary of our hopes.

Such are the queftions with which we fhall terminate the laft divifion of our work. And how admirably calculated is this view of the human race, emancipated from its chains, releafed alike from the dominion of chance, as well as from that of the enemies of its progrefs, and advancing with a firm and indeviate ftep in the paths of truth, to confole the philofopher lamenting the errors, the flagrant acts of injuftice, the crimes with which the earth is ftill polluted ? It is the contemplation of this profpect that rewards him for all his efforts to affift the progrefs of reafon and the eftablifhment of liberty. He dares to regard thefe efforts as a part of the eternal chain of the deftiny of mankind ; and in this perfuafion he finds the true delight of virtue, the pleafure of having performed a durable fervice, which no viciffitude will ever deftroy in a fatal operation calculated to reftore the reign of prejudice and flavery. This fentiment is the afylum

lum into which he retires, and to which the memory of his perfecutors cannot follow him : he unites himfelf in imagination with man reftored to his rights, delivered from oppref- fion, and proceeding with rapid ftrides in the path of happinefs : he forgets his own misfor- tunes while his thoughts are thus employed ; he lives no longer to adverfity, calumny and malice, but becomes the affociate of thefe wifer and more fortunate beings whofe en- viable condition he fo earneftly contributed to produce.

THE END.